political movements in Mexico, Brazil, Argentina, and Cuba that were responding to similar modernization phenomena.

This study is based not only on a large body of official party literature and local newspapers for the period, but also on the newly discovered records of the Archivo de la Cámara de Comercio, Agricultura e Industria of the Department of La Libertad for the years 1904–1932.

Peter F. Klarén was awarded the Ph.D. degree from the University of California at Los Angeles. He received a Foreign Area Fellowship for field work in Peru and was awarded an ACLS-SSRC postdoctoral fellowship for 1973–1974 to continue his research in the field of socioagrarian history and political change in Peru. He is assistant professor of history at George Washington University.

Modernization, Dislocation, and Aprismo

Origins of the Peruvian Aprista Party, 1870-1932

Latin American Monographs, No. 32
Institute of Latin American Studies
The University of Texas at Austin

Modernization, Dislocation, and Aprismo

Origins of the Peruvian Aprista Party, 1870-1932

By Peter F. Klarén

PUBLISHED FOR THE INSTITUTE OF LATIN AMERICAN STUDIES
BY THE UNIVERSITY OF TEXAS PRESS · AUSTIN AND LONDON

Library of Congress Cataloging in Publication Data

Klarén, Peter, 1938-
  Modernization, dislocation, and Aprismo.

  (Latin American monographs, no. 32)
  Bibliography: p.
  1. Partido Aprista Peruano. I. Texas. University
at Austin. Institute of Latin American Studies.
II. Title. III. Series: Latin American monographs
(Austin, Tex.) no. 32.
JL3498.A6K53   329.9'85   73-4915
ISBN 0-292-76001-9

CONTENTS

MAPS

TABLES

FIGURE

INTRODUCTION

The pink-stuccoed, oval Plaza de Acho, adjacent to the Rimac River in the heart of old Lima, had on many previous occasions been the scene of great pageantry and drama. There were the times during the colonial period when the viceroy, attended with great pomp and ceremony by his court, would turn out in all his dazzling finery during the Feria del Señor de Los Milagros to view—along with all Lima—the tauromachian skills of the world's best bullfighters. On a gray, overcast Sunday afternoon in the winter of 1931,[1] however, Acho was witness to a unique and totally different sort of drama. For on that day before a huge throng of working and middle-class Limeños, it was not a torero who received the ringing approval of the crowds, but rather a handsome, young, aspiring provincial politician—barely thirty-six years old and a candidate for president. His voice, occasionally cracking with emotion, pierced the heavy Lima mist with stinging attacks on the old order and exhortations to the crowd to join with him to forge a new, revolutionary Peruvian society. As he reached the end of his speech, he paused briefly and then, to the delight of the mass, closed with the words "solo el Aprismo podrá salvarnos" (only Aprismo can be our salvation).

To thousands of Peruvians in 1931 that emotion-packed phrase touched a vital cord. Unsettled by the impact of the depression and moved by the constant revolutionary rhetoric of Víctor Raúl Haya de la Torre, the spellbinding orator that winter afternoon in Acho, they flocked in ever increasing numbers to the banners of his fledgling Peruvian Aprista party (Partido Aprista Peruano—PAP). A few months later they would give his new political movement, in a bitterly fought electoral campaign, what almost amounted to a stunning upset at the polls. The election launched

[1] August 23, 1931.

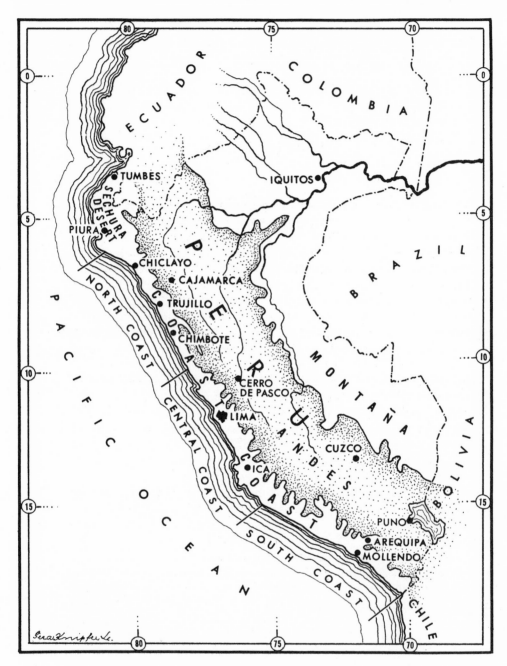

The physical divisions of Peru

both APRA[2] and Haya on a stormy career that would make each a major, if not decisive, power on the Peruvian political panorama for the next thirty-five years.

Over the years political commentators and scholars have grappled with the perplexing problem of explaining the sudden rise and longstanding power of the Aprista movement within the Peruvian polity. Many, in perhaps the most commonly accepted interpretation of APRA, have argued that the party was simply the manifestation of the world-wide depression, which brought down Latin American governments with impunity and set into motion a period of social upheaval perhaps unequaled, except for the Mexican Revolution, in modern Latin American history. While this fact no doubt considerably aided the party's recruitment in the early 1930's, it does not adequately explain the longevity of a party in a nation where, with often monotonous frequency, political groupings have suddenly appeared only to vanish with equal rapidity from the nation's political map. The fact of the matter is that nowhere in Latin America did a lasting political movement approaching the scope and size of APRA emerge solely out of the ashes of the 1929 Wall Street crash, and Peru was to prove no exception.

The roots of the Aprista movement, on the contrary, lie much deeper in the Peruvian sociopolitical milieu and are in fact closely related to the decidedly regional character that has been the hallmark of the party since 1931. Since that year the party has consistently drawn its principal electoral strength from the northern part of the country, leading Peruvian

---

[2] Founded in 1930 shortly after the overthrow of the Legíua government, the Partido Aprista Peruano (PAP) was conceived by Haya as the Peruvian counterpart to his Alianza Popular Revolucionario Americano (APRA). The latter had been founded by Haya in Mexico in 1924 as a broad, continental-wide political movement whose objectives were summed up in a five-point maximum program (*programa máximo*):

1. Action against Yankee Imperialism
2. Political unity of Latin America
3. Nationalization of lands and industry
4. Internationalization of the Panama Canal
5. Solidarity of all oppressed peoples and classes of the world

Initially Haya envisioned that APRA would serve as a catalyst for the formation throughout Latin America of various national Aprista parties, which would work for the achievement of these goals. At the same time each of these parties would compose a specific program (*programa mínimo*) designed to meet local conditions and problems. While there had been some attempts to form Aprista parties in several Latin American countries during the 1920's, the Peruvian party of 1930 was the first successful effort to attract a substantial popular following.

political commentators to refer to the area politically as "el sólido norte Aprista." In 1931, for example, APRA polled approximately 44 percent of its total vote from the six northern departments of the country. On the other hand, the sixteen remaining departments, excluding Lima (30 percent), contributed only 26 percent to the party's total vote. This regionalization of the party is even more striking in certain specific cases. In the same election the party polled a huge 74 percent of the total votes cast in the northern department of La Libertad and 60 percent in adjacent Lambayeque, while drawing only 21 percent in both Arequipa and Cuzco in the south. To a large extent this regional pattern of APRA has persisted down to the present. In the 1962 and 1963 elections, for example, APRA continued to show marked electoral strength in the north and widespread weakness in the south.

A closer examination of these voting patterns reveals that this regionalization of the party, roughly along a north-south axis, has tended to coincide broadly with a fundamental economic division within the country. Very generally, the party has traditionally found its electoral strength in the more economically developed north, where, since the turn of the century, agriculture and mining have steadily been modernized for export purposes. Thus, since 1931 APRA has attracted a very large number of followers from the sugar-producing belt of the north coast and the mining centers of the northern and central sierra.

Conversely, the party's appeal has traditionally lagged in the poorer, more backward and traditional central and southern agricultural sections of the country, where the economy has developed no ties with foreign markets and production has remained oriented toward local consumption. Such departments as Arequipa, Cuzco, Ayacucho, Moquegua, and Puno, to name a few areas, have rarely contributed more than 20 percent of their vote to the party. One major exception to this pattern has been the department of Ica, where cotton, since the early part of the century, has been produced for a foreign market and where APRA has had a considerable impact.

Rather than focusing on what we shall call this "geoeconomic" pattern of APRA and its possible significance, many Aprista analysts, pointing to this regionalization, have argued that the party can be explained in terms of the traditional Hispanic-Peruvian personalism and particularism that have long dominated the history of this Andean republic. For them the key to APRA lies in the figure of the charismatic northerner, Haya, the personification of the modern-day caudillo whose sheer personal magnetism succeeded in forging a mass party in the north. In a similar vein and reinforcing this older view, a more recent interpretation of APRA holds that, politically, the Peruvian electorate does not respond to concrete programs or ideology, but rather only to the mystique and charisma of the caudillo. Again Haya is seen as the central and dominant factor in the rise of APRA. In short, APRA, in something of a variation of the "great man" theory of history, is viewed as just another example in a long tradition of Peruvian political movements whose clientele has been localized and brought together by the sheer personal force of, so to speak, a hometown favorite.

This interpretation no doubt holds a certain validity considering the historic interaction of personalism and regionalism in the Peruvian body politic. However, it is far too facile and simplistic a theory to explain such a complex political movement. The main difficulty is that it ignores a fundamental political axiom—that political leaders do not act in a vacuum and, consequently, no matter what the extent of their charisma, these leaders must have at hand certain basic or "gut" issues with which they appeal to the people, if indeed they are to be successful. It is my contention that Haya, a man of brilliant intellect and consummate political skill as well as great charisma, was indeed of paramount importance to the rise of APRA, but not its raison d'être. His importance within the total spectrum of APRA lay in his genius for identifying and articulating certain solutions to basic problems, which in recent decades had become increasingly acute throughout the north-coast region. These problems revolved around the development in the north of a modern, export-oriented economic structure, dominated by a dynamic and rapidly expanding sugar industry. Haya, along with other fellow northerners, became the political spokesman for various segments of the population in that area who in one way or another were dislocated and frustrated by the rapid break-up of the traditional society. It is precisely these fundamental structural changes that at root created the Aprista movement and that explain the persistent phenomenon of "el sólido norte Aprista."

Sugar planting had been an economic mainstay of north-coast agrarian society ever since the Spaniards first settled Trujillo in the early sixteenth century. Over the centuries the industry underwent numerous changes and alterations that often affected the surrounding countryside. While technological innovations, as with the development of modern cultivation methods, occasionally spurred expansion and change, such other developments as the impact of the wars for independence or Ramón Castilla's manumission of Negro slaves (1854) had, from time to time, equally important, if not wholly salutary, effects upon the industry. In more recent times the agrarian upheavals occasioned by the War of the Pacific (1879-1883) inaugurated a period of intense and far-reaching change in the entire north-coast sugar complex. During the next several decades, as the region struggled to rebuild from the ravages of the war, the sugar industry, spurred by large infusions of foreign capital, entered a period of reorganization and modernization that radically recast the industry in a new, more up-to-date mold. The hallmark of this modernizing process was the general concentration of land throughout the north coast, as the modern, corporate, capital-intensive plantation gradually absorbed scores of relatively small, old-fashioned, and less efficient haciendas. Ultimately, it was the rise of the corporate estate that was to alter so radically the traditional fabric of the northern countryside.

The first crack in the old structure appeared within the ranks of the planter class, which had long dominated the social and political life of the region. Unable to compete with their more modern corporate rivals, the old planters gradually disappeared from the face of the land, their haciendas taken over and merged into the new industrial plantation. This group was followed in short order by the once prosperous and independent class of small farmers, who were likewise displaced from their lands by the expanding corporate estate. Even the urban commercial structure of the region was not spared the general disruptions of this new, dynamic force, as the corporate plantations extended the range of their activities into the commercial realm and ultimately displaced the area's old merchant class. At the same time as these fissures were occurring in the area's social structure, a new rural proletariat, composed largely of Indians from the nearby sierra, emerged on the new plantations. By the 1920's much of the north-coast society from Trujillo to Chiclayo only remotely resembled its former, prewar character.

At first these changes affected the area's population in what seemed to be a unique and personal manner. Each family, dislocated in one way or another by these changes, confronted *alone* the urgent need to find a new position in a suddenly altered and largely unpredictable world. As they sought to reconcile their new circumstances with old traditions, beliefs, and most importantly former expectations, they only encountered mounting frustrations and insecurities. In time these seemingly personal difficulties took the shape of class grievances, which were subsequently articulated by the group's more politically aware members, led by Haya but also including other able men, such as Antenor Orrego Espinoza, Carlos Manuel Cox, and the Spelucín brothers. By the 1920's the bare outlines of a new and unique political movement began to form in the north, a movement that was eventually to revolutionize the traditional cast of Peruvian politics.

While the popular base, leadership, and general frame of reference of the new Aprista movement focused largely in the north as a response to local conditions, the party's impact nevertheless reached out beyond its immediate geographical and historical confines. In fact the social and economic dislocations in the sugar belt that fueled the rise of APRA in the north were also being repeated at the same time in other areas of the country where economic modernization was likewise transforming and dislocating the traditional caste of society. These changes in the national economy, in turn, were part of a much wider process of economic transformation that saw the Peruvian economy, a potentially lucrative source of raw materials, pulled increasingly into the broader economic structure of the industrializing nations of Europe and the United States. In this wider context, involving essentially the revival of the old colonial-metropolis relationship of the past, foreign capital quickly became the motor force for converting the Peruvian economy into a modern, export-oriented capability. Indeed, the rapid increase in American capital, along with British investment, during the period 1895-1930 was no less than astonishing.

This infusion of foreign investment capital had the effect of slowly carving out pockets of economic modernization in various parts of the country. In addition to the sugar belt of the north, the mining district of the central sierra, the oil-producing area of Piura, the cotton-growing litoral of Ica, and, of course, the general manufacturing and trading sector of the capital all began, by the turn of the century, to stand out, in something of a patchwork design, on the Peruvian economic map. In isolated pockets of the central highlands, for example, the mining industry, in decadence for most of the nineteenth century, was rapidly revived and reorganized with American capital as the principal driving force. The most notable of the new mines was, of course, the huge copper complex that was opened up in 1903 by the American-owned Cerro de Pasco Mining Company. Likewise, in Piura and Ica similar developments soon occurred as oil and cotton production were modernized to meet growing international demand. A major magnet for the attraction of foreign investment at this time also proved to be the capital itself. Here, by the turn of the century, banking, insurance, food processing, textile manufacturing, certain light industries, and urban transportation and utility facilities were all beginning to dot the city's economic landscape. Accompanying these developments was the appearance of several large, foreign-dominated companies, such as Grace and Company and Gildemeister and Company, which not only provided a powerful stimulus for this economic change but also contributed toward the general disruption of the traditional economic structure.

The development of these pockets of economic modernization, with their tendency to create new economic and social relationships as well as to disrupt and destroy old patterns of life, served eventually to broaden the political appeal that APRA was first to make in the sugar belt of the north coast. Buffeted by the dislocative winds of rapid economic change, many would turn to APRA in an effort to protest against what seemed to them to be a suddenly topsy-turvy world. Indeed, the political rhetoric and program of APRA in the north proved to have broader meaning and applicability to Peruvians in widely divergent corners of the country.

At the same time the movement further extended its political focus by indirectly addressing itself to all those Peruvians of the middle and lower classes who harbored resentment against the existing system. Specifically demanding satisfactions for northern grievances, the party in a much broader sense awakened a national interest by loudly proclaiming that the time had come for similar meaningful structural reform throughout the country. In this vein APRA represented a new link in a long and distinguished chain of reform, which led back to Manuel González Prada, who, after the War of the Pacific, had so eloquently raised his voice against the corruptions and inadequacies of the system. Unlike previous efforts to reform the country, however, until the formation of APRA, no well-organized, mass political party had prior to 1931 dared to directly challenge and confront the traditional power structure. The year 1931, then, was in many respects a true watershed in Peruvian history, for from that date forward the *possibility* of translating individual or group dissatisfaction into political channels increasingly became a part of everyday Peruvian life.

For a number of reasons the Trujillo region, which embraces as one economic unit the Chicama and Santa Catalina valleys, was selected to test the geoeconomic hypothesis of the origins of APRA. First, the broad time period under examination, roughly from shortly before the War of the Pacific to the early 1930's, made it virtually impossible to include the

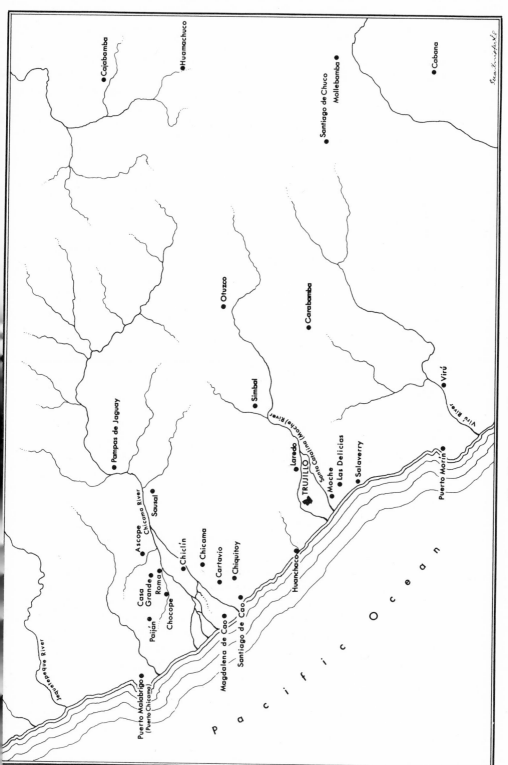

The Chicama and Santa Catalina valleys

entire north coast without sacrificing the detail that was deemed essential in making the study worthwhile. In addition, source material was much more readily available for these two valleys than for their counterparts in other parts of the coast. Most importantly, however, it was felt that what happened in the Chicama-Santa Catalina region, where over 60 percent of the sugar industry came to be concentrated, represented a microcosm of what transpired in other sugar-producing areas along the coast.

The Chicama Valley is located several miles north of Trujillo and agriculturally has always been considered the wealthiest valley of the entire north coast, if not all Peru. Watered by the Chicama River, which originates some one hundred miles due east in the high Andes, the valley is approximately thirty miles broad at its widest point and comprises some four hundred square miles, one-quarter of which is cultivated. Its ecological importance dates back to pre-Columbian times, when it was a major center of the Chimú civilization. Several towns dot the valley, including Ascope, Magdalena de Cao, Santiago de Cao, Chicama, and Malabrigo, several of which were the sites of former *comunidades indígenas*. Although at one time the inhabitants of the valley cultivated a wide range of food crops, in recent times the ecological balance of the valley has been sharply altered as sugar-cane production has come to dominate the economy of the area.

The Santa Catalina Valley, by comparison, is considered agriculturally less important than its adjacent counterpart and is smaller, occupying only about one-quarter of the land area of the Chicama Valley. However, the fact that the city of Trujillo, the capital of the department of La Libertad and at one time the second largest city in Peru, is located in the valley adds considerably to its economic importance. Like all of the river valleys of the coast, the Santa Catalina Valley is dominated by the river of the same name, which provides life-giving water for its agriculture. The valley has long ranked second of all the sugar-producing valleys of the country.

Since both the Chicama and Santa Catalina valleys have traditionally been considered among the richest agricultural areas in the nation, source materials for their study have not been lacking. Data for the economic development of the region, for example, were readily culled from a variety of sources, including accounts of travelers, agricultural journals, local newspapers, memoirs and writings of various planters, and numerous government reports. Moreover, as the sugar industry in the region developed and became the principal contributor to the export economy of the nation, greater attention, in the form of articles and monographs, was focused on the area by those interested in improving its productive capacity. Thus, the government as well as the area's sugar companies from time to time undertook exhaustive studies to determine ways of improving the agricultural yield of the valleys. Although many of these studies are concerned primarily with technological aspects of cane cultivation, they do, in the process of describing the region, shed considerable light on general economic and social conditions in the area. Probably the single most useful source on the changing economic environment of the region, however, was the archives of the Cámara de Comercio, Agricultura e Industria del Departamento de La Libertad. Located in the Chamber of Commerce offices in Trujillo, the archives yielded some seventeen bound volumes of correspondence, minutes, reports, and policy statements of the Chamber from 1904 to 1932.

As for the political aspects of the study, a large amount of material on the rise of APRA was located in both Lima and Trujillo. Since the party has traditionally been mass oriented, its leaders have taken care, over the years, to make available to the public the party's general aims and program. Aprista presses have, therefore, always turned out a wide variety of official literature, including newspapers, journals, books, documents, and other assorted campaign materials—most of which are still preserved in the National Library. In cases in which specific information was lacking, I resorted to personal interviews with party leaders who were active in the early days of the movement. Finally, an examination of the State Department Serial Files on Peru (1910-1937), which include the diplomatic dispatches of the American ambassador and embassy staff in Lima, proved most useful on matters relating to the election of 1931.

Despite the general availability of materials for the study, however, some research difficulties were encountered. First, Peruvians, at least since independence, have for a variety of reasons generally been a very unhistorically minded people. As a result, they have in many cases been notoriously lax in collecting, preserving, and cataloguing the documentary evidence of their history. Some sources, particularly those of government agencies, which might have been useful for this study have been either lost, destroyed, or so badly preserved that their use was impossible. This unfortunate situation has been further compounded by the fact that provincial archives, if they exist at all, are generally in a worse state of disrepair than those in the capital.

A second difficulty involved the inaccessibility of the archives of the major sugar plantations. This situation was due in large measure to the apprehension among company officials, in the main foreign, that the publication of historical data on these firms might provoke a serious political reaction in the country, thereby jeopardizing their future operations. Given the widespread, underlying hostilities against foreign interests in Peru by large segments of the population, this reluctance to allow researchers access to company files, at least prior to the present Velasco government, is perhaps understandable. Now that several of these companies have been nationalized by the new government, an effort has been made to make these archives available to the scholarly community. In fact, many of these documents have now been transported to Lima and deposited in the newly organized Center for Agrarian Documentation (Centro de documentación agraria). Despite some serious organizational and cataloguing shortcomings, several Peruvian and North American scholars are presently working in these sources, a fact that in time should considerably broaden and deepen our knowledge of the nation's agrarian history.

Finally, a search was made for any fictional works of the coastal sugar belt that might have illuminated some of the social processes dealt with in this study. Lamentably, only one was located, a series of short stories by an obscure Trujillo writer. There unfortunately does not exist the equivalent in Peruvian letters of a José María Arguedas, a Mario Vargas Llosa, or a Ciro Alegria for northern plantation society.

I should like to thank a number of Peruvians and Americans without whose generous assistance this book could never have been written. In this regard I wish first to express my sincere thanks to Félix Denegri Luna, who not only graciously allowed me the use of his formidable private library, but also extended to me his friendship, encouragement, and professional advice. My debt to him is indeed a large one. I am also grateful to a number of other Peruvians whose kindness and aid to me can never really be repaid. They include Ingeniero Carlos Moreyra Paz Soldán of Lima, don Carlos Orbegoso Barua of the Sociedad Nacional Agraria, Ingenieros Raúl Montesinos of the Instituto de Planificacion and Miguel Angel Castro of the FAO, Sta. Graciela Sánchez Cerro of the Biblioteca Nacional, Drs. Vicente Eduardo Rosell de Cárdenas and Víctor Cuadro Parodi of the Cámara de Comercio de La Libertad, Dr. Julio Gutiérrez Solari and don Jaime de Orbegoso of Trujillo, Leopoldo Pita V. of the Confederación de Trabajadores del Perú, ex-Senator Carlos Manuel Cox, ex-Deputy Luís Cáceres Aguilar, Sra. Carmela Spelucín de Orrego, and Dr. Jorge Basadre. A special word of thanks goes to don Víctor Raúl Haya de la

Torre, who, although he sometimes disagreed with my interpretations, patiently and graciously endured several hours of questioning.

Thanks also should go to Julio Cotler, Anibal Sánchez Reulet, Edward González, James Lockhart, Earl T. Glauert, Carl Solberg, Shane Hunt, Marysa Navarro, and Liisa North, all of whom read and criticized portions of the manuscript. Needless to say, any faults in fact or judgment are my sole responsibility and should not be attributed to those who have so generously given of their time and effort in criticizing the manuscript. In addition, I would like to acknowledge the Foreign Area Fellowship Program for its financial support at UCLA and in Peru, as well as Washington State University for providing me with a summer faculty research grant. Above all I owe a large debt of gratitude to Robert N. Burr for whose counsel and constant encouragement I shall always be grateful.

P.F.K.

Modernization, Dislocation, and Aprismo
Origins of the Peruvian Aprista Party, 1870-1932

1. The Modernization of the Sugar Industry and the Concentration of Land in the Chicama Valley

The early 1870's had been an unusually prosperous time for the twenty-five sugar planters of the rich and fertile Chicama Valley of northern Peru. Labor was cheap, credit was plentiful, the price of sugar on the world market was high, and the country, thanks to Ramón Castilla, no longer suffered from the endemic internal strife and civil war that had plagued the economic and political development of the nation since independence. Now, perhaps more than at any time since the early eighteenth century, the planter aristocracy of the valley—the Iturreguis, the Pinilloses, the Bracamontes, the Puentes, and the Orbegosos—were able to enjoy the seignorial life that had long been the ideal of Hispanic-Peruvian society. Like their landed counterparts in other regions of the country, they lived part of the year in their elegant town houses in Trujillo, sent their sons off to Lima or Europe to be educated, and sometimes traveled abroad themselves.

Some four decades later, however, almost all of these prominent planter families had disappeared from the valley. Gone were the splendid *casa haciendas* and ornate chapels that had dotted the valley for so many years. Gone, too, were the rolling pastures and multicolored meadows of rice, cotton, and alfalfa that had once intermingled with the patches of tall, green cane stalks. Now, from the foothills of the Andes to the very edges of the Pacific, all that greeted the visitor's eye was an immense, uninterrupted sea of cane and two jet black stacks that belched smoke into the brilliant, blue sky. Two giant, industrial sugar plantations now dominated the economic and social life of the valley. This virtual revolution in the agrarian structure of the valley, which saw land concentrate into a very few hands, began to unfold in the late 1870's, when a series of domestic and foreign disasters rocked the sugar planters of the north coast.

Until that unfortunate decade coastal agriculture had, ever since the mid-1850's, enjoyed a sharp resurgence from the chaotic and depressionary postindependence era.[1] Agrarian prosperity had been largely rekindled during these two decades as a result of both the agricultural policies of Ramón Castilla and the impact of the guano boom of the 1840's. Castilla took over the political reins of the country in 1854 and proceeded to impose peace and order in the countryside, a condition that had eluded the creole statesmen of the new nation ever since the disasters of the wars for independence. In addition, Castilla moved to finally free the coastal peasantry, a key element in the return of agrarian prosperity, from the colonial legacy of taxation, which, despite earlier efforts, had continued to weigh heavily on the Indian and mestizo sectors of the population.

More important for the resurgence of coastal agriculture during this period, however, was the guano boom of the 1840's and 1850's, which for the first time since independence produced large amounts of capital for reinvestment in the agrarian sector.[2] Profits from this "new industry" rapidly soared, enriching in the process the old creole families and parvenue landholders of the independence period—many of whom now turned to the problem of reorganizing and revitalizing coastal agriculture. As a result of these two developments, cotton and sugar cane, boosted by heavy

[1] For the main outlines of Peruvian agrarian development since the advent of the republic see Jean Piel's highly suggestive article, "The Place of the Peasantry in the National Life of Peru in the Nineteenth Century," *Past and Present*, no. 46 (February 1970), pp. 108-133.

[2] On the guano industry's capital contributions to the sugar industry, see also Jonathan V. Levin, *The Export Economies: Their Pattern of Development in Historical Perspective*, pp. 120-121.

foreign demand caused by the American Civil War, as well as staple production experienced a sharp resurgence during the 1850's and 1860's on the old coastal haciendas.[3] With the arrival of the 1870's, however, this cycle of agrarian expansion was suddenly cut short and a period of sharp contraction ensued.

The first blow to the new coastal prosperity occurred in 1875, when suddenly the guano boom collapsed. The revitalized sugar industry of the north, like other areas of the economy, immediately suffered a serious reversal. Deeply endebted to Lima banks and other financial institutions, the planters of the north coast quickly saw their recent profits evaporate under the impact of the immediate recall of outstanding loans.

As the economic crisis deepened, events abroad further complicated the planters' plight. After almost a decade of historic highs, the international price of sugar on the Liverpool exchange dropped sharply. Coming as it did on the heels of the loan recalls, the price decline plunged the industry into the throes of depression. When this setback was followed by a serious labor shortage occasioned by the closing of the Portuguese Far Eastern port of Macao, a major source of Chinese labor, many planters wondered if things could indeed get very much worse.[4]

The outbreak of the War of the Pacific in 1879 soon answered their question. Like other areas of the Peruvian economy, the industry was virtually paralyzed by the war. During its latter stages, the invading Chilean armies systematically razed large sugar-producing areas of the north coast. The Chicama Valley plantations not put to the torch were saved only by the herculean financial efforts of a few wealthy planters who paid large cash indemnities to the Chilean General Lynch.[5] By the time peace was finally restored in 1883, agriculture in the valley, as elsewhere along the coast, had been largely reduced to a subsistence level.[6]

---

[3] For a discussion of prosperity in the sugar industry during this period, see Federico Moreno, *Las irrigaciones de la costa*, pp. 4-5; Alejandro Garland, *Reseña industrial del Perú*, pp. 51-53; and "El azúcar peruano," *Informaciones Comerciales*, 2 parts, nos. 8-9 (August-September 1950), pp. 11-16, 8-17.

[4] Alejandro Garland, *La industria azucarera en el Perú*, pp. 12-13.

[5] For a good discussion of Lynch's march through the north, see Jorge Basadre, *Historia de la república del Perú*, V, 2475-2476 (hereafter cited as *Historia del Perú*). See also Emilio Romero, *Historia económica del Perú*, pp. 411-412; and Carlos Camino Calderón, *Tradiciones de Trujillo*, pp. 148-154.

[6] Sugar exports had dropped nationally from a peak of 80,000 tons in 1879 to a low of 34,478 in 1884 (Moreno, *Las irrigaciones*, p. 144, and Garland, *Reseña industrial*, pp. 51-53).

Recovery during the immediate postwar years was painfully slow. The lack of credit facilities, a severe shortage of braceros, and the need to rebuild and replace valuable machinery all posed difficult and often insurmountable problems to the planters of the valley. Moreover, the postwar years saw the price of sugar on the world market drop sharply once more, this time from thirty-six to eleven shillings the hundred pounds.[7]

Under these circumstances the valley's once proud and prosperous planters struggled vainly to rebuild. Yet, in all too many cases bankruptcy and foreclosures were the end result. One observer in the valley later wrote: "Very few were those who saved themselves from the shipwreck of bankruptcy and were able to conserve their lands. . . . The quickly made fortunes of the past decades disappeared as fast as they had been made while the once deafening roar of the numerous sugar mills in the valley was now replaced by silence. Bankruptcies became the order of the day as banks and other financial institutions took possession of the valley's plantations and mills, now in total decadence."[8]

As is sometimes the case in times of economic adversity, however, a few planters, all of foreign origins and relative newcomers to the valley, were able to profit from such dire conditions. Such was the case of the immigrant Larco brothers and a wealthy Lima financier named Juan Gildemeister, all of whom, shortly after the war, began to buy up the landholdings of the valley's bankrupt planters. By the late 1880's a marked trend toward foreign intrusion and land consolidation was clearly visible throughout the valley.

The Larco brothers, Andrés and Rafael, had arrived in Peru from Italy in the early 1850's. After apparently prospering in commercial endeavors in Lima, the two brothers moved to Trujillo in the late 1860's, planning to purchase lands in the adjacent Virú Valley in order to cultivate cotton. Subsequently, they bought the hacienda San Ildefonso, but soon found that the cotton business did not afford the same financial opportunities as did the now booming sugar industry. Thus, in 1872 the two brothers

---

[7] Basadre, *Historia del Perú*, VI, 2697.

[8] Raúl E. Haya, "Trujillo industrial de 1870 a 1920," *La Industria*, January 6, 1921, my translation. For a further discussion of this, see also Gustavo de la Torre, "Relación hecho el 23 de mayo de 1888 por el sub prefecto de Trujillo," May 23, 1888, p. 5, and "Memoria del prefecto del departamento de La Libertad" (Trujillo, 1898), pp. 13-14, in the manuscript collection of the Sala de Investigaciones de la Biblioteca Nacional del Perú.

rented the huge 1,250-fanegada (one fanegada = 1.59 acres) hacienda Chiquitoy, located in the Chicama Valley. Considerably expanding the 200 fanegadas that the previous renter had devoted to sugar cane, the Larcos quickly reaped large financial dividends, which they used in 1878 to buy the haciendas Tulape and Cepeda and to rent the *fundo* Mocollope, all in the Chicama Valley.[9]

Like other planters in the valley, the Larcos were economically jolted by the war and the subsequent drop in the world price of sugar in the immediate postwar years. Fortunately, the family had developed strong financial ties with the English commercial and banking house Graham, Rowe, and Company, which provided the necessary funds to weather the crisis.[10] Indeed, it was not long before the enterprising Larcos, backed financially by Graham, Rowe, were turning the crisis into personal advantage. Arguing that the only way to counteract the crisis of falling prices was to expand production as rapidly as possible,[11] Andrés Larco began to purchase adjacent plantations. During the next decade, the Larcos acquired or rented eight major haciendas, which were incorporated into the original plantation Roma. The new lands doubled the size of Roma (formerly Tulape and Cepeda) from two thousand to four thousand fanegadas.[12]

While Andrés Larco's plan to overcome the crisis of the early 1880's worked well for those, like himself, who were fortunate enough to be able to tap large reserves of credit and thereby expand operations, it was simply unrealistic for most of the remaining planters of the area. During the prewar sugar boom (1861-1875), they had been able to secure large loans from the guano-rich Peruvian banking houses with relatively little difficulty.[13] However, the end of the guano boom and the war had virtually

[9] Hermilio Valdizán, *Víctor Larco Herrera: El hombre, la obra*, pp. 16-22. Rafael took charge of the management of Chiquitoy, while Andrés administered Tulape and Cepeda, which he renamed Roma after the capital of his homeland (Santiago Vallejo, *Trujillo en estampas y anécdotas*, p. 173).

[10] Of Graham, Rowe, and Company's role in the fortunes of the Larcos, Rafael Larco Herrera, the son of Andrés's brother Rafael, wrote: "During more than fifty years, the respectable commercial firm Graham, Rowe, and Co. in Lima maintained close and cordial relations with the members of the Larco family, contributing . . . capital in moments of crisis and providing avenues of distribution for our sugar crops by way of their commercial establishments in Liverpool, Valparaiso, and New York" (*Veintisiete años de labor en Chiclín: Reminiscencias y apuntes*, p. 171).

[11] *Boletín de la Sociedad Nacional de Agricultura*, April 1900, pp. 369-373.

[12] Valdizán, *Víctor Larco Herrera*, pp. 23-24; see also Rafael Larco Herrera, *Memorias*, p. 12.

[13] Garland estimated that the total debt contracted by the sugar industry in Peru in

dried up all sources of national credit. The only other readily available capital to which planters might turn was held by foreign banking firms. Yet, in general, they were willing to extend credit only to those planters, like the Larcos, who had exhibited in the past the entrepreneurial and technological skills necessary for success in this increasingly sophisticated industry.[14] In the Chicama Valley, this lack of easily obtainable credit, which might have allowed the average planter to endure the crisis postwar years, played a key role in the concentration of the landholding structure that unfolded in the area in the late 1880's.[15]

While the Larcos were rapidly acquiring increasing predominance in the valley, the newcomer Juan Gildemeister was also beginning to make his presence felt. Born in Bremen, Germany, in 1823, Gildemeister migrated to Brazil as a merchant seaman in his early teens. In Rio he worked for a commercial establishment until accumulating enough cash to purchase a small 180-ton schooner, which he loaded with wood destined for market in Chile. Arriving at Valparaíso after what must have been a hazardous voyage around Cape Horn, the enterprising German sold his cargo and ship and headed for Peru. In Lima, after an unproductive trip to California during the gold rush, he established an importing business, which soon prospered. With the profits he accumulated over the years in imports, Gildemeister began to invest in the by now blossoming nitrate business in the south.[16] Temporarily ruined in his new endeavor by the disastrous earthquake and the tidal wave that destroyed much of his holdings in Iquique in 1868, the undaunted Gildemeister turned calamity into success by subsequently cornering the nitrate market through a remarkable financial maneuver.

Taking advantage of the fact that a submarine cable did not yet exist between the Pacific coast and New York, Gildemeister, in a splendid example of the financial ways of his age, hurriedly dispatched an agent to Hamburg to buy a large supply of nitrate on credit at the old rate. Arriving before the news of the disaster reached Europe, the agent succeeded in buying a huge quantity of nitrate before the price skyrocketed, thereby

---

1875 amounted to some thirty million soles (five million pounds sterling), which he felt was entirely too high (*La industria azucarera*, p. 12).

[14] Ibid., p. 13.

[15] For a valuable glimpse into the postwar state of the sugar industry in the Chicama Valley as well as the difficulties in obtaining credit, see *Exposición documentada, . . . de "El Cañal" . . . Pinillos*, pp. 5-6.

[16] Oscar Bermúdez, *Historia del salitre desde sus orígines hasta la guerra del Pacífico*, pp. 266-268.

remaking his fortune in its resale several days later.[17] By 1874 Gildemeister had reconstituted and expanded his nitrate business by buying out his competitors, who had gone bankrupt after the earthquake—a process he would soon repeat in the sugar industry in the north. Some years later, in 1889, foreseeing eventual hard times for the industry, he divested his entire holdings to an English firm for 1.2 million pounds sterling. A year earlier he had begun to acquire haciendas in the Chicama Valley.

Over the course of the next decade the firm Gildemeister y Cía, also known as the Sociedad Agrícola Casa Grande Ltda., bought various plantations in the valley, including Casa Grande, which became the center of its sugar operations. By the time of his death in 1898 ten years later, Gildemeister had acquired eight major sugar plantations and ranked as the second-largest landholder in the valley behind the Larco family. A year later the total assets of the company were valued at approximately 270,000 pounds sterling.[18]

In addition to the Larcos and the Gildemeisters, a third important landholding element, the Cartavio Sugar Company, arose in the valley in the 1890's. The basis of the company was the 910-fanegada hacienda Cartavio, which the powerful Lima commercial firm W. R. Grace and Company had acquired in 1882 in return for the cancellation of a debt owed the company by Cartavio's owner, one Guillermo Alzamora.[19] Apparently, Grace, whose major business interests at that time lay in commercial endeavors, did not decide what to do with the new property until nine years later when, with a capital of 200,000 pounds sterling, the Cartavio Sugar Company was formed to exploit the holdings as a subsidiary of Grace.[20]

The intrusion of foreign capital into the Chicama Valley was not an isolated phenomenon in Peru during this period. On the contrary, it marked the beginning of what was to become a veritable flood tide of investment into widespread areas of the country during the first decades of the twentieth century.[21] While foreigners, particularly the British, had

[17] Basadre, *Historia del Perú*, VII, 3202-3203; see also VIII, 3915-3916.
[18] Sociedad Agrícola Casa Grande, *Estatutos 1899*, p. 3. For a list of the haciendas purchased, see Carlos M. Alvarez Beltrán, *El problema social-económico en el valle de Chicama*, pp. 25-38. This is a useful though often incomplete historical survey of the landholding patterns in the Chicama Valley compiled from the records of the Registro de Propiedad Inmueble in Trujillo.
[19] Enrique Centurión Herrera, *El Perú en el mundo*, p. 410.
[20] Moreno, *Las irrigaciones*, pp. 137-138.
[21] Precise foreign investment statistics for the late nineteenth century in Peru, unfortunately, are unavailable. However, several sources, which focus on a later

long found Peru a fertile field for the implantation of investment capital,[22] the recent war-time destruction of the Peruvian economy, which
now opened the way toward more rapid economic modernization, as well
as the general outward thrust of European economic imperialism in the
latter part of the nineteenth century, substantially heightened foreign
interest in capital investment in Peru. Encouraged by the nation's political
leadership, this infusion of foreign capital flowed mainly into rebuilding
and modernizing the export sector of the economy, which, by the turn of
the century, was becoming increasingly connected to the European capitalist system. Even American investors, relative latecomers compared to their
British counterparts, were beginning to eye the future potential of the
Peruvian export economy. By 1897 American capital invested in Peru
stood at a modest 6 million dollars, a figure that would increase over
thirtyfold during the next three decades.[23] Thus, from the late 1880's
onward, foreign funds gravitated into such export-related areas as road and
rail building and port modernization, as well as directly into mining and
sugar and cotton production.

A major landmark in this investment process was the so-called Contrato
Grace, which was concluded in 1889 between the Peruvian government
and the nation's principal British creditors. According to this agreement,
Peru's foreign debt was totally refinanced in return for which the British
group assumed direct control and operation of the state railroad system. A
year later, the group formed the Peruvian Corporation Ltd., a holding
company charged with the task of operating the nation's railroads. In
effect, the Grace Contract set the stage for a large-scale expansion of
foreign investment in Peru over the next four decades while further linking
the nation's economy to Great Britain.[24]

Although reflective of foreign activity in Peru at this time, the appearance of these three new, foreign sugar producers—the Larcos, the Gildemeisters, and the Cartavio Sugar Company—in the Chicama Valley posed

---

period, indicate that substantial investment activity was already beginning to occur in
Peru at this time. See, for example, James C. Carey, *Peru and the United States,
1900-1962*, pp. 21-22. Also, Frederic M. Halsey, *Investments in Latin America and
the British West Indies*, p. 322; Max Winkler, *Investments of United States Capital in
Latin America*, p. 148; and Robert W. Dunn, *American Foreign Investments*, p. 82.
  [22] See Winkler, *Investments of United States Capital*, p. 146.
  [23] U.S. Congress, Senate Committee on Foreign Relations, *United States-Latin
American Relations*, p. 296.
  [24] Jesús Chavarría, "La desaparición del Perú colonial (1870-1919)," *Aportes*, no.
23 (January 1972), pp. 131-132.

difficult competitive problems for the area's few remaining planters who had somehow managed to survive the postwar years of crisis. Intent upon applying modern, capitalist techniques to a heretofore traditionally operated industry, the newcomers gradually, beginning in the 1890's, commenced to reorganize and modernize the entire process of sugar production. They introduced new growing techniques, imported the latest machinery from Europe and the United States, and arranged—through world-wide contacts—efficient and direct methods of distributing and selling their product. All this, of course, was made possible by the large reserves of foreign credit available to the new capitalists.[25] The upshot of these events was the development of a decidedly uneven economic struggle between the surviving "old-fashioned" planters in the valley and the more competitive, fast moving, and modern-oriented newcomers.

The older planters were severely handicapped in this struggle for survival by two factors, the aforementioned lack of readily available credit and a tradition-bound mentality, which eschewed modern, capitalist techniques. As a result, they continued to use antiquated machinery and old-fashioned production systems, which proved no match for their modern competitors. Recognizing the generally backward attitude of the majority of coastal planters, Alejandro Garland related the reactions of a visitor to Peru's north coast in 1894: "A few months ago a correspondent on assignment for the *Times* [of London] toured the Peruvian coast. In one of his subsequent articles the reporter expressed his complete surprise at the thoroughly backward state in which he found the area's sugar mills. He went on to say that these *ingenios*, except for a few, had not been altered in over 25 years, despite numerous innovations that had been made during this time in Europe. He concluded that the general agricultural progress realized in the last quarter century in other parts of the world has seemingly not reached Peru."[26] Another observer concurred in this assessment, adding that on the numerous small sugar plantations of the north coast administrative and productive procedures were appallingly inefficient and inadequate.[27]

While such backwardness contributed mightily to the eventual demise of

[25] Garland, *Reseña industrial*, pp. 51-53; also, Haya, "Trujillo industrial de 1870 a 1920."

[26] Garland, *La industria azucarera*, p. 36, my translation.

[27] Arthur R. Rosenfeld, *La industria azucarera del Perú*, pp. 11-12. Regarding the inability of the older planters to adapt to the new methods, see José Carlos Mariátegui, *Siete ensayos de interpretación de la realidad peruana*, p. 27.

the old planters in the valley, the prosperity of the 1890's momentarily slowed the tendency toward consolidation. The first major wave of concentration had occurred between the years 1885 and 1890, a period when the industry was still struggling to regain its prewar prosperity and many landowners were simply unable to survive.[28] When the industry finally entered a period of marked growth and prosperity beginning roughly around 1892, the consolidation process slowed down substantially, with no major property transfers occurring in the valley between 1895 and 1900.[29]

However, in keeping with its inherent oscillations, the industry was once again thrown into depression around the turn of the century due to world-wide overproduction, which sent sugar prices plunging. By 1902 prices on the Liverpool market had dropped from twelve to six shillings the hundred pounds (see Fig. 1).[30] As a result, a second and more pronounced cycle of bankruptcy and land consolidation was initiated all along the sugar-producing coast. The inefficient, traditional planters, now unable to turn a profit, were forced increasingly to sell to the new capitalists, who, desirous of accelerating production in order to offset the price decline, quickly bought up all available sugar haciendas.[31] In the Chicama Valley between the years 1900 and 1910, no less than fourteen large haciendas were acquired by the two emerging giants of the industry in the region—the Larco brothers and the Gildemeisters.[32]

[28] Alvarez Beltrán, *El problema social-económico*, pp. 25-38.

[29] Although sugar exports did not approach prewar levels until 1896, they did rise steadily after 1892, reaching a postwar peak in 1898 (Moreno, *Las irrigaciones*, p. 144). See also the export tables in Ministerio de Hacienda y Comercio, Dirección Nacional de Estadística, *Extracto estadístico del Perú, 1940*, pp. 308-309.

[30] "El azúcar peruano," no. 8, p. 14. The crisis of 1900 was caused by the following factors: "Competition of beet sugar, stimulated during the nineteenth century by nationalistic policies in many European countries, was felt keenly [in Peru] since it affected the price of cane sugar. Technical progress and protectionist legislation forced up the output with little interruption until, at the end of the century, two-thirds of the sugar consumed in the world was derived from beet and only one-third from cane. The price of sugar suffered a 50% drop in 1902 as compared with 1900, but it increased shortly after the International Conference of Brussels in 1902 which established to a certain extent a *modus vivendi* between beet and cane sugar producers" (Pan American Union, *The Peruvian Economy*, p. 68).

[31] Rosenfeld, *La industria azucarera*, pp. 11-12; also Haya, "Trujillo industrial de 1870 a 1920."

[32] Alvarez Beltrán, *El problema social-económico*, pp. 25-38; see also Table 1. This figure does not include the expansion of the Cartavio Sugar Company, for which data were unavailable. However, according to one source, Cartavio, too, around 1898, was beginning to buy additional haciendas in the valley (Santiago Rebaza Demóstenes,

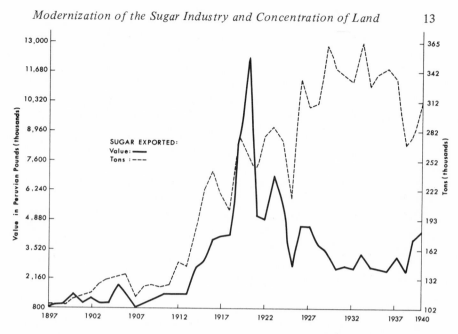

Fig. 1. Annual value and tonnage of Peruvian sugar exports
(Prepared from *Extracto Estadístico* pp. 308-309.)

During the prosperous 1890's the sugar interests of the Larco family had
continued to expand and thrive, though the family business had been split
into two branches in 1888. This division had resulted from the death of
Rafael in 1882. The final settlement of his legacy gave the hacienda Roma
to his brother Andrés, while the remaining holdings—the renting rights to
the hacienda Chiquitoy—went to Rafael's widow and six sons, who formed
the firm Viuda de Larco e Hijos. Rafael's oldest son, Víctor, assumed the
management of the new firm.[33]

Conferencia pública: La agricultura en el valle de Chicama, pp. 6-7). It should also be
pointed out that in addition to the crisis of 1900 the severe drought of 1906-1907
probably contributed substantially to the process of land concentration. Rafael Larco
Herrera stated that during this crisis he lost 38,000 pounds sterling and was himself
on the verge of bankruptcy. Other planters with fewer financial reserves than the
Larcos had were probably unable to survive this crisis and sold out (*Memorias*, p. 37).
[33] R. Larco Herrera, *Memorias*, p. 12, and Valdizán, *Víctor Larco Herrera*,
pp. 21-23.

The year 1901 marked a further turning point in the development of the family holdings. The firm Viuda de Larco e Hijos was liquidated in that year because of disputes over the operation of the business that had been smoldering for several years between Víctor, the firm's administrator, and Rafael, a younger brother who had been entrusted with the management of the hacienda Chiclín.[34] The ensuing settlement gave the renting rights of Chiquitoy to Víctor, while the haciendas Chiclín and Molino de Bracamonte went to the widow Larco and the remaining five children, with Rafael assuming the direction of the new firm.[35]

Later the same year the ambitious Víctor Larco Herrera purchased Roma from Andrés Larco, who had decided to retire. With the acquisition of Roma, which in land area alone totaled over 4,000 fanegadas, Víctor Larco unquestionably became the largest and, for the moment, most powerful landholder in the Chicama Valley. Over the next five years, aided by the depression in the sugar industry, which lasted until 1903, he increased the size of his domain by purchasing nine more haciendas from bankrupt planters.[36]

While Víctor Larco was busy constructing a virtual sugar empire in the valley, the Gildemeisters were beginning to encounter some temporary difficulties. Juan Gildemeister, the founder of the family fortune, died in 1898, leaving his sons to continue the family businesses. Unable to cope with the economic crisis of the turn of the century, Gildemeister's heirs called in a distant cousin, Enrique Gildemeister, to take over the management of Casa Grande. Don Enrique, a man of consummate business skill, subsequently corrected the financial ills that had been causing the trouble at Casa Grande,[37] and, beginning in 1903, he commenced to expand the plantation's operations by purchasing four large haciendas in the valley

[34] Carlos Larco Herrera, *Hacienda Chiclín: Transferencia indebida de una acción social*, p. 9. This legal tract gives valuable data on the rise and development of the Larco family holdings from 1888. The dispute between the two brothers, which was to grow with the years, was probably due primarily to personality differences. Víctor was gruff, impetuous, opinionated, and aggressive, while Rafael was more refined, polite, and well mannered, though a bit eccentric like his brother (interview with Ronald M. J. Gordon, a long-time official of the British Sugar Estates in Peru who was acquainted with the Larcos, Lima [San Isidro], April 14, 1967).

[35] Valdizán, *Víctor Larco Herrera*, pp. 23-24.

[36] See Vallejo, *Trujillo en estampas y anécdotas*, p. 182; also Alvarez Beltrán, *El problema social-económico*, pp. 25-38.

[37] Enrique Gildemeister had been born in Iquique, where his father, Juan Gildemeister's brother, had continued in the nitrate business (interview with Carlos Moreyra Paz Soldán, vice-president under Prado and former manager of the sugar plantation Santa Barbara, Lima [San Isidro], April 2, 1967).

over the next seven years.[38] During this period Casa Grande consolidated its position as the second-largest plantation in the valley.

Meanwhile, nationally, the first decade of the twentieth century witnessed a concerted effort by the country's remaining planters to modernize their operations. Forced to compete with an industry abroad that was rapidly becoming more efficient and technologically modern, the planters were increasingly anxious to find ways of improving their agricultural techniques. They took a giant step in this direction in 1901 by convincing the government of the efficacy of establishing a national school of agriculture. The founding of the new school in Lima the following year and also the establishment of a sugar experiment station near Lima in 1906 marked the beginning of a new era of technological innovation in the nation's agrarian export complex along the coast.[39]

Nowhere was this modernizing trend more clearly evident than in the Chicama Valley. The Larco brothers, who had traditionally been among the most progressive planters in the area, soon initiated a series of changes designed to improve overall operations. Rafael, for example, installed in 1907 a seventeen-kilometer railroad system at Chiclín so that cane could be more efficiently transported from field to sugar mill to port for export. Three years later he also hired several full-time agronomists, presumably graduates of the new school in Lima, to institute the latest production techniques at Chiclín.[40]

Likewise, the Gildemeisters moved during this period to modernize their operations. A major turn in this direction was taken in 1910, when the family merged with a large German syndicate. The German company provided the necessary funds for expansion and modernization while also sending a host of German technicians from Bremen to improve efficiency at Casa Grande. Among other things, they brought with them an enormous, modern sugar mill, which, when completely installed, processed some three thousand tons of sugar a day. The additional capital made available by the German firm also enabled Casa Grande to purchase more land in the valley.[41]

[38] Moreno, *Las irrigaciones*, pp. 137-138, and Alvarez Beltrán, *El problema social-económico*, pp. 25-38.

[39] Rosenfeld, *La industria azucarera*, p. 11; Garland, *Reseña industrial*, pp. 52-53; and H. C. Prinsen Geerligs, *The World's Cane Sugar Industry: Past and Present*, p. 271.

[40] R. Larco Herrera, *Memorias*, pp. 43-47.

[41] The sugar mill was so large that it took four years to install ("La gran industria azucarera del Perú," *La Industria*, August 7, 1915).

In a technological sense the industry in the valley as well as all along the coast was in an excellent position to exploit the new demands for sugar created by the advent of World War I. Like other Peruvian and Latin American raw-material producers, the sugar industry during the war years experienced a new era of boom. Sugar exports rose somewhat modestly in tonnage between 1914 and 1919 (176,670 to 272,099), but skyrocketed spectacularly in value during the same period (2.6 to 8.3 million Peruvian pounds) as the scarcity occasioned by the war caused prices to jump from ten to thirteen shillings in 1913 to the astronomical height of sixty-five in 1920 (see Fig. 1).[42]

During the war years the modernization process was accelerated. With more money now available for reinvestment in plant and equipment, the process of vertical integration, which had begun earlier, was virtually completed. Casa Grande even acquired from the government the rights in perpetuity of the port of Malabrigo in 1915 and proceeded to construct elaborate facilities to accelerate the export of its sugar. One observer commented: "The plantations are now complete units, that is to say, they produce their own cane, process it in their factories, and transport it by their own railroad or road system to their own ports for transhipment to market. They thus control the production of cane from planting to final sale abroad."[43]

The war years also witnessed the final demise of the smaller planters in the valley. By 1918 Casa Grande had absorbed some twenty-five haciendas and *fundos* totaling 7,216 fanegadas, making the German-Peruvian-owned plantation the largest in all of Peru. Likewise, Roma, owned by Víctor Larco, comprised some twenty-four units totaling 6,244 fanegadas (see Table 1). One final merger remained to be consummated, and this time it was between the two giants—Roma and Casa Grande.

Shortly after the end of World War I, Víctor Larco had begun to encounter financial difficulties. Like other planters who had profited from the war boom, Larco now had to assign a substantial percentage of his profits to amortize the large debts incurred by Graham, Rowe during the lean prewar years.[44] At the same time, pressured by growing labor unrest

[42] Ministerio de Hacienda y Comercio, *Extracto estadístico del Perú, 1940*, pp. 308-309. The European nations in 1912 accounted for 8.3 million of the 9 million tons of sugar produced in the world. During the war this production fell to 2.5 million tons, leaving a tremendous void that the world's other producers, like Peru, tried to fill ("El azúcar peruano," no. 8, p. 14).

[43] Gerardo Klinge, *La industria azucarera en el Perú*, p. 16, my translation; see also Basadre, *Historia del Perú*, VII, 3470.

[44] Alberto Salomón, *Peru: Potentialities of Economic Development*, p. 63.

Table 1. Concentration of Rural Property in the Chicama Valley

Fundo	Fanegadas ca. 1850	1918	1927
Sausal	528		
Gasnape	597		
Chicamita	380		
Cañal	140		
Pampas	194		
Santa Rosa	300		
Santa Clara	390		
Mocán	1,200		
Facalá	750		
Potrero	100		
Aljovín	50	Casa	
Casa Grande	250	Grande	
Lache	200	(7,216)	
La Viña	150		
Licapa	300		
Churín y Estancia	130		
Vizcaíno	160		
Mayal, Bazarrate, y Terraplán	80		
Chacarilla	8		
Cereaga	80		
Veracruz	80		
La Pampa	140		
Lucas González	40		
Ingenio Lazo	79		
Comunidad (Tierra de)	890		
			Casa Grande
Garrapón	80	I. Solís	(13,460)
Pampas de Ventura	100		
Tesoro	300		
Troche	100		
San José Bajo (I)	300		
Cepeda	120		
La Constancia	300		
El Porvenir	100		
Las Gavidias	160		
San José Alto	400		
La Libertad	90	Roma	
San José Bajo (II)	300	(6,244)	
La Victoria	11		
Roma (Tulape)	500		

(*Continued on p. 18*)

Table 1 (*continued*)

Fundo	Fanegadas ca. 1850	1918	1927
Bazán	360		
Montejo	150		
La Viñita	150		
La Comunidad (Ascope)	110		
Las Viudas	120		
Palmillo	180		
La Virgen	56		
Farias	100		
Tutumal	100		
Mocollope	1,510		
Molino Galindo	215		
Molino Larco	212		
Cajenleque	200		
La Fortuna	500		
Sintuco	300		
Cartavio	360		
Hacienda Arriba	116		Cartavio
Sonolipe	400		(2,206)
Cartavio Viejo, Yacutinamo, y Nepén	670		
Comunidad (Tierra de)	90		
Chiclín	670		
Molino de Bracamonte	120		
Salamanca	1,000		Chiclín
Toquen	45		(1,835)
Chiquitoy	1,250		

Source: Reprinted from *Tenencia de la tierra y desarrollo socio-económico del sector agrícola: Perú*, prepared by the Comité Interamericano de Desarrollo Agrícola (CIDA), Organization of American States, Washington, D.C. 20006.

that had culminated in several recent strikes throughout the valley, Larco decreed a general wage increase of some 33 percent for his labor force, something most planters elsewhere had resisted. A year later he traveled to Europe to purchase new equipment for his mill and aging rolling stock.[45]

[45] In order to finance these purchases, Larco contracted a series of loans, among them one for the huge sum of 2.5 million soles from the Banco del Perú y Londres (Comité Interamericano de Desarrollo Agrícola [CIDA], *Tenencia de la tierra y desarrollo socio-económico del sector agrícola: Perú*, pp. 20-21).

As events soon proved, Larco had chosen precisely the wrong time to undertake both of these moves, which greatly overextended his financial resources at a time when sugar prices were beginning to decline.

With the end of the war and gradual economic recovery of the European combatants, the production of sugar on the world market began once again to rise sharply. Sugar producers in Peru, as elsewhere, now found it necessary to readjust their production schedules to coincide with a reduced share of the world market. Total export sales plummeted radically from a historic high in 1920 of 12.5 million pounds to a more modest level of 4 million the following year (see Fig. 1).[46] Although the latter figure was still the third largest in Peruvian history, Larco's share was not enough to offset his recent expenses.

Realizing that he had overextended himself, Larco tried to remedy the situation by rescinding his earlier decree increasing wages. This move occurred exactly when the valley's sugar workers, feeling the pinch of postwar inflation, were beginning to organize into unions. The news of the wage reduction helped to further mobilize the discontented mass of sugar workers at Roma, acting as a catalyst for the new union. While Larco was returning with his newly purchased equipment from Europe in 1921, Roma was struck by a massive labor walkout, which completely crippled the production capacity of the plantation.

Larco, a stubborn and whimsical man,[47] who, like other planters in the valley, equated the rising labor movement with Socialism and the specter of the Russian Revolution,[48] reacted to the strike by first resorting to the use of force. When this tactic failed, the owner of Roma, rather than bargain with the strikers, decided to close down permanently the plantation's sugar mill, contracting with the Gildemeisters to process Roma cane in the mills of Casa Grande and dismissing the large number of mill workers on his own plantation. Even this move failed to put an end to the strike, however, and only succeeded in further strengthening the resolve of the strikers.[49]

[46] Ministerio de Hacienda y Comercio, *Extracto estadístico del Perú, 1940*, pp. 308-309.

[47] Larco at one time, in a peak of rage because his mechanics were unable to operate properly some new tractors that he had purchased at considerable expense, ordered the equipment hauled off to the docks of Huanchaco and dumped into the sea (conversations with Carlos Orbegoso Barua, Carlos Moreyra Paz Soldán, and Ronald M. J. Gordon—all of whom related the same story).

[48] Lauro A. Curletti, *El problema industrial en el valle de Chicama*, p. 16.

[49] The entire strike is discussed in Chapter 2.

The strike at Roma was finally broken in 1922 by the use of government troops, but the financial damage that it had caused Larco was considerable. Thus weakened, Larco was unable to weather a series of misfortunes that struck the entire sugar industry along the coast during the 1920's. Most damaging was the recuperation of the European beet sugar industry, which by 1925 was once more matching prewar output. Furthermore, the British government for the first time began to subsidize the creation of a domestic beet sugar industry. In a few short years, Britain, formerly Peru's major foreign sugar market, was producing some 500,000 tons of beet sugar annually while simultaneously erecting a high tariff to protect the infant industry. Finally, as if these events were not enough, much of Peru's sugar crop in La Libertad and Lambayeque was destroyed by the freakish, torrential rains that struck the north coast in the fall of 1926.[50] Larco, whose financial position had been debilitated with each succeeding misfortune, was finally bankrupted and forced to sell his entire holdings in 1927 to Casa Grande for some thirteen million Peruvian soles.[51]

The demise of Roma virtually completed the concentration of the main haciendas in the Chicama Valley. Of some twenty-two sugar mills that had existed in the valley prior to the War of the Pacific, only two were now operating (see Table 2). Casa Grande, which after the purchase of Roma owned approximately 13,460 fanegadas, now dominated the landholding structure of the valley. Only Rafael Larco at Chiclín (1,835 fanegadas) and the Grace interests at Cartavio (2,206 fanegadas) remained independent of the German-Peruvian firm (see Table 1).

[50] "El azúcar peruano," no. 8, p. 15; see also Jorge M. Zegarra, *Las lluvias y avenidas extraordinarias del verano de 1925 . . . Libertad*, pp. 29-34.

[51] CIDA, *Tenencia de la tierra*, pp. 20-21. According to the Peruvian historian Dr. Félix Denegri Luna, Larco by now was so heavily indebted, not only to Graham, Rowe but also to the powerful Banco del Perú y Londres, that the then president of Peru, Augusto B. Leguía, personally intervened in Larco's financial predicament. Leguía was understandably concerned that a Larco bankruptcy would seriously damage the government's credit rating abroad—a key factor in Leguía's blueprint for Peruvian development in the 1920's. In addition, Larco's precarious financial position threatened the already shaky foundations of the nation's most important industry. As a result, Leguía apparently put pressure on Agusto Gildemeister to accept the offer proposed by Larco to sell out to Casa Grande, at a sum no doubt considerably higher than the Gildemeisters would have liked to pay. Presumably, the owners of Casa Grande would have been more than content to wait for Larco's financial misfortunes to deteriorate further so that they could virtually dictate any eventual purchase terms (letter from Denegri, June 9, 1969).

Table 2. Major Sugar Mills in Peru ca. 1925

Mills	Location	Owners
Tumán	Chiclayo	Negociación Tumán (Pardo Bros.)
Pucalá	Chiclayo	Sociedad Agrícola Pucalá Ltda.
Patapo	Chiclayo	Compañía de Azúcar de Chiclayo
Pomalca	Chiclayo	Sociedad Agrícola Pomalca Ltda.
Almendral	Chiclayo	Alejandro Galloso
Cayaltí	Chiclayo	Negociación Agrícola Cayaltí y Talpo (Aspíllaga Hermanos)
Cavour	Pacasmayo	Luis Biffi
Buenos Aires	Pacasmayo	Juan V. Larrañaga
Casa Grande	Trujillo	Empresa Agrícola Chicama Ltda.
Cartavio	Trujillo	Cartavio Sugar Co. Ltd. (W. R. Grace & Co.)
Roma	Trujillo	Negociación Roma (Larco Herrera Hnos.)
Laredo	Trujillo	Negociación Laredo (J. Ignacio Chopitea)
Tambo Real	Chimbote	Sociedad Agrícola Tambo Real Ltda. (Thorne & Co.)
San Jacinto	Samanco	British Sugar Co. Ltd. (W. & J. Lockett)
Paramonga	Supe	Sociedad Agrícola Paramonga Ltda.
Huaito	Supe	Cañevaro & Co.
San Nicolás	Supe	Sociedad Agrícola San Nicolás
El Ingenio	Huacho	Santiago Fumigalli e Hijos
Ingenio Central de Huaura	Huacho	Ingenio Central Azucarero de Huaura
Andahuasi	Huacho	Andahuasi Estate Co. (Fraser Luckie & Co.)
Infantas	Lima	Sociedad Agrícola Infantas Candivilla
Chacra Cerro	Lima	Ernesto y Oscar Davescovi
Puente Piedra	Lima	Sociedad Agrícola Puente Piedra
Pro	Lima	Eulogio E. Fernandini
La Estrella	Lima	Pow Lung & Co. (Sociedad Industrial La Estrella)
Buen Pastor	Lima	Sociedad Agrícola San Agustin (Prado y Ugarteche)
Naranjal	Lima	Sociedad Agrícola Naranjal
Carapongo	Lima	Sociedad Agrícola Carapongo Ltda.
Monte Rico	Lima	Compañía Monte Rico Grande (César Soto & Co.)
Chuquitanta	Lima	Garcia & Hermano
Santa Bárbara, Cañete	Lima	Sociedad Agrícola Santa Bárbara
Pampa Blanca	Mollendo	Víctor F. Lira
Chucarapi	Mollendo	Carlos L. de Romaña

Source: William Edward Dunn, *Peru: A Commercial and Industrial Handbook*, p. 107.

This process of consolidation was largely rooted to a series of national and international events that radically altered the traditional man-land relationship of Peru's north coast. It began in the 1870's with the collapse of the guano boom, which, during the previous decade, had freed large amounts of loan capital for the development of the north-coast sugar industry. While planters struggled with the problems of the sharp credit restrictions that followed, the war with Chile erupted. The invading Chilean armies, reminiscent of Sherman's devastating march through the American South during the Civil War, put the torch to numerous plantations, bringing the industry to a complete standstill by 1882. The process of rebuilding during the postwar decades proved a herculean task for many planters. Credit was all but impossible to obtain, the world price of sugar turned down, labor was scarce if at all available, and, finally and most importantly, the character of the industry began to change. Abroad, mechanization along with the introduction of new methods and technology were already showing signs of the revolution that would shortly alter the entire face of the industry.

All these factors tended to produce a Darwinian-like process of the survival of the fittest among the beleaguered north-coast planters. Only the most resourceful and forward looking, such as the immigrant Larcos, were able to survive the crisis, and in their case it meant virtually mortgaging their holdings to foreign banks. Later Víctor Larco was, on more than one occasion, heard to curse the British banking firm Graham, Rowe, and Company for continuing to exact their "pound of financial flesh" long after the war years. Yet, unlike the other more tradition bound planters the Larcos had exhibited the aggressive, tough-minded entrepreneurial qualities that made them atuned to the changes in the industry abroad. Foreign credit institutions were willing to bankroll such men during the crisis, postwar years as well as later during the bad years when the industry suffered from the endemic, cyclical oscillations of the world market.

The Larcos, however, were by no means alone in proving a match for the traditional planter aristocracy of the region. Other wealthy newcomers in the person of the Gildemeisters and the Grace interests, sensing the entrepreneurial weaknesses of the older planters and the possibilities of profitably remaking the industry along modern lines, moved into the region. With large quantities of capital and technological know-how, they ultimately proved the downfall of the Pinillos, Iturreguis, Bracamontes, and other members of the old planter class who could not adjust to a fast-changing world. With their demise the social structure that had long prevailed in the Chicama Valley and that was characteristic of much of the north coast became a closed chapter in Peruvian history.[52]

[52] With some local variations, this same general pattern of modernization and consolidation occurred in the other major sugar valleys along the north coast from Lima to Chiclayo. (For a list of these plantations and their locations see Table 2.) For example, in the smaller, adjacent Santa Catalina Valley, José Ignacio Chopitea, beginning with the 200 fanegada hacienda Laredo in the 1880's, came to dominate the landholdings of the valley by 1921, having increased his holdings to some 1,300 fanegadas (see George Vanderghem et al., *Memorias presentadas al Ministerio de Fomento . . . república*, p. 92, and *El Perú centenario*, pp. 99-100). Similarly, in Lambayeque the Dall'Orzo and De la Piedra families vastly expanded and modernized their plantations at Tumán (3,733 hectares, ca. 1920) and Pomalca (880 fanegadas, ca. 1920), as did the Aspillaga Andersons at Cayaltí (3,750 hectares, ca. 1920); see particularly Carlos J. Backmann, *Departamento de Lambayeque*, pp. 140-209, which gives a wealth of valuable data on both the general agrarian structure and sugar industry of Lambayeque around 1920.

2. The Rise of a Rural Proletariat

While the growth of the sugar industry between the years 1870 and 1930 wrought profound changes in the landholding structure of the Chicama and Santa Catalina valleys, it also produced far-reaching alterations in the social fabric of society in this region. Responding to the critical shortage of labor needed to stoke the fires of the newly emerging sugar industry, the planters began, shortly after the War of the Pacific, to draw upon the heretofore neglected reserve of Indian labor in the northern sierra. By the late 1890's a steadily increasing stream of Indians was pouring into the region's sugar-producing valleys. Over the next several decades this migratory flow, periodically swelling to floodlike proportions or receding to a trickle, depending on the fortunes of the sugar industry, provided the basis for the emergence of a new rural proletariat in the north.

An adequate supply of labor had traditionally been a major problem for the region's sugar planters. At first largely dependent on Negro slaves, the planters had been forced to turn to the importation of Chinese coolies, particularly after Castilla's manumission decree of 1854.[1] Between 1850 and

[1] The majority of Chinese went to work on the cotton or sugar plantations, while the remainder were utilized in the guano industry or for the construction of railroads (Basadre, *Historia del Perú*, V, 2074-2075).

1874, some 87,247 Chinese were brought to Peru, with a large percentage assigned to work in the cane fields of the departments of Lima and La Libertad. Although this solution to the chronic scarcity of labor within the industry proved only moderately successful, a series of problems, not the least of which was an international incident over the treatment of coolies en route to Peru, cut short the utilization of this source of labor, particularly after 1876.[2]

With the gradual recuperation and subsequent expansion of the sugar industry after the War of the Pacific, the labor problem became increasingly critical. Gerardo Klinge, a prominent sugar planter in the early decades of the twentieth century, for example, wrote: "Labor was . . . at one time [after the War of the Pacific] the great problem of coastal agriculture. When the author was a boy, he heard this problem constantly discussed every-where—in the university, parliament, the national press, and wherever two hacendados or persons interested in national economic development came together."[3] Denied access to traditional foreign labor sources, many planters increasingly began to turn to the sierra Indian to meet their rising labor needs.

In both valleys there had always existed a small number of Indians and *cholos*,[4] who worked as braceros on the region's sugar plantations. Their numbers, however, up until the late 1890's were considerably reduced, a small minority compared to the large number of Chinese who had been brought decades before to work the department's sugar fields. Rafael Larco Herrera wrote that when he first went to work on the hacienda Chiquitoy in 1889 "the field tasks were done by a few Indian braceros and several hundred Chinese."[5] Another Liberteño of the period stated that as late as 1894 "the number of Indian peons who were brought to the coast, for the most part from Sihuas, Cabana, Chota,[6] and other areas of the sierra was still very small."[7] Evidently, after 1895, the number of Indian

[2] Watt Stewart, *Chinese Bondage in Peru: A History of the Chinese Coolie in Peru, 1849-1874*, pp. 48-53.

[3] Gerardo Klinge, *La industria azucarera en el Perú*, p. 14, my translation.

[4] The word *cholo* is used in Peru to describe a person whose racial background is either Indian or mestizo and who, by virtue of his having acquired the accouterments of Western-Hispanic culture, is considered to have attained a status in society higher than that of an Indian. The term generally conveys a degree of contempt or conde-scension. However, while readily employed as an insult, paradoxically, on a personal or an intimate level it can also be used as a term of affection or endearment.

[5] Rafael Larco Herrera, *La obra social de Chiclín*, p. 6, my translation.

[6] Towns in the Sierra of La Libertad.

[7] Santiago Vallejo, *Trujillo en estampas y anécdotas*, p. 177, my translation.

migrant workers to the coast rose sharply, for the Dutch agronomist George Vanderghem, who traveled along the north coast around the turn of the century, observed that the bulk of the sugar industry's labor force was composed of Indians from the sierra regions.[8]

To tap this large source of Indian labor in the highlands, the planters of La Libertad, as elsewhere along the coast, turned in the 1890's to the *enganche* system—a method of contracting indigenous labor first developed in the mining regions of Peru. In broad outlines this system worked in the following cruel, but efficient, manner.[9] Periodically, the planter approached the local *enganchador* or *contratista*, a sort of labor agent whose job was to provide the planter with an adequate supply of braceros. On informing him of the exact number of workers that he would need for the coming season, the planter forwarded the *enganchador* a substantial amount of money, usually in gold, which was to be used as an advance payment to the future bracero.

Next, either the *enganchador* himself or his agent, the *subenganchador*,

---

[8] George Vanderghem et al. *Memorias presentadas al Ministerio de Fomento . . . república*, p. 61. However, the appearance of numerous treatises urging greater utilization of the bracero from the sierra during the first decade of the twentieth century indicates that the planters' acceptance of this new source of labor was not as rapid as one might have expected. While repeatedly stressing the critical shortage of braceros during this period, the authors of these tracts often called for government action to alleviate the labor crisis. See, for example, the following: Sociedad Nacional Agraria, *Provisión de brazos para la agricultura*; Pelayo Puga, *Un proyecto de ley electoral: La falta de brazos para la agricultura de la costa del Perú*; Daniel V. Taboada, *La inmigración en la costa*; A. M. Rodríguez Dulanto, *El primer problema de la agricultura nacional*; and Carlos A. Atoche, "El problema de una escasez de brazos . . . en nuestros campos." Moreover, many planters continued to import foreign braceros, primarily Japanese, well into the twentieth century. Augusto B. Leguía, at the time manager of a large northern sugar plantation, imported, for example, some 790 Japanese braceros in 1898. Subsequent importations of Japanese occurred in 1900, 1903, 1906, and 1907. For a good discussion of Japanese immigration to Peru, see Toraje Irie, "History of Japanese Migration to Peru," *Hispanic American Historical Review* 31 (August 1951): 437-452. The slow acceptance of the highland Indians as a source of cheap labor may be in part explained by the facts that they were often struck down by illness after descending to the coast and that they usually wanted to return to their lands in the sierra after sixty or ninety days in the sugar fields.

[9] The following sources were used in explaining the *enganche* system: Felipe de Osma, *Informe sobre las huelgas del norte . . . Osma*, pp. 6-8, and Alberto Ulloa y Sotomayor, *La organización social y legal del trabajo en el Perú*, pp. 91-93, both of which deal specifically with the *enganche* and its workings in the Chicama Valley. More general references were taken from Francisco Mostajo, *Algunas ideas sobre la cuestión obrera: Contrato de enganche*, pp. 45-50; Moisés Poblete Troncoso, *Condiciones de vida y de trabajo de la población indígena del Perú*, pp. 80-90; and Hildebrando Castro Pozo, *Nuestra comunidad indígena*, pp. 117-124.

undertook the arduous journey to the highlands, visiting such provincial towns and villages as Huamachuco, Santiago de Chuco, Chota, and even Cajabamba, which was located in the southern sierra of Cajamarca. In each area he systematically made the rounds of the local *comunidades indígenas,* or Indian communities, where the prospective bracero lived and worked.[10] The *enganchador* usually took care to arrive either well before or shortly after the local harvest when the Indian would probably be free to migrate to the coast to work.[11] Using the gold as a lure, the *enganchador* then offered the prospect a job, painting the benefits to be gained, both pecuniary and otherwise, in the most attractive manner. The Indian, attracted by the immediate prospects of receiving a rather formidable sum of gold,[12] usually agreed to the offer and signed a contract, which in most cases he could not read. This contract ordinarily called for the Indian's services for a specified number of months, usually two or three, indicating specifically his obligations during this period.[13] After this time, according

[10] It was not uncommon for local authorities to aid the *enganchador* in rounding up prospective braceros, a service for which, of course, they were well paid. In some instances, the authorities themselves acted as *enganchadores,* delivering Indians within their jurisdictions to *hacendados* in need of braceros. Ulloa y Sotomayor reported: "It has not been many years since the subprefect of Luya was forced to release a bracero that he had bought for 200 soles and forceably taken to the hacienda Bagua Chica. It is by no means unusual that the authorities, in concert with the *gamonales,* personally take or send dozens or hundreds of Indians to *fundos,* where they are forced to work. In many cases, the unfortunate Indians are forced to abandon their lands in the process, leaving them undefended in the face of those anxious to grab them" (*La organización social y legal,* p. 93, my translation). For additional information on this aspect of the *enganche,* see also Pelayo Samanamud, "El contrato de enganche," *Revista Universitaria* 2 (1912): 62.

[11] Castro Pozo wrote: "In the north, October and November . . . are the months of liquidation and *enganche.* Since during this period the first rains begin to fall and the harvest is usually finished, the masculine population [of the *communidad*], which now has little to do, signs up for the *enganche* and heads for the mines or the coastal plantations. This migration generally occurs en masse with entire communities joining the *enganche.* Only the old people and a few children remain to prepare the fields for the spring planting" (*Nuestra comunidad indígena,* pp. 100-102, my translation).

[12] According to Vanderghem, the amount varied usually from 30 to 100 soles (*Memorias,* p. 58).

[13] The following, a copy of an *enganche* contract from Jauja in 1910, indicates the extent of the obligations undertaken unknowingly by the illiterate peasant: "Be it known by the present document that I ____ resident of the town of ____ and legally free to make any type of contract, receive to my satisfaction the sum of ____ soles from B. and A. Salazar as an advance payment to be canceled by my work on the hacienda ____ of the Chanchamayo Valley, obligating me to work ____ work days. I will honor the present contract and agree to pay back the advancement that I received as well as the *enganche* commission, which is paid at said hacienda, and any

to the contract, the bracero was free to leave the plantation, provided that all debts he may have contracted during his stay had been canceled. The latter provision very often proved devastating to the Indian's interest, for, once he accepted the amount of gold forwarded by the *enganchador*, he legally became indebted with little prospect, as will be seen, of immediately being able to pay off his original debt.

Several factors explain the Indian's willingness to accept what proved to be a blatantly unfair contract. Francisco Mostajo, who wrote his doctoral thesis on the *enganche* system in 1913, best summed up these factors in the following passage:

... generally the Indian from the sierra submits to the *enganche* in order to obtain a monetary advance so that he can satisfy his momentary necessities, without really concerning himself about what might come later. The money is used either for religious expenses, which for him means alcoholism, or for the interminable litigation to which he is often subjected or for the payment of debts which he has contracted on his property. At other times he agrees to the *enganche* in order to escape conscription, which is another plague for him. Rarely does he sign up for the laudable aim of getting money to improve his farm.[14]

Aided by the efficiency of the *enganche* system, the coastal sugar planter increasingly resorted to the use of Indian braceros to solve his labor problems. By the turn of the century the migratory stream of Indians from the highlands to the coast had swelled to the point where *La Industria*, the leading newspaper of the departmental capital, Trujillo, was calling on authorities to increase the size of the rural constabulary in order to ensure the maintenance of law and order among this new segment of the population. *La Industria* further reported that the *permanent* bracero population of the five major plantations in the Chicama Valley had reached an esti-

---

expenses and damages that may be incurred, for which I designate as co-signer ____ resident of the town of ____. We jointly agree to forfeit our present and future possessions, including all rights to our homes and whatever rights under the law we might be entitled to in any subsequent legal suit. So that this contract may be public, we sign jointly and *in solidum* before the following witnesses. Signatures of the labor contractor ____, subcontractor ____, contracting party ____, co-signer ____, and witnesses ____ " (from Dora Mayer de Zulen et al., *Conferencias pronunciades en el centro unión hijos de Cajacay—julio, 1914*, p. 6, my translation).

[14] Mostajo, *Algunas ideas sobre la cuestión obrera*, pp. 48-49, my translation.

mated one thousand, a figure that continued to rise steadily throughout the next decade.[15]

For the newcomer, plantation living and working conditions were harsh and oppressive, as might be expected. First, the *enganche* system continued to hold him tightly within its web. Upon his arrival on the plantation, the Indian soon found himself wholly responsible to the *enganchador* and had virtually no dealings with the planter. In essence, the *enganchador* acted as a third, independent party in the system. The planter paid the bracero through the *enganchador*, who collected a 20 to 30 percent fee on each salary while at the same time he controlled the worker's daily ration by receiving it directly from the planter for redistribution. Generally, the *enganchador* also obtained the right from the planter to establish on the plantation an *almacén* or *bodega*, a sort of general store, to sell goods, usually at inflated prices, to the bracero. By means of the *bodega* the *enganchador* was able to keep the bracero further entangled in a system of debt peonage.

The bracero was commonly paid by the *enganchador* in script valid only at his store.[16] During the first few weeks of the bracero's employment, the *enganchador* readily sold him goods on credit. Once the bracero received his first wage payment, in script, he found that at the *enganchador's* shop, where inflated prices prevailed, it was barely enough to purchase the following week's provisions. Having spent the advancement paid him upon signing the contract in the highlands, the bracero now discovered that by week's end he had nothing left from his wages to pay off his initial debt. Moreover, the *enganchador* predictably charged a high interest rate for both the original gold payment and his credit accounts at the store, so as time progressed the bracero often sank further into debt. Since his contract specified that he could not abandon his work after termination of the agreed-upon period unless all his debts were canceled, the bracero was thus frequently forced to continue working on the plantation indefinitely or at least until he could pay off his debts.

[15] *La Industria*, April 3, 1900.
[16] Often part of the salary was paid in coca or alcohol (Poblete Troncoso, *Condiciones de vida y de trabajo*, pp. 84-85). Partial payment in rum was apparently quite common on several coastal sugar plantations, since the *enganchador* received from the planter large amounts of molasses, which he converted into the beverage (Víctor Marie, "La agricultura y la economía rural—valle de Chicama: Memoria presentada al Ministerio de Fomento," *Boletín Agrícola*, nos. 10-11 [April-May 1905], pp. 282-283).

In order to further ensure that the bracero was caught in the *engan-chador*'s net he was also prohibited from leaving the hacienda to buy from shops in nearby villages. In this way he was forced to buy exclusively from the *enganchador*, who was thus able to perpetrate all kinds of unfair practices on his captive clientele. For example, the *enganchador* usually stocked inferior, low-quality goods, often rejects from nearby retail shops in adjacent towns. Another common practice was for the *enganchador* to limit the length of time his script money was valid for redemption in his store. Thus, the bracero was forced to purchase goods unnecessarily so as not to lose a portion of his wages through the expiration of the script.

The general conditions under which the bracero labored, like the *enganche* system, were just as oppressive. Writing after his extensive tour of the Chicama Valley in 1902, Vanderghem painted a bleak picture of plantation realities for the recently arrived bracero:

They work by the hour from 6 A.M. to 6 P.M., with a short interval for rest at 11 A.M. However, it is more common for them to be assigned a fixed amount of work or *tarea* to be finished in the space of one day. . . . The peons are paid approximately 50 centavos a day or by *tarea* and they are given in addition their room and board. The latter generally consists of 1/2 pound of meat, 1 1/2 pounds of rice, and an ounce of salt. The *enganchador*, in this system, earns a commission which varies from 15-20% of the total number of *tareas* . . . done.[17]

In addition to the long hours, low wages, and abuses of the *enganchador*, the lot of the bracero was further aggravated by his propensity to contract malaria and other serious "coastal" illnesses. Having inherited no defenses against tropical diseases after living his entire life in the healthy, cool climate of the sierra, the bracero—once at sea level—easily fell victim to malaria, which was most common in the hot, humid valleys of the coast. Probably the first major malaria epidemic to affect the recently migrated *serranos* in large numbers occurred in 1897. The outbreak was first reported in the province of Zaña in the department of Lambayeque, where the large sugar hacienda Cayaltí was located. From there it spread as far south as the Chicama Valley as braceros, desperately trying to escape from the dreaded disease, carried the germ to other nearby areas. With medical facilities on most sugar haciendas around the turn of the

---

[17] Vanderghem, *Memorias*, pp. 58-59, my translation.

century practically nonexistent, the disease decimated the ranks of the region's sugar workers.[18]

While the Indian migrant found the new coastal environment fraught with dangers and difficulties unknown in the highlands, he also began to experience changes in his traditional life style. Exposed to a radically different cultural milieu on the coast, he soon began to undergo in varying degrees the process of acculturation to coastal, creole society. Outwardly the manifestations of these changes were sometimes striking. Spanish words and phrases picked up from overseers or the local *bodeguero* gradually began to creep into his lexicon until ultimately he approached a bilingual state. Rice soon replaced the traditional corn as the central component of his diet. *Cañazo*, not totally unknown or alien to his taste, became increasingly pleasurable, until it vied with the traditional *chicha* as the Indian's favorite alcoholic beverage. As the process accelerated, differences in clothing could be noted, the traditional seventeenth-century Spanish pants giving way to the more modern Western style trousers commonly worn on the coast.

For those who stayed for longer periods on the plantation, unable or unwilling to return to the sierra, the outward manifestations of acculturation were accompanied by subtle changes in attitudes and general world view. Visits to the wonders of the nearby Trujillo market on a lazy Sunday afternoon, accompanied by a co-worker who himself had already become experienced in such matters, opened up a whole new world and social order to the newcomer, a world in which people lived and interacted according to very different patterns and mores. Indeed, it was not long before the outlines of a wider entity known as Peru with its capital in Lima became visible. A myriad of new modes of behavior and thought bombarded the consciousness of the Indian migrant, and, as he gradually absorbed them into his life style, he changed from Indian to *cholo*.

Not that he openly embraced the new culture without hesitation and some reluctance. The conservative nature and general resistance to change on the part of peasants the world over is a well-known fact. The *serrano's*

---

[18] Previous epidemics of malaria, such as the one in 1888-89, struck down the more numerous Chinese braceros, who composed the majority of the sugar work force in those days (Sociedad Nacional Agraria, *Provisión de brazos*, p. 50). The Sociedad itself criticized the living and working conditions to which its member sugar planters subjected their workers.

original idea had been to migrate temporarily to the coast, where plantation work would give him a chance to pick up his sagging fortunes or the
monetary where-with-all to rescue his land from the clutches of unscrupulous landgrabbers. Under these circumstances there was certainly no
pressing urgency to adapt and conform to his new surroundings, although
some degree of change was likely to occur. However, as his dream of
immediate return to the sierra faded under the harsh reality of the
enganche system, the need to belong and adapt to the new culture became
stronger. The traditional Indian suspicion of and resistance to the new now
gave way to an open willingness, often driven by the sheer desire for
survival, to adopt the local patterns of life.

While by no means all of the Indian migrants and probably only a
relatively small proportion underwent total acculturation, as time went on
their numbers on the region's plantations steadily grew, particularly as a
permanent work force came into existence. More open to the currents of
change blowing in the world outside the plantation, the acculturated element of the work force began to respond to the calls of a few for changes
in the oppressive work regimen and general living conditions on the plantations. In time this new development would lead to the formation of labor
unions, which would serve as the principal vehicles for achieving a more
equitable work system. However, while the character of the labor force
remained, for the moment at least, culturally Indian, the response of the
braceros to the exploitative conditions under which they were forced to
live and work varied between long periods of passivity punctured suddenly
by spontaneous outbreaks of violence and bloodshed.

As the first decade of the twentieth century drew to a close, the growing
concentration of sugar braceros, coupled with the oppressive circumstances to which they were subjected, did begin to create optimum conditions for the outbreak of labor unrest in the region. Although sporadic
labor troubles had traditionally been a part of life in the valley, the first
widespread and serious disturbances of this century occurred in the year
1910 and multiplied with increasing frequency during the next few years.

None of these early disturbances were strikes in the modern sense. With
labor unions and even mutual societies still unknown in the valley, these
outbreaks were generally spontaneous eruptions of violence, devoid of any
extensive planning or organization. Usually they were quite short and were
characterized by a period of violence that quickly "burned itself out."
Joaquín Díaz Ahumada, one of the first labor organizers in the valley and

witness as a boy to many of these early explosions of violence, described them in the following manner:

There were cases, for example, when only a partial walkout occurred, usually in protest against the size of the *tarea* or the abuses of the *mayordomo*. When this happened the workers threw down their tools, sometimes physically attacked the *mayordomo*, and returned to their houses. Often, however, because of the partial nature of the walkout, the *patrón* was able to break it by having the ringleaders arrested and jailed or expelled from the plantation. But in the case of a massive walkout, things were different. The peons abandoned their labors in the field and returned en masse to the hacienda shouting, "Viva la huelga." Running through the streets of the living quarters with their machetes waving and lamps held high, they shouted threats against the *patrón* and the employees who had committed the abuses against them. For the moment masters of the situation and thoroughly agitated, they would head for the *almacenes*, or bazaars, of the hacienda ... which they would sack and then set on fire. Once these acts of destruction had been accomplished, the strikers generally would get drunk without even attempting to present their demands to the *patrón*.[19]

It is important to note here that the type of labor unrest described by Ahumada was typical in the sierra, where there existed large concentrations of Indians on haciendas and in mining enclaves, a fact that points up the largely Indian character of the plantation work force on the coast at this time.

An example of this early type of labor trouble in the Chicama Valley and probably the most serious outbreak of labor violence in the history of the country occurred in 1912.[20] The disturbances erupted with a fury on the morning of April 8 on the German-Peruvian owned plantation Casa Grande, which had become one of the largest industrial centers in Peru, employing between four and five thousand workers. Angry at a company

[19] Joaquín Díaz Ahumada, *Historia de las luchas sindicales en el valle de Chicama*, p. 17, my translation.

[20] The labor trouble in the Chicama Valley invariably spilled over into the adjacent Santa Catalina Valley, usually engulfing the hacienda Laredo. The following account of the strike was taken from the Trujillo daily *La Industria*, April 9 to April 26, 1912. Editorially, the paper took a moderate position regarding the outbreak, supporting the demands of the strikers and criticizing working conditions on the valley's plantations while condemning the violence to which the braceros resorted.

order increasing the size of the *tarea*[21] and demanding an increase in daily wages from fifty to sixty centavos, the largely unorganized workers exploded into an orgy of violence. While some braceros set fire to the ripening cane fields, others directed their wrath against the hated *enganchador*, looting and then burning the plantation's major *bodegas*. Special care was taken to destroy the *enganchador*'s credit records, which effectively kept the braceros shackled in debt peonage. By the end of the first day of rioting, several persons had been killed, and the rural troops that had been called in to restore order had been put to flight.

Over the next few days the violence spread to adjoining plantations until the entire Chicama Valley was aflame. A major confrontation between strikers and the authorities soon occurred when some sixty heavily armed troops from the region's Cuartel no. 7 met several thousand angry, machete-wielding braceros on the hacienda Sausal, an annex of Casa Grande. Opening fire on the approaching bracero mass at a range of 150 feet, the troops killed some fifteen but failed to stem the attack and were forced to abandon the hacienda, leaving it to the complete mercy of the rioters. Subsequently, the *casa hacienda* was looted and burned.

Similar scenes were repeated on the other large plantations in the region, such as Chiquitoy, Cartavio, and Laredo, forcing the evacuation of technicians and managers. By the seventh day of disorders considerable concern began to be manifested among city officials and merchants in Trujillo lest the rioting braceros march on the city, which was virtually unprotected. On the morning of the fourteenth, a meeting of the city's hierarchy was held in the Prefecture to discuss the formation of a *guardia urbana* designed to defend the city against any mass invasion of braceros. Although it was later decided that such a force would not be necessary, since a large detachment of troops was en route to Trujillo from Lima, most merchants suspended business operations and bolted their doors.

The following day a cruiser arrived at the port of Salaverry and some three hundred troops and artillery pieces destined for the valley were disembarked. Meanwhile, in Trujillo several arrests were made for allegedly "inciting disorder" among the braceros, including the respected Benjamín Pérez Treviño, editor of the liberal daily *La Razón*, who was charged with contributing to the disorders by publishing "inflamatory statements" regarding the strike. Actually Pérez had been arrested for thoroughly

---

[21] A predetermined amount of land that the bracero was assigned to work on a piece-work basis.

castigating the heavy-handed tactics of city officials and the planters, whom he charged had completely mishandled the disorders from their inception.

Once the large numbers of government troops arrived at the valley's major trouble centers and repressive tactics were instituted, the disturbances were quickly suppressed. Gradually, order was restored and a relative calm returned to the valley. Final estimates of casualties and damages caused by the violence were extremely high. Although the government *informe* published later conspicuously made no mention of either, a private report issued by the Pro Indian Society stated that at least 150 strikers had been killed and many more wounded.[22]

Probably the most reliable report on the strike, it cited low wages, the abuses of the *enganche* system, wretched living conditions, and long working hours as being the principal reasons for the outbreak of violence. Indeed, according to the report's author, the longstanding existence of these conditions had made the day when large-scale rioting would erupt in the region inevitable.[23] Another fundamental cause for the disturbances was to be found in the mounting tensions between Peruvian and German employees at Casa Grande months before the fatal outbreak. Earlier in the year a new German administrator had arrived at the plantation along with several German technicians. Evidently the new administrator began immediately to institute reforms in the management of the plantation, changes that were not well received by some of the company's Peruvian employees. Tensions intensified when the new management dismissed several of the disgruntled Peruvians, replacing them with some of the newly arrived Germans. Several incidents were soon reported of clashes between Peruvian employees and their German superiors. At about this time it was also decided to introduce certain "economies" into the plantation's operations, including an increase in the size of the *tarea*—a move that alienated the large number of cane cutters employed by the planta-

[22] For the government account, see Osma, *Informe que sobre las huelgas.* Rómulo Cuneo Vidal, *La huelga de Chicama: Informe aprobada por la Sociedad Pro Indígena sobre los sucesos de Chicama y las medidas que deben ponerles repara*; also appeared in *La Prensa*, October 10, 1912.

[23] Cuneo Vidal, *La huelga de Chicama.* Osma, in his official report, placed almost the entire blame for the strike on the *enganchador* and virtually absolved the planters themselves of any wrong. He went to some lengths to show that the braceros were making satisfactory wages and living under reasonable conditions, facts that both *La Industria* and the Cuneo Vidal report denied. *La Industria*, however, does place considerable fault for the strike on the abuses of the *enganche* system.

tion. Thus, when another incident occurred between Peruvian and German, the tinderbox atmosphere that reigned at Casa Grande exploded into a violent wave of rioting.[24]

These immediate causes for friction were probably further exacerbated by certain underlying tensions characteristic of plantation societies. Eric Wolf and Sidney Mintz, both of whom have extensively studied the social dynamics of plantation life in the tropics, have suggested that conflict is very common in the corporate plantation between the dominant, foreign-born technical and managerial staff and the native work force. Usually the former views local problems in terms of outside interests rather than in the context of the local environment and tends toward what they call in-group cohesion and group self-consciousness. The foreign technicians, the authors contend, identify strongly with the parent country and often view themselves as intellectually and racially superior to the native work force. This attitude generally leads to a polarization between the two groups, one foreign and the other native, that focuses on nationalist or racialist sentiments.[25] No doubt these factors played an overriding role in the violent outbreak at Casa Grande and later at the other foreign-owned plantations in the region.

After the reestablishment of peace in the valley, some attempts were made by the planters to correct the conditions that had caused the strike. Some planters, convinced that the abuses of the *enganchador* had indeed played a key role in precipitating the disturbances, proceeded to take the advice of the government report, which called for his elimination and the institution of direct dealings between planter and bracero. In addition, the owners of Casa Grande began to consider the idea of directly importing its own goods and establishing company stores that would sell to the bracero at lower prices.

Despite these seeming improvements, however, general conditions on the valley's plantations remained much the same as before the strike. Indeed, on some matters a hardening of attitudes on the part of the planters toward the braceros seemed clearly visible. Reports appeared in the local press, for example, calling for an increase in the number of rural troops stationed at Chocope and elsewhere throughout the valley in order, it was said, to "prevent" such disturbances from erupting in the future. More-

[24] See Rafael Larco Herrera, *Memorias*, pp. 59-60; Cuneo Vidal, *La huelga de Chicama*; and *La Industria*, April 8, 1912.
[25] Eric R. Wolf and Sidney Mintz, "Haciendas and Plantations in Middle America and the Antilles," *Social and Economic Studies* 6, no. 3 (1957): 406.

over, the previously moderate daily *La Industria*, which had traditionally tended to reflect planter opinion, increasingly took a harder line on questions relating to the labor problem.[26]

While planter attitudes tended to "harden" on most labor issues after 1912, another and potentially more disruptive factor was appearing in the already explosive labor scene of the region. By the second decade of the century the process of cultural *mestizaje*, long at work on the area's plantations, was beginning to substantially transform the traditional Indian cast of the work force. Large elements of this work force, particularly at the upper levels of skilled and semiskilled workers but also at the bracero level, were now largely composed of *cholos*. No longer passive or submissive to what they considered injustices in the plantation regimen, they were more than willing to challenge and attempt to change the existing order of things, something they or their fathers decades earlier had never risked doing. Breaking down the resistance of the older workers and the remaining Indian element of the work force, the *cholos*, located principally in the plantation work shops and factories, began to organize small *gremios*, or guilds, on the region's plantations and to declare limited work stoppages in support of their demands. Although these efforts, generally isolated and lacking in any widespread adhesion, were rarely successful, they did represent the first embryos of organized labor in the valley.

It was not until the full effects of World War I had been felt in the valley, however, that modern unions began to take shape.[27] The outbreak of war in Europe signaled the commencement of an economic boom for the export-oriented economy of Peru, as elsewhere in Latin America. Among the main national recipients of this bonanza was the sugar industry, which during the next few years expanded production and reaped profits in an astonishing manner.[28] Responding to such favorable conditions, landowners throughout the country plowed up acreage formerly devoted to the production of staples and substituted such high-value cash crops as sugar or cotton. The upshot of this trend was a subsequent scarcity of staples, which caused food prices throughout the country to climb sharply. During the period 1913 to 1920 food prices more than doubled.

[26] In later years labor violence in the valley was given minimal and usually biased coverage by the newspaper. Editorials invariably supported the position of the planters.

[27] Díaz Ahumada, *Historia de las luchas sindicales*, p. 21.

[28] See the previous chapter dealing with the rise of the sugar industry. For the general effects of the war on the Peruvian economy, see Hernando Lavalle, *La gran guerra y el organismo económico nacional*.

Particularly hard hit by this rising cost of living were the Peruvian laboring classes, which did not receive a compensating increase in wages during this period.[29] Such conditions ultimately fueled the discontent of not only Peru's emerging urban working classes,[30] but also the salaried sugar workers of the north coast.

Although wages on the valley's main plantations increased some 40 percent during the war years, such boosts were insufficient to keep pace with the rapidly climbing costs of living.[31] By 1917 a rising tide of discontent among the sugar workers began to sweep through the valley. Attempts to harness this discontent through the further organization of labor on the plantations now met with more success than previously. Again the skilled workers of the *talleres*, or work shops, led efforts to organize *gremios*, and a series of strikes were called on the valley's large haciendas. However, most of these *gremios*, like their predecessors, tended to break up and disappear after the strikes had terminated and a settlement had been reached. Apparently, only one such organization survived, becoming the first permanent labor organization established on the valley's plantations. The founder was a mechanic named Eduardo Chávez Terrazas, a fiery young radical who only shortly before had gone to work in the shops of the plantation Cartavio. Chávez, who evidently had gained some knowledge of labor organization while working in Trujillo, quickly set up the Sociedad de Auxilios Mutuos y Caja de Ahorros de Cartavio (Mutual Aid and Savings Society of Cartavio) and led a work stoppage that succeeded in obtaining the eight-hour work day among the plantation's shop and factory workers, the first such victory in the valley.[32]

It was not until two years later, however, when labor agitation erupted once again, that labor organization made further progress in the valley. This new outbreak of trouble was due to two fundamental causes. First, as the European combatants began to recover from the effects of the war and the world sugar production gradually began to augment, the price of sugar on the world market dropped sharply, forcing the valley's planters to

[29] Polete Troncoso, *Condiciones de vida y de trabajo*, p. 114.

[30] See Basadre, *Historia del Perú*, VIII, 3904-3908.

[31] See the following chapter, which deals with the effects of the process of land concentration upon the small landholding structure in the Chicama Valley and how this affected staple production in the region.

[32] Díaz Ahumada, *Historia de las luchas sindicales*, pp. 24-27. Also interview with Leopoldo Pita Verdi, an early labor organizer in the Chicama Valley and now an official of the Confederación de Trabajadores del Perú (CTP), in Lima, March 21, 1967.

readjust their production schedules and cut down on costs. In an effort to accomplish the latter, many planters either "froze" or lowered wages, a move that—coupled with the steadily rising cost of living—made the position of the sugar workers untenable. Second, Peru was beginning to receive some of the ideological currents sweeping across Europe by the close of the war. These ideas, arriving first in Lima, quickly filtered out to the provinces, where their impact, as in the capital, was considerable among elements of the discontented middle and lower classes.

By 1921 the Chicama Valley had become a veritable hotbed of discontent. Periodic strikes and outbreaks of violence had been constant occurrences since the end of the war,[33] and attempts to organize were gradually gaining ground. Until 1921, however, organizing activities had been generally confined to the class of semiskilled and skilled workers who labored in the shops and factories of the plantation. Deciding that the time was ripe to organize all types of plantation employees—office clerks, plant workers, and braceros—into one single union, two youthful mechanics on the hacienda Roma, Joaquín Díaz Ahumada and Artemio Zavala, began in early 1921 to lay plans for the creation of a general *sindicato* at Roma.[34]

Díaz and Zavala had become acquainted while working in the work shops of Roma. Díaz gives the following account of their growing sense of social consciousness and adhesion to the labor movement:

At that time I lived on the hacienda Roma with a work partner named Artemio Zavala, a *muchacho* from Santiago de Chuco who was the same age, twenty-three, as myself. For reasons of work we had become good friends and used to get together often to read about and discuss the labor movement and Socialism generally. . . . In our eagerness to know more about the labor agitations and revolutionary socialism which were then sweeping the world, we bought books written by socialists like Lenin, Trotski, Malatesta, Kropotkine, Gorki, Marx, Vasconcelos, Palacios, etc. We read with great desire once our interest and concern for the new revolutionary ideals was awakened.[35]

Since both Díaz and Zavala knew very little about the practical aspects of

---

[33] In addition to periodic work stoppages, two major strikes occurred in the valley, one in 1917 and the other in 1919. For a brief account of the 1917 strike, see Roberto Maclean y Estenos, *Sociología del Perú*, p. 145. According to Maclean, the strikers won a wage increase and some concessions for better living conditions. I was unable to locate a satisfactory account of the 1919 strike, though some aspects of it were reported in *La Industria*.

[34] Díaz Ahumada, *Historia de las luchas sindicales*, pp. 33-34.

[35] Ibid., pp. 32-33.

organizing a union, they decided to establish contact with Eduardo Chávez, who, it will be recalled, had successfully organized the mutual aid society in 1917 at Cartavio. Working together with Chávez, they made plans to organize not only Roma but also the other important plantations in the valley. Other leaders were sought out and a recruitment campaign was quietly initiated among the mass of sugar workers. According to Díaz, the most difficult segment to convince to join the new union at Roma were the *empleados*, who were reluctant to collaborate with the braceros whom they considered inferior. However, most were finally persuaded that only by such united action could concessions be gained from the owner.[36]

On the other hand, it is likely that the Indian braceros responded more readily to the new union. Cut off from his family and relatives in the sierra, the recently arrived bracero probably looked upon the union as a convenient substitute for the more traditional kinship ties he had left behind. Further, the union was the first community-wide structure to which the Indian bracero, traditionally the lowest caste on the coastal social structure, was allowed entrance and in which he was given limited participation—even if on a somewhat unequal basis. This fact doubtless increased the new union's appeal to this numerically important plantation group.[37]

Once the recruitment phase of the plan had been largely completed, a general meeting was called for the night of March 17 in order to elect officers and formulate a series of complaints and demands to be presented to the Larcos. At the meeting statutes for the new union, which had been drawn up by Díaz and Zavala in collaboration with Chávez and which adhered very closely to the Cartavio model, were accepted by the workers present. Next it was decided to use the name Sociedad Obrera de Auxilios Mutuos y Caja de Ahorros instead of the word *sindicato*, for the former had generally been accepted by the valley's planters as "inoffensive" (Díaz described these *sociedades* as intensely conservative organizations whose ends were always only to cure the sick and bury the dead), while the latter

---

[36] Concerning these clandestine meetings with Chávez, Díaz writes: "Several times we had to travel on saddleless horses, which we got secretly from the cattle watchman of the plantation. We traveled at night, met with Chávez, and the following day showed up on time for work. From these nocturnal meetings with Chávez, we learned the theory and tactics of the labor movement and what each of us should do" (ibid., pp. 33-34).

[37] Solomon Miller, "Hacienda to Plantation in Northern Peru: The Process of Proletarianization of a Tenant Farmer Society" in *Contemporary Change in Traditional Societies*, ed. Julian H. Steward, p. 206.

was considered "revolutionary" in character and therefore totally unac-
ceptable. In this way, according to Díaz, the leaders of the new union
hoped to provoke, at least at the outset, as little resistance from the
planters as possible. Elections were also conducted, with Zavala being
elected president of the new union, and a list of demands was composed
and approved.[38]

The announcement of the formation of a new labor organization on the
hacienda Roma was greeted enthusiastically by Trujillo labor groups as
well as by elements of an increasingly discontented middle class. The
newspaper *La Libertad*, which was published by a group of reform-
oriented intellectuals who belonged to the "Trujillo Bohemia,"[39] for
example, came out in full support of the new union. Edited by the respected Antenor Orrego, *La Libertad*, since its foundation a few years
before, had directed its appeal toward discontented elements of the
Trujillo middle class, which included skilled workers, merchant groups,
and students. Although often sympathetic to the problems of labor, it was
not considered an organ of organized labor in the department. Likewise,
local labor unions, which had long ignored the plight of the bracero and
had shown little interest in attempting to organize the valley's mass of
sugar workers, now came out wholeheartedly in support of the new syndicate.[40] This new-found urban support for the valley's fledgling labor movement was largely due to the fact that the postwar economic crisis, aggravated as will be shown later by various local factors, had considerably
worsened the conditions of the middle classes in and around Trujillo,
thereby causing them to become more radical politically.

Shortly after the announcement of the formation of the Roma union,[41]
the plantation's management announced the intention of eliminating the
33 percent wage increase that Larco had decreed in 1917. This news,
according to Díaz, fell hard on the workers of Roma and considerably
aided the recruitment of new members for the union. With opinion at

[38] Díaz Ahumada, *Historia de las luchas sindicales*, pp. 34-35.

[39] More will be said about the "Bohemia" in later chapters.

[40] Díaz Ahumada, *Historia de las luchas sindicales*, pp. 34-35. During the strike of
1921, the dock workers at Salaverry, railroad workers of Trujillo, and the Sociedad
Unión de Empleados de Trujillo also struck in support of the sugar workers (ibid., pp.
56-59).

[41] The following account of the 1921 strike is taken primarily from the pages of
Díaz Ahumada, ibid. However, *La Industria* and the government account of the strike
by Lauro A. Curletti, *El problema industrial en el valle de Chicama*, were also con-
sulted. There is a brief treatment of the strike in Maclean y Estenos, *Sociología del
Perú*, pp. 145-150.

Roma now galvanized into opposition to the plantation management, the leadership of the union decided to present formally its list of grievances and to call a strike within forty-eight hours should the demands not be met. In addition to the suppression of the newly decreed wage reduction, the list of demands included the establishment of the eight-hour day, abolition of the *enganche* system, elimination of corporal punishment, union control of the weighing process of cane, indemnification by the plantation in case of accidents or sickness, extension of medical services, suppression of the plantation's private police force, and, finally, full recognition of the new union. Predictably, management categorically rejected these demands, and on an April morning at 8 A.M., the entire work force at Roma walked off the job.

In contrast to the chaotic and disorganized strikes of previous years, the strike of 1921 was generally well directed by the new Roma union. Extensive preparations, for example, had been made for the initial rebuff that was expected from the plantation management. A strike fund had been established prior to the walkout, and immediately attempts to solicit further aid from the major Trujillo unions were successfully undertaken. Likewise, other well-planned tactics were employed in order to evade the methods traditionally used by the planters to break strikes and also to put further pressure on management to accede to the demands of the strikers. For example, partly in response to the closing of all market facilities on the plantation to the strikers[42] and also in order to dramatize their demands, the leaders organized a protest march to the nearby town of Ascope. Denied permission to enter Ascope by municipal officials who were allegedly in the pay of the Larcos, the marchers, numbering in the thousands, proceeded to Chicama, where by the day's end they were finally given permission to camp on the outskirts of town. For the next thirty days several thousand strikers and their families remained on the improvised camp site on the edge of town while negotiations among management, government officials, and strikers were conducted.

Soon after the march to Chicama, local authorities, prodded by the new government of Augusto B. Leguía, began to try more pacific and concillia-

---

[42] Díaz writes: ". . . the sources of drinking water and even the sewers were closed, as were the food market, bakery, and milk stores. Also, the gates of the plantation were barred to prevent outside venders from entering to sell these items. Finally, troops were deployed to prevent the use of the common kitchen that had been set up by the unions to feed the strikers. In addition, soldiers entered the houses of the peons to force them to go to work, an act that provoked violent clashes between both groups" (*Historia de las luchas sindicales*, pp. 39-40, my translation).

tory methods to solve the strike. In part the new tactics were a result of the failure of repressive methods to break the strike. However, more importantly, they were due to the momentary political exigencies that the new president faced.

Leguía had come to power via an army coup in 1919 after a disputed election in which he claimed victory over the government-backed, Civilist party candidate, Ramón Aspillaga. Fearing that the elections might be annulled by a Civilist-controlled Congress, Leguía resorted to the traditional military means to assure his ascendancy to the presidency. Up to this point Leguía's political career had been a rather checkered one. A middle-class businessman from Lambayeque, he had risen rapidly within the ranks of the aristocratic Civilist party, which was to rule Peru continuously, except for a brief interlude, from 1895 to 1919.[43] After serving ably as treasury minister in the regime of Manuel Candamo (1903-1904) and later prime minister under José Pardo (1904-1908), Leguía was tapped by the party to be its next presidential candidate and was easily elected to the office in 1908.

As president, however, Leguía exhibited a marked degree of personalism and arbitrariness, which subsequently embroiled him in a sharp dispute with both Congress and his own party. The ensuing quarrel ultimately divided the party so severely that it ended Leguía's ambitions for a second term and paved the way for the election of the reform-minded ex-mayor of Lima, Guillermo Billinghurst, in 1912. Forced into exile, Leguía ostensibly retired from politics and spent the next several years pursuing business interests in New York and London.

However, his political fortunes soon rose again toward the close of World War I when the Civilist party, which had regained power in 1915, began to show signs of crumbling in the face of rising urban pressures from an emerging and increasingly restless and vocal middle and laboring class. Realizing that conditions were ripe for a successful return to politics, Leguía sailed for Peru in 1918 to campaign actively for the presidency. Soon the former president was adroitly directing his campaign appeal to Lima's emergent middle and popular classes, whose formation had been given a sharp boost by the economic progress brought on by World War I. This new sociopolitical grouping, which by 1918 was clearly casting about for political leadership and greater representation in the body politic, was

---

[43] Basadre calls this period of virtually uninterrupted Civilist rule "la República Aristocrática."

composed of elements of a new bourgeoisie of more modest origins than
the old Civilist aristocracy. It included in addition an ever proliferating
number of government employees and teachers, whose positions had been
carved out of a rapidly expanding national budget that had risen fivefold
from 14.2 million soles in 1900 to 70 million in 1920 and that would
double again during the *oncenio*.[44] Joining this political array, which was
shortly to coalesce behind the candidacy of Leguía, were members of a
growing urban laboring sector, which ever since the onset of the war had
been increasingly flexing its newly found political muscles in a bewildering
number of work stoppages and strikes against the *ancien régime*. Finally,
the movement included a large number of disenchanted middle-class
students who were populating the nation's oldest universities in ever increasing numbers and a small, but restless and vocal group of intellectuals
whose militantly reformist and often Socialist views found expression in
the Lima newspaper *Germinal*. To all these elements, in one way or
another restless for a change in the old order, Leguía quickly became the
man of the hour. Presenting himself as a would-be reformer interested in
the welfare of student, merchant, and worker alike and obliquely attacking
the political bankruptcy of the old ruling Civilist oligarchy, Leguía succeeded in easily defeating his lackluster opponent at the polls.[45]

Once ensconced in the Presidential Palace, Leguía, in a skillfully conceived effort to capture the new spirit of the times, symbolically dubbed
his new regime "la Patria Nueva," then moved quickly to further solidify
his support among the popular classes. Under his leadership, a Constituent
Assembly proceeded to frame a new constitution, which, on the surface at
least, promised a new era in Peruvian politics. The 1920 Constitution not
only elaborately protected individual rights, but also provided for a host of
reform provisions that, among other things, committed the state to such
novelties as price controls, progressive taxation, protection of the rights

---

[44] See Emilio Romero, *Historia económica del Perú*, p. 442.

[45] Basadre states that, "from a social point of view, Leguiismo was propelled by the
middle classes, a phenomenon analogous to the rise of Alessandri and Irigoyen to
power in Chile and Argentina, respectively" (*Historia del Perú*, IX, 4218). See also his
Perú: Problema y posibilidad, pp. 173-174. That Leguía's electoral campaign was to a
large extent oriented toward capturing the Lima middle-class vote is illustrated by the
following remarks he made in an address to the Federación de Estudiantes del Perú
(FEP) in early 1919: "It is necessary to save the desperate situation of the middle
class . . . which like the proletariat has unjustly been forgotten and has been denied
the benefits of a social security plan designed to take care of them in accident,
sickness or retirement" (*Historia del Perú*, IX, 4178).

and welfare of organized labor, broadened programs in the field of public education, and protection of Indian rights, including the inviolability of the nation's *comunidades indígenas*. The latter provision was followed by several legislative acts, including the creation in 1921 of a new Indian Affairs Bureau of the Ministry of Development, designed to protect the nation's *comunidades indígenas*, which since the turn of the century had been threatened by the inexorable advance of commercial agriculture. While ultimately a failure, Leguía's efforts in behalf of the Indian communities served for a time to capture the support of a small but influential group of intellectuals, headed by Hildebrando Castro Pozo, who were spearheading the Indigenista movement in the country.[46]

Leguía's desire to retain middle-class support was clearly evident, moreover, soon after his election when he stepped in to negotiate a dispute between the Empleados de Comercio de Lima and local employers. The government-appointed negotiators succeeded in winning for the *empleados* a substantial wage increase as well as a number of fringe concessions, such as longer lunch hours and the like.[47] Other visible acts favorable to the popular classes were implemented by Leguía early in his regime. A decree promulgated in March, 1920, created a new Labor Section in the Ministerio de Fomento (Economic Development), which would be the basis for a future independent ministry. Also, several measures relating to rent control were passed by Congress the same year.[48]

Leguía's reformist stance continued during the first two years of his regime. Faced with strong opposition from elements of the now deposed Civilist party—some of whom were actively conspiring to bring down his government, Leguía found it expedient to pursue his initial policy of catering to the middle and working classes. This situation largely explains his rather liberal approach to solving the labor disturbances that had paralyzed the Chicama Valley. In spite of widespread opposition from Liberteño planters who favored a "hard line" toward the strikers at

[46] Basadre, *Historia del Perú*, VIII, 3947-3950. On the matter of Leguía's policy of protecting the nation's *comunidades indígenas* from outside encroachments, a sharp reversal from the attitude of previous governments, see François Chevalier's excellent article, "Official Indigenismo in Peru in 1920: Origins, Significance, and Socioeconomic Scope," in *Race and Class in Latin America*, ed. Magnus Mörner, Chapter 9. In this article Chevalier also provides a good account of the Indigenista movement, which had gathered considerable support in middle-class circles during this period (see particularly pp. 187-189).

[47] Basadre, *Historia del Perú*, IX, 4179-4180.

[48] Ibid., p. 4182.

Roma,[49] Leguía, at least during the early stages of the strike, tended to support the position of the strikers. He sent Agustín Haya de la Torre, the locally popular brother of the later founder of Aprismo, to Trujillo with orders to bring about a peaceful and just settlement of the strike.

On his two conciliatory missions to Trujillo as the government trouble-shooter, Agustín, according to Díaz, made a very favorable impression on the strikers. Upon his first arrival he ordered union leaders, imprisoned earlier by the local authorities, released, visited the campsite of the strikers where he promised a just settlement, and established an arbitration board composed of representatives of labor, government, and the plantation Roma. After several meetings, agreement was ostensibly reached to end the strike, with Roma officials reluctantly giving in to most of the strikers' demands. However, soon after Agustín's return to Lima new troubles erupted once again in the valley.

The new disturbances occurred for two reasons. First, during the thirty days in which the Roma workers were camped outside Chicama, widespread efforts were made to organize unions on the other plantations in the valley. According to Díaz, "brigadas de agitación y propaganda" were nightly sent out from the Chicama encampment and soon new "sociedades" sprang up at Chiclín, Sausal, and Casa Grande. Once the strike was seemingly settled to the benefit of labor at Roma, these new unions began to present similar demands on the remaining plantations in the valley, thus igniting a new series of work stoppages throughout the region.

Second, soon after the outbreak of these new strikes, the management of Roma announced that its sugar mill was to be closed down permanently and that a contract had been signed with the owners of Casa Grande to have the sugar cane of Roma processed in the latter's mill. Since the closing of the mill at Roma meant the immediate dismissal of a large number of former strikers, the syndicate immediately interpreted the move, coming as it did shortly after the arbitration agreement and Agustín Haya de la Torre's return to Lima, as a breach of faith on the part of the plantation officials, and a new strike was called.[50] This time the strike was not confined to Roma, and efforts to unite the entire movement through-

---

[49] Rafael Larco Herrera, the brother of the owner of Roma, for example, was thoroughly outraged at the position that Leguía took early in the strike in favor of the strikers (*Memorias*, pp. 63-66).

[50] The decision by Larco seemed calculated to break the new union, although it may also be argued that it was motivated by the precarious financial state of Roma at that time. See Chapter 1.

out the valley were quickly undertaken by labor leaders anxious to forge a united labor front in order to strengthen their position. As a result, the Sindicato Regional de Trabajo, composed of unions established on the main plantations in the valley, was founded in Trujillo—the first such regional agricultural labor organization in Peru.

The renewed outbreak of trouble initiated a more serious wave of violence throughout the valley. New attempts to conciliate the disputes were made during the course of the next few months by Agustín Haya and then Minister of Fomento Lauro Curletti, but, after short periods of peace, both missions ended in failure with the resumption of violence. In December, Leguía, acting upon the recommendations of Curletti, decreed an end to the strike, which, although favorable in some respects to the strikers, by no means met their most pressing demands.[51] For example, the decree made no mention of the need for pay raises, while only partial recognition was given to the new unions. Dissatisfied with the December decree, the new unions continued to call work stoppages that plagued the valley well into 1922.

The new trouble coincided with a hardening of Leguía's previously liberal attitude toward the nation's urban working classes as well as the student and intellectual components of his 1918 coalition. In part this seeming shift away from labor was more apparent than real, for much of Leguía's early support of the worker had turned out to be largely rhetorical. Little in the way of tangible aid had actually been accomplished for this sector during the first years of the regime. Nevertheless, it became increasingly clear by late 1921 that what little interest Leguía had previously expressed in meeting labor's demands was fast waning as the political basis of the new regime shifted.

Although still catering to his middle-class clientele, Leguía had increasingly begun to favor only the interests of that portion of the 1918 coalition which represented the new, monied class of entrepreneurs originating during the profitable war years. This group, as well as elements of the middle class and coastal exporters, profited immensely from Leguía's policy of attracting to Peru huge amounts of foreign capital and loans.[52] Such an

[51] Leguía, in the decree, declared the *enganche* illegal and to be eliminated within nine months from the valley, ordered the eight-hour day with certain exceptions, and called for a general improvement in living and health services. See Curletti, *El problema industrial*, pp. 31-33, for a copy of the December Decree.

[52] By 1925 United States investments in Peru had reached a record 100 million dollars, second only to Great Britain's 125 million (Robert W. Dunn, *American*

infusion of capital, which Leguía saw as the means to modernize and expand coastal Peru's incipient capitalist structure, provided the basis for a general acceleration in the pace of economic activity of the country. Since the growing demands and aggressiveness of labor threatened his blueprint for developing the nation, Leguía began to crack down on this sector, a policy that was reflected in his handling of the continuing disturbances in the Chicama Valley region.

Early in 1922 a large detachment of federal troops arrived in Trujillo by ship from Lima. Soon labor leaders were being rounded up and jailed while the Sindicato Regional del Trabajo was forcibly dissolved. Once the leadership had been eliminated, the movement quickly degenerated into isolated incidents of violence, which included cane burning and other acts of vandalism. Finally, order was restored and life in the valley returned to normal.

During the balance of the Leguía regime, the labor movement in the valley remained largely moribund. From time to time minor disturbances erupted, but they were quickly quelled by newly stationed troops in the nearby valley towns, the product of one provision of Leguía's December decree. Of the early labor leaders in the valley, few remained, for they had been blacklisted from work on the plantations of the region. Leopoldo Pita, for example, the organizer of Chiclín during the strike, found work in Lima and later participated in the anti-Leguía demonstrations in 1923.[53] Artemio Zavala, the former head of the Roma union, returned to the highlands shortly after the end of the strike in 1922 and died a few months later of tuberculosis.

The severity of the 1921 strike in the valley clearly reflected the profound changes that had occurred in the region's labor force since the first trickle of Indian labor had begun to descend from the highlands of La Libertad in the 1890's. In response to the rise and industrialization of the valley's sugar industry, a rural proletariat had, by the turn of the century, begun to emerge on the major plantations in the region. Subjected to oppressive living and working conditions and bolstered by increasing numbers, this previously dormant mass began to grow increasingly restless. By the end of the first decade "spontaneous" outbreaks of labor violence

---

Foreign Investments, p. 82). For the best general treatment of United States investments in Peru during the *oncenio*, see James C. Carey, *Peru and the United States, 1900-1962*, Chapters 4 and 5. Fredrick B. Pike (*The Modern History of Peru*, pp. 228-229) states that Peru's foreign debt rose from around 10 to 100 million dollars between 1918 and 1929.

[53] Interview, Leopoldo Pita Verdi, Lima, March 21, 1967.

were commonplace occurrences throughout the valley. However, it was not until the end of World War I that a semblance of organization began to appear within the ranks of the region's sugar workers.

The end of the war saw the influx of new revolutionary ideas to Peru as well as a sharp decline in the country's export-oriented economy. The effects of the latter on the nation's popular classes produced additional discontent among the valley's sugar workers, while the former provided modern examples of how the shackles of oppression might be broken. Thus, between 1917 and 1921 labor throughout the Chicama Valley organized, and, in the face of planter intransigence, bloody strikes became the order of the day. Though the planters, with the help of the national government, ultimately succeeded in breaking the longest and most violent of these strikes in 1921, such a solution to the problem could only be a temporary one in the long run. For by the 1920's the Chicama Valley, together with the adjacent Santa Catalina Valley, had become one of the largest industrial centers in the country, employing a work force of twenty thousand persons.[54] As the 1921 strike demonstrated, such a force, when organized, could perhaps overturn the existing political and social system in the region, a fact that was not to go unnoticed among a group of young, reform-minded Liberteños in the years ahead.

[54] William Edward Dunn, *Peru: A Commercial and Industrial Handbook*, p. 442.

3. Plantation vs. *Pequeño Agricultor*:
The Decline of the Small Farmer

Prior to the War of the Pacific, the Chicama Valley was dotted with several small, but flourishing towns. Formerly the sites of large, prosperous Indian communities, which during the wars for independence had been severely ravaged, these towns had, by the 1850's, begun to recover some of their former prosperity. A stable population, varying from several hundred to a few thousand inhabitants, worked the surrounding lands and tended to a small but growing commercial life. The landholding structure of these towns, communal under Spanish rule, had, by mid-century, become substantially divided, with each *agricultor* in possession of plots ranging from a few to several hundred acres.[1] As the century progressed, these scattered

[1] With the advent of independence, Simón Bolívar, in a policy designed to stimulate economic recovery in the countryside, abolished the communal landholding system of the *comunidades indígenas*. In its place the "liberator" ordered all community lands to be redistributed on a private-property basis to those who had formerly worked the lands. As Jean Piel has pointed out in a recent article, this new land policy was something of a disaster from the point of view of the Indian population. "In their credulity, passivity and ignorance, the peasants of the communities were in a weak defensive position when it came to the redistribution of land. Those in charge of the operation, the surveyors, the lawyers, the *caciques*, the village notables, the *mestizos* and the tax officers, made sure they secured the best plots and in this way

villages and towns continued to grow and prosper, as general prosperity gradually returned to the countryside. However, by the first decade of the twentieth century these same towns had entered onto a collision course with the region's expanding sugar plantations, which increasingly began to strangle the urban, agricultural, and commercial life of the valley.

According to Antonio Raimondi, the well-known Italian explorer who traveled extensively throughout Peru in the 1850's and 1860's, two of the valley's most prosperous towns in the 1850's were Santiago de Cao and Ascope. Raimondi noted that Santiago was "quite a large town" whose prosperity was indicated by the "solid adobe and neatly whitewashed houses" that stood in sharp contrast to the more common reed and mud structures found along the coast. The inhabitants of Santiago were prosperous, independent farmers who cultivated corn, wheat, rice, and other staples.[2] The Italian traveler found Ascope enjoying an even greater state of prosperity:

Over the last few years Ascope has grown and continues to grow very rapidly. One notes everywhere the cement of new constructions. The town today has more than three thousand inhabitants, and it is widely believed that within a short time it will become one of the largest cities in Peru. The town has well-built houses and a large, handsome square. Among its principal families are the Flores, Vargas, and Guerras, and there is not lacking among these and other families a small social club where members can pass a moment of merrymaking. Ascope even has two pianos. The principal inhabitants of the town are *hacendados* who own farms both in the immediate vicinity and in the sierra. The rest of the population own small parcels of land on which they cultivate corn and rice.[3]

---

they built up for themselves overnight estates of thousands of hectares at the expense of the communal lands" ("The Place of the Peasantry in the National Life of Peru in the Nineteenth Century," *Past and Present*, no. 46 [February 1970], p. 118). As a result of this process of change, the landholding pattern of the *comunidades* over the next several decades gradually began to resemble that of the society at large. Indeed, by the 1850's the old *comunidades* had become something of a microcosm of the surrounding countryside, containing within their old boundaries a general mix of large and small, privately owned holdings. Some idea of the general landholding structure of these coastal communities, as they probably appeared in the second half of the nineteenth century, can be gleaned from John Gillin's excellent study *Moche: A Peruvian Coastal Community*, pp. 8-12. Moche, which Gillin studied in the 1940's, was one of the only coastal Indian communities to survive the rise of the modern, commercial estate and retain, for the most part, its traditional structure well into the twentieth century.

[2] Antonio Raimondi, *Notas de viajes para su obra "el Perú,"* I, 189.

[3] Antonio Raimondi, *El Perú*, I, 194-195, my translation. Another contemporary wrote: "Thirty years ago Ascope was a simple *fundo*; today it is a town of great

Thomas Hutchinson, another foreign traveler, made some similar observations on the agrarian life around Trujillo when he visited the area in 1872. Referring to the *agricultores* of Moche, an Indian community of about two thousand near Trujillo, he wrote: " . . . they are the marketgardeners for Trujillo, as it is from their little farms that the town is supplied with maize, melons, alfalfa, potatoes, and other vegetables."[4]

Following these excursions, George Vanderghem, the Dutch agricultural specialist under contract to the Peruvian government, visited the Chicama Valley in 1900 on an inspection tour of the northern coast. After noting the prosperity of the valley's towns, Vanderghem went on to comment on the well-being of the independent farmers of Ascope, Santiago, and Paiján who worked the rich and extensive lands surrounding these towns. He further observed that these lands yielded a wide range of produce from traditional staples like corn and wheat to assorted varieties of fruits and vegetables.[5]

Two decades later, however, this prosperous picture of the valley's towns had all but disappeared. Once flourishing towns like Santiago and Ascope now stood empty and barren, their commercial life dead and their once largely divided lands invaded by a sea of sugar cane. Commenting on the decayed state of Ascope and Santiago as well as Chocope, Paiján, Magdalena, and others, a Trujillo labor journal in 1917 stated: ". . . those who have seen these towns recently come away with a very sad impression; houses with only their walls standing while others are ready to collapse. Now only traces of the former life of these towns are visible, and the visitor is greeted with nothing but gloom and total silence. A slight distance away sugar cane, like an invasion, advances inexorably and triumphantly toward these last vestiges of urban life in the region."[6] The cause for this precipitous decline lies in the social and economic impact of the expanding sugar industry throughout the valley during the first decades of the twentieth century.

The rise of the valley's sugar industry, as has been noted, brought about a widespread concentration of the landholding structure in the area, with

————
importance and it is becoming considerably more prosperous because of the rich lands that surround it" (Mariano Felipe Paz Soldán, *Diccionario geográfico estadístico del Perú*, p. 78, my translation).

[4] Thomas J. Hutchinson, *Two Years in Peru with Exploration of Its Antiquities*, II, 145.

[5] George Vanderghem, et al., *Memorias presentadas al Ministerio de Fomento . . . república*, p. 63.

[6] "Memorial que en defensa de las clases trabajadoras presentarán al Parlamento Nacional las Sociedades Obreras de Trujillo," *El Derecho Obrero*, September 23, 1917, my translation.

the medium-sized haciendas being absorbed by the rising sugar empires of the Larcos, the Gildemeisters, and the Grace interests (Cartavio). While the traditional planters were adversely affected by this process, so, too, were the small independent farmers who owned plots in and around the main towns in the area. By the turn of the century a violent conflict between planter and independent farmer had erupted throughout the valley. Waxing hot over the next several decades, this conflict, which ultimately brought about the demise of the region's *agricultores*, was waged primarily over the vital question of water rights.[7]

Owing to climatic and geographical factors, water has traditionally been a problem for the inhabitants of the coastal valleys of the north. Due to the influences of the Humboldt Current, rain rarely falls in these valleys, a fact that obligates farmers in the region to rely almost entirely upon either subsoil well water or river sources to irrigate their crops. Moreover, river water, the more abundant of the two, is insufficient to meet the agrarian needs of the region. This lack is due to the fact that the rains in the highlands, which water the rivers flowing to the coast, fall only seasonally (roughly from November to April)—leaving a long dry season when the volume of these rivers is considerably reduced.[8] Periodically, the coastal region is also subjected to drought conditions when even these annual rains fail, for extraordinary climatic reasons, to materialize, thus depriving the coastal-flowing rivers of their normal supply of water. Because of these peculiar regional factors a system of rationing, or *sistema de riego*, which limits the amount of water that each planter or farmer is entitled to extract from the valley's rivers, has long been a necessity.

In the Chicama Valley the water-rationing system dates back, at least in modern times,[9] to 1699, when Antonio de Saavedra y Leyva, the dean of

---

[7] This conflict was not limited to the Chicama Valley, but was a widespread phenomenon that occurred all along the northern coast during the second half of the nineteenth century (Manuel A. Mesones P., "El uso del agua, en relación con su valor jurídico-social," in *Anales del Primer Congreso de Irrigación y Colonización del Norte*, I, 749-750).

[8] The average monthly discharge of the Chicama River, calculated over a ten-year span from 1948 to 1957, can be seen in the following table (figures in millions of cubic meters):

Jan.	68.6	May	61.2	Sept.	8.8
Feb.	122.7	June	26.6	Oct.	13.0
March	236.1	July	17.5	Nov.	16.3
April	185.1	Aug.	11.7	Dec.	15.7

(David A. Robinson, *Peru in Four Dimensions*, p. 168).

[9] In pre-Columbian times water-use regulations were probably common in the valley.

the Trujillo Cathedral as well as *juez superintendente del juzgado de aguas* for the crown, composed the first water code for the region.[10] It included the following regulations:

The code allowed one day of water for each fifty fanegadas; determined the amounts which corresponded to Indian communities; prohibited Spaniards, mulattoes, mestizos, and other castes who used to rent the lands of these communities from continuing to do so; and established that in the distribution of water for irrigation purposes the water administrators should take care not to deprive the towns in the area of their drinking water. The penalty for abusing any of these regulations was a fine of one hundred pesos for *hacendados* and a year's exile in the presidios of Chagres and Valdivia for the guilty *mayordomo*. If the guilty party was Negro, mulatto, mestizo, or a mixture, the penalty was one hundred lashes administered in a public place.... Finally, the code set regulations for the regular cleaning and repair of irrigation ditches and canals.[11]

These regulations remained in effect without substantial alteration for the next two hundred years.[12] During this time the code was administered by local *jueces*, or judges, often strongly under the influence of the powerful landed interests of the valley. But since the region's water supply was largely sufficient to meet crop demands, the valley's smaller landed interests were by and large not compromised and general harmony prevailed. However, the sharp expansion in cane cultivation, a crop that needed three times the amount of water required by other staples for adequate growth, altered the basic crop-water relationship, causing severe water shortages. As a result, the administration of water, which by the last decade of the nineteenth century was in the hands of the valley's emerging sugar barons, increasingly tended to favor the large landed interests to the disadvantage of the region's smaller farmers.

The planters used various forms of economic coercion, including outright bribery, to ensure that their claims for water were recognized by the

---

[10] The title of the 1699 Code was *El código de aguas o de la repartición de las aguas de esta ciudad y valle de su provincia, que reglamente el uso, el derecho y el beneficio de las aguas de los ríos Santa Catalina, Moche, Virú, Chicama y Jequetepeque.*

[11] Enrique Patrón, *Leyes, decretos, resoluciones, reglamentos y circulares vigentes en el ramo de justicia: Legislación de aguas*, pp. xxiv-xxv, my translation.

[12] Attempts either to frame a general water code for the whole of Peru or to revise the Saavedra Code were made in the years 1841, 1855-1856, 1866, and 1870—all without effect. An excellent brief survey of these attempts can be found in the introduction to Patrón's work (ibid., pp. xxv-xxx).

valley's water administration. In such a system the middle and small land-holders found themselves powerless to defend their own claims to the *riego*. Although not specifically accusing the sugar planters of manipulating the *riego* for their benefit, Enrique de Guimaraes, *juez privativo de aguas* for the province of Trujillo from 1900 to 1906, nevertheless implied this when he wrote: "When I took charge of the jurisdiction of water rights in this province, I found that those who administered the rights were invariably the employees of the region's farmers, on whom they depended for their monthly salaries. Such an arrangement, as can be imagined, tended to compromise their independence in carrying out their official functions, for, since they earned their wages from individual farmers, they were reluctant to denounce any abuses committed by their employers. If they did report such abuses to the authorities they simply lost their jobs."[13]

An example of the type of water dispute that arose in the valley as a result of such an unjust situation occurred at the hacienda Cartavio in 1886. In that year a dispute erupted between the administrator of Cartavio and the *comuneros* of Santiago de Cao over the use of local water sources. Apparently, the administrator forcibly tried to prevent the *comuneros* from drawing water for their lands from a traditional water source. Before the dispute degenerated into bloodshed, it was brought before the departmental prefect, who ultimately resolved the conflict by ostensibly fining Cartavio for attempting to violate the water rights of Santiago.[14] Whether or not Cartavio ever paid the fine or, more importantly, stopped abusing the *comuneros*' rights was not recorded, though the latter is unlikely.

The absence of a national water code and the increasing strain on water reserves from the general expansion of sugar and rice production along the coast ultimately forced the central government to reexamine the long-ignored problem of water administration along the coast. Largely due to the initiative of Eleodoro Romero, professor and former dean of the San Marcos law school who was named minister of justice in 1899, a commission composed of large landowners and several prominent lawyers was

---

[13] *Memoria presentada al supremo gobierno por el juez privativo de aguas de la provincia de Trujillo Dr. D. Enrique de Guimaraes correspondiente al año 1905,* pp. 8-9, my translation; hereafter cited as *Guimaraes memoria.*

[14] It is probable that the fine was never paid and Cartavio continued to usurp the community's water supply ("Expediente promovido ante la prefectura del departamento de La Libertad sobre administración de las aguas del común de Santiago de Cao," Trujillo, September 21, 1886, in the manuscript collection of the Sala de Investigaciones de la Biblioteca Nacional del Perú).

formed to frame a national water code. A year later the commission presented its recommendations, which were to a large extent taken from the Spanish Code of 1879.[15] After undergoing several revisions by a Congress dominated by the powerful landed interests of the coast, the proposed code was adopted in 1902.[16]

The part of the code that directly concerns this study established a rather cumbersome administrative system for the nation's major river valleys. The linchpin of the system was the creation of local *comunidades de regantes*, or district water boards, composed of no less than three landholders in the region. Each district (the Chicama Valley eventually had five) elected a full-time water administrator whose function was to see that the local and national ordinances in the district were executed properly. In addition, the board also elected a three-man executive committee, or *sindicato regional*, whose job was to oversee the work of the administrator as well as to inflict punishment on those in the district who violated the water laws. Legal disputes were generally resolved in the nearest law court, where either a special judge (*juez privativo de aguas*) especially trained in water law or a regular judge, both appointed by the government, heard and decided cases involving water rights.[17]

The new system, though it did establish a better defined administrative structure, by no means prevented the same abuses common in the past from reoccurring. This inadequacy was due to the fact that the large landholders could now legally control the administrative apparatus, for voting for the office of administrator and membership on the *sindicato regional* was carried out according to the amount of water (*riegos*) alloted to or the extension of land cultivated by each landowner in the district. Thus, the large landholders, with more votes at their disposal, could generally control the election of these officials and thereby manipulate the administration of water according to their particular interests.[18] In the Chicama Valley the presidents of the water districts of Magdalena de Cao

[15] See the textual comparisons between the new code and the Spanish Code in Manuel S. Pasapera, *La ley de aguas con sus antecedentes*, pp. 13-124.

[16] Juan Vicente Nicolini, *La policía de las aguas en el Perú*, pp. 30-31.

[17] A complete text of the 1902 Code as well as later decrees affecting its execution can be found in Guillermo de Vivanco, *Legislación agrícola del Perú*, pp. 315-540; see particularly pp. 373-388 and 397-406 on the functioning of the Comunidad de Regantes. The Comunidad de Regantes was also empowered to revise or create new local ordinances, providing that they were approved by the Ministerio de Fomento in Lima. In this way, local variations, so important in any general water code, were accommodated (see Article 232 of the Code on p. 374).

[18] Article 235 outlines voting procedures (ibid., p. 375).

and Paiján in the year 1904, for example, were none other than Víctor Larco and Alfredo Gildemeister, the two largest sugar planters in the valley.[19]

Commenting on the injustices of the new law and particularly Article 235, which established voting practices, Gustavo de la Torre, a medium-sized landholder in the valley who on several occasions had clashed with the powerful Larco interests over the question of water rights and who often defended the interests of the smaller farmers in the valley, wrote the following: "Nobody is really fooled by the aforementioned Article 235. It simply tends to confirm the domination of the water system by the large planters to the detriment of the region's small farmers. This domination is notorious in the valleys of this province and it results in great injustice as well as irreparable harm to the small farmer. . . . The way in which the votes are computed according to the present law [Article 235] is the means by which the interests of the small farmers, if they conflict with the large landowners, are completely submerged."[20] De la Torre, who wrote this in a letter to the Cámara de Comercio, Agricultura e Industria of the department of La Libertad, went on to implore that this body use its influence to try and change the inequities of the law.

A similar assessment of the injustices of the 1902 Code was made some years later by one of the participants of the Lambayeque Congress on Irrigation and Colonization. After stating that the *comunidad de regantes* was controlled by large landowners who selected the administrators and members of the *sindicatos regionales* as well as formulated the local ordinances governing the *riego*, he wrote, "One has to conclude that these administrators, sindicates, and regulations simply did not protect the collective interests of the water districts of the region, but only the private interests of individual landowners."[21]

The seemingly hopeless position of the small farmer, who could not expect a just and equitable administration of water rights, even under the new code, led in many instances to his resorting to violence. Cases of armed attacks by aggrieved farmers on officials charged with the administration of the system apparently occurred frequently in many parts of the

[19] *Guimaraes memoria*, Appendix 6.

[20] Gustavo de la Torre, Trujillo, to Alfredo A. Pinillos, President, Trujillo, March 3, 1909, a.l.s., 2 pp., Archivo de la Cámara de Comercio, Agricultura e Industria del Departamento de La Libertad, my translation. The latter will hereafter be cited as Archivo de la Cámara.

[21] Mesones, "El uso del agua," p. 754, my translation.

country. Indeed, on occasion such outbreaks of violence became severe enough for local officials to call on the national government to send special troops to quell the disturbances.[22]

With the all important apparatus of water administration in their hands, the large planters virtually assured themselves of available water resources for their ever expanding fields of sugar cane. It was particularly during periods of scarcity that the planters exercised this control to their benefit, extracting without sanction more water than the law permitted from the Chicama River and thus leaving the small farmers grouped around the towns in the valley virtually waterless. A typical example of this action was reported by a government engineer investigating the conditions in the valley during the severe drought of 1906-1907. He stated that "the farmers of the Indian Community Santiago de Cao protest that, while they are prohibited from drawing water for their fields in times of scarcity, the *hacendados* who receive water from the same source continue to draw their regular amounts. From what I have seen their complaints are justified." He went on to record the disastrous effects of this abuse on the *agricultores* of the town in the following way: "The favorite crop of Santiago de Cao is Egyptian wheat, which its farmers produce very well. The community also grows barley and has some thirty fanegadas devoted to sugar cane, which is processed in the mills of Cartavio. All this has now disappeared. The scarcity of water has made the town a virtual ghost town. But by the looks of the construction of the houses, which are today in ruins, one can see that the town was at one time prosperous and thriving."[23]

The position of the valley's small landholders, as the sugar plantations continued to expand, became increasingly untenable. Unable to resist a crop loss for one or two seasons because of a lack of savings or the difficulty of contracting loans,[24] the small farmers in the valley gradually were forced to abandon their lands—often selling out to the planters who were eager to obtain these plots not so much for the added acreage they afforded for cane cultivation, but for the water rights themselves. How-

---

[22] Alberto Ulloa y Sotomayor, *Lineamientos de una legislación rural*, p. 57. Ronald M. J. Gordon, an Englishman who in 1907 came to Peru to work for the British Sugar Estates in Nepeña, said that disputes over water rights very often degenerated into armed conflicts (interview, Lima [San Isidro], April 14, 1967).

[23] Pedro C. Venturo, *Estudio de los ríos Chicama y Moche*, p. 25, my translation.

[24] The question of loans to small farmers is an interesting one, although information on it is very limited. Mariátegui stated that small landholders found it very difficult if not impossible to contract loans unless they devoted their lands to the

ever, some farmers were able to resist for longer periods of time, in which case the planters resorted to more direct means of gaining control of the land. It was common, for example, for the planter to initiate a legal claim to the land in the local court, claiming that the farmer possessed no legal title to the land he worked. This accusation was true in many cases, for the old colonial titles that had belonged to the Indian communities had not always been officially passed on after independence to the *comuneros* who worked the lands. Thus, even though the land in question had probably been worked by the farmer's family for several generations, the absence of any clear title of ownership made his case untenable in the courts. To make matters worse, the planter, employing a skilled lawyer, could present a far better case in court than the defenseless farmer. Finally, if this was not sufficient to wrest control of the land, the planter could, and often did, resort to the not uncommon practice of bribing the local judge in order to obtain a favorable decision.[25]

The planters were also able to gain control of the lands owned by the municipalities of the region, which also adversely affected the area's small farmers. These lands had formerly formed part of the old Indian communities, but upon their disintegration during the nineteenth century some of their lands had passed into the hands of the *municipios*. As such they were rented out to the farmers of the area in small parcels. When the planters began to expand, they found no difficulty in purchasing such lands, for by the turn of the century their increasing economic power had spilled over into the political arena so that they exercised considerable influence over the municipal officials. Thus, many small farmers who had rented municipal lands for generations were also forced to abandon what they considered to be "their" lands.[26]

Over the next few decades, aided by periodic droughts and the inexorable expansion of sugar cane, this process of absorption of the small landholdings in the valley gradually unfolded. The valley's two principal

---

production of such cash crops as sugar or cotton. He attributed this to the fact that the financial institutions in the country were primarily in the hands of foreign interests who wanted Peru to concentrate on the production of lucrative export crops (*Siete ensayos de interpretación de la realidad peruana*, p. 83). It might be added that interest rates were probably prohibitive to the small farmer, who operated on a highly limited and precarious budget.

[25] Interview with Luis Cáceres Aguilar in Lima on June 10, 1967. Cáceres was born in 1908 in Santiago de Cao of a family of small farmers. He was an Aprista deputy to Congress from La Libertad. This process is further described in a short story entitled "Latifundio," by Nilo Gutiérrez Vargas in his *Cuentos de Trujillo*, pp. 58-61.

[26] Interview with Cáceres.

newspapers, the liberal-oriented *La Razón* and the more conservative *La Industria*, both recorded and lamented the disappearance of the small farmers of the region. An editorial in the former, for example, in 1913 called on the small farmers to form an agricultural organization to protect their interests while at the same time deploring the fact that "the old towns of the Chicama Valley are disappearing one after the other, sacrificed to the insatiable thirst for water and gold of that great octopus that is sugar cane."[27] In a similar vein, *La Industria*, in an editorial calling for the government to impose taxes on the sugar industry, stated:

It should be added that even a water code was composed for the benefit of the planters. This code permitted them to dominate completely the small farmers of the region, obligating them to sell their property or submit to the dictates of the district water board, which is always controlled by the large planters. Our region is a perfect example of this entire process. Our valleys of Chicama and Santa Catalina are today in the hands of very few planters, who are able to manipulate the law to serve their own interests. So while these *grandes* have been able to progress in their business very rapidly, the towns which are located near the plantations are gradually disappearing. It can actually be said that today these towns are of little importance and mere dependencies of these plantations.[28]

The sugar boom of World War I, moreover, sharply accelerated the disappearance of the small farmer from the region. Even Trujillo, the departmental capital, was not spared from the absorption process. In an article entitled "La Caña Invade Trujillo," the editorial writer for *El Norte*, the reform-oriented successor of *La Razón*, wrote that, due to the huge sugar profits obtained during the war, "the small farmers who traditionally dedicated their fields to the cultivation of staples have been despoiled of their small plots . . . and the *latifundio* extends its covetous tentacles to the very heart of the city."[29]

Apparently, the protests raised by some newspapers, both local and national, against the absorption of the small landholders led to some

[27] *La Razón*, June 13, 1913, my translation.

[28] *La Industria*, August 21, 1915, my translation. For further evidence of this process of absorption, see the following references, which represent only a small portion of letters and articles dealing with this question: *La Industria*, March 8, 1909, and April 3, 1912; Presidente del Sindicato de Poroto y Pedregal, Trujillo, to Presidente de la Cámara, Trujillo, January 17, 1912, a.l.s., 3 pp., Archivo de la Cámara; *La Razón*, October 18, 1912; *El Derecho Obrero*, February 1, 1920; E. Espejo, Trujillo, to Presidente de la Cámara, Trujillo, December 18, 1917, a.l.s., 2 pp., Archivo de la Cámara; and *El Norte*, June 2, 1923.

[29] *El Norte*, October 25, 1924, my translation.

attempts to reform the 1902 Code. In 1918, for example, a new law was decreed taking the administration of water completely away from the local *comunidades de regantes* and placing it in the hands of the newly created *comisiones técnicas de irrigación*, which were composed of government-appointed engineers.[30] However, there is no evidence that this change from a decentralized to a centralized administration eliminated the abuses of the powerful local landed interests and brought about a more impartial and just administration of the *riego*. Indeed, one agrarian authority has written that in practice the new law changed very little and that the "spirit" of the 1902 Code was largely retained in most coastal valleys.[31] Regardless of the new law, the absorption of the region's small farmers continued well into the 1920's.

While not concerned directly with preserving the existence of the area's small farmers, the Leguía government did make some efforts in the 1920's to arrest the destruction of the nation's dwindling Indian communities. Anxious to attract the political support of an influential group of Indigenistas, intellectuals who had long been voicing their concern for the plight of the Indians, Leguía reversed the policy of previous governments and undertook some specific measures to ostensibly protect their interests. For example, several pro-Indian features were written into the Constitution of 1920, including a provision recognizing the legal existence of the Indian community, a fact largely ignored by the state since independence. In addition, the constitution declared that such communal corporations were hereafter to be considered an inalienable part of the state domain.[32]

Soon after its promulgation, Leguía formulated a number of laws designed to implement the spirit of the new constitution. Thus, in 1921 a special Indian Affairs Bureau within the Ministry of Development was established, and a year later the Foundation for the Protection of Indians (Patronato de la Raza Indígena), headed by the archbishop of Lima, came into being. The Foundation, which was subdivided into a series of separate provincial committees, was designed to adjudicate cases involving land disputes between local *hacendados* and neighboring Indian communities. Such disputes had traditionally been settled by local judges, who for the

[30] See Nicolini, *La policía de las aguas*, pp. 39-41.

[31] Edgardo Seoane, *Surcos de Paz*, p. 147; also see Nicolini, *La policía de las aguas*, pp. 61, 64, in which the author quotes two critics of the new law. Both say that it continued to undermine the position of the small farmer.

[32] See particularly Article 58, which can be found in translation in Graham H. Stuart, *The Governmental System of Peru*, p. 142.

most part were dominated by large landowners and who therefore handed down the expected verdict. In 1925 a further effort to halt the disintegration of the Indian communities was undertaken when the government ordered engineers of the Ministry of Development, under the supervision of the local committees of the Patronato, to register and survey all existing Indian communities in the country. By 1923, however, it had become clear that Leguía, now firmly tied to the nation's large landowning class, had no intention of enforcing or pushing his pro-Indian policies at their expense. This fact led to a large-scale defection of such young Indigenista supporters of the regime as J. A. Encinas, Hildebrando Castro Pozo, and Alberto Solís, all of whom were subsequently jailed or deported from the country for their outspoken opposition to the regime.[33]

During the remainder of the *oncenio*, the destruction of the Indian communities, with their small-farmer class, accelerated, not only on the coast where sugar and cotton meant increased export profits, but also in the highlands. José María Arguedas, in his moving novel *Yawar Fiesta*, has vividly portrayed the struggle for survival of one Indian community, Puquio, in the highlands of Ayacucho during this period. He shows how many highland communities in the south were being victimized by neighboring ranchers, who, because of lucrative profits from the growing urban demand for beef, leather, and other cattle products, were encroaching and enclosing Indian pasture lands in order to expand their own ranching operations. This process of despoilation led to several serious Indian rebellions in the province of Azangaro on the shores of Lake Titicaca in the period 1921-1923.

Unfortunately, because of the lack of adequate statistics, no figures are available on the exact number of small landowners in the north who lost their lands during the first three decades of the century. However, Claude Collin-Delavaud, a French scholar working on this question for a more recent period, estimates that over the last thirty years some 2,500 families in the department of La Libertad have been dispossessed of their property.[34] Considering the widespread depopulation of the towns around the

[33] For an excellent discussion of Leguía's Indian policies, see François Chevalier, "Official Indigenismo in Peru in 1920: Origins, Significance, and Socioeconomic Scope," in *Race and Class in Latin America*, ed. Magnus Mörner, particularly pp. 186-192.

[34] Claude Collin-Delavaud, "Consecuencias de la modernización de la agricultura en las haciendas de la costa norte del Perú," *Revista del Museo Nacional* 33 (1964): 276. The encroachments of the plantations into the *comunidades*, as Collin-Delavaud indicates, has continued in varying degrees right up to the present day (see Gillin, *Moche*,

turn of the century, as well as the extent of land consolidation, it would seem reasonable to conclude that at least as many and probably far more families, perhaps as high as 5,000, were uprooted from their lands between 1890 and 1930. Politically speaking, this, of course, was no mean figure, particularly in light of the fact that it was representative of a once solid and flourishing rural, mestizo middle class in the region.

Moreover, if one were to include the number of *yanaconas*, or share-croppers, who likewise were pushed off the land during this period, these figures would have to be revised sharply upward. Although data again are lacking on the extent of *yanaconaje* in the region, it seems to have been utilized to a considerable extent as a form of land exploitation by planters in the valleys.[35] Such a system had always been favored by landowners, particularly in the sierra, who, for a lack of capital, among other reasons, preferred to employ the cheapest (and most inefficient) form of land exploitation possible. Thus, in addition to the peonage or bracero system, *yanaconaje* was probably used by many of the traditional planters of the region, particularly when labor and capital were scarce, as during and immediately after the War of the Pacific.

However, as the process of mechanization and modernization unfolded in the region after 1890, such a system became increasingly anachronistic. Vestiges of it were retained by the new sugar companies in some of the less productive areas of the valleys, which were deemed inadequate for cane cultivation.[36] But in the main, what sharecropping had existed gradually declined in the region.

This process of dispossession, which evolved during the first decades of the twentieth century, produced a classical case of the general proletarization of a formerly landed or semilanded sector of north-coast society. Deprived of their lands, both the region's small farmers and the *yanaconas* were forced to seek employment on the area's large sugar plantations. From respectable independent or semiindependent farmers, they therefore

pp. 5, 72, and passim). The Peruvian sociologist José Sabogal W., who is doing a similar study of the *comunidad* Santiago de Cao, also near Trujillo, has related the persistent struggles this community has experienced, even in recent times, with its giant, corporate neighbor Cartavio (interview, Lima, February 20, 1967).

[35] See Roger Alcantara Mostacero, "El yanaconaje en los valles de Chicama y de Santa Catalina," pp. 42-70. Solomon Miller, in his recent study of the plantation Laredo near Trujillo, states that some 3,000 of the plantation's 7,800 cultivable acres are still rented out to sharecroppers ("Hacienda to Plantation in Northern Peru: The Process of Proletarianization of a Tenant Farmer Society" in *Contemporary Change in Traditional Societies*, ed. Julian H. Steward, p. 193.

[36] Miller, "Hacienda to Plantation in Northern Peru," p. 193.

either dropped into the miserable ranks of sugar braceros, as in the case of the *yanaconas*,[37] or became *empleados* or skilled wage earners, ironically now dependent for their existence on those who had usurped their lands. Full of resentments against the valley's sugar companies, they contributed to the creation of an explosive social climate throughout the region that ultimately would have widespread political ramifications.

[37] It should be noted that, since the *yanaconas*, culturally speaking, were for the most part Indians, their transformation into the emerging plantation proletariate in the region evolved slowly as they gradually became exposed as braceros to the process of acculturation. See the discussion of the Indian, acculturation, and proletarization in Chapter 2.

4. Urban Decline and the Commercial Crisis of the 1920's

While the plantation system continued to expand along the north coast to the detriment of the small farmer and the sharecropper, signs of its adverse effect on urban life in the region began to appear. The traditional *latifundio* in Latin America has, by its very nature, been antiurban. Its tendency to be an entirely self-sufficing community, producing all the physical and even spiritual necessities of life, resulted, more often than not, in the retardation of city growth. This was to a large extent the case along the northern coast of Peru during the early nineteenth century. Cities and towns were small and relatively unimportant, while life was primarily focused on the still small and economically self-sufficient haciendas and plantations of the region.

The rise of the more modern sugar plantation toward the end of the century, however, tended to stimulate urban life all along the new coastal sugar belt from Trujillo to Chiclayo. No longer primarily concerned with maintaining a more or less self-contained economic unit, *hacendados* and new entrepreneurs, responding to European demand, increasingly began to convert the area's cultivatable land to sugar cane. With the ensuing emergence of a monocultural economy, trade and commerce quickly expanded to fulfill the needs of the growing plantation complex. It was not long before urban centers all along the coast were pulsating with economic activity and a new petite-bourgeois class was born.

The interconnection between town and plantation, however, was relatively short lived. During the first decades of the century the modernizing process on the area's plantations entered a new, corporate phase, which tended to clash with the developing urban structure of previous years. Sidney Mintz, commenting on the Cuban experience of the early twentieth century, has written "that the plantation (or latifundium) is an urbanizing force. As such it urbanizes while it proletarianizes. By creating towns, by appropriating large areas within which the rural population must concentrate itself densely, by bringing improvements in transportation and communication, by standardizing work practices, by establishing company stores, the latifundium does its powerful best to create a factory situation, albeit a rural one."[1] Mintz might have added that the competitive nature of the plantation vis à vis the established town was precisely due to its evolving corporate structure. The aim of the corporation was complete vertical integration, the elimination of all secondary or middle men from its operations and, thus, the consolidation of the entire system, so to speak, under one roof. Under such a philosophy, the adjacent town or city became a superfluous entity to the plantation. The latter simply assumed, as Mintz suggests, all the functions previously reserved to the town.

Casa Grande soon came to be the leading exponent and practitioner of this corporate design in the Trujillo region. In its quest for vertical integration the German-based firm moved in the second decade of the twentieth century to control all aspects of sugar production from field to market.[2] Vertical integration, however, did not stop here. It also involved developing ancillary enterprises designed to provide cheaply the necessary food and consumer goods for the plantation work force. Thus, Casa Grande purchased a number of haciendas in the nearby highlands and proceeded to convert and modernize their production schedules to meet inexpensively the plantation demands for foodstuffs. Likewise, the company pressed the national government to lease Casa Grande the nearby port of Malabrigo so that it might be used not only to facilitate the export of sugar to market but also to import directly from abroad consumer items for resale to its plantation work force. In 1915 the Gildemeisters secured

---

[1] Sidney Mintz, "The Industrialization of Sugar Production and Its Relationship to Social and Economic Change," in *Background to Revolution: The Development of Modern Cuba*, ed. Robert Freeman Smith, p. 182.

[2] See Chapter 1.

this concession and began to import large quantities of low-cost merchandise to stock the plantation's newly constructed company store. This new policy, coupled as it was to the suffocating effects of the expansion of sugar cane into staple-producing areas around the region's towns, crippled the urban life of the area over the following decade.

The boom in the sugar industry in the region during the decade of the 1860's first stimulated the growth and economic activity of towns throughout the region. Two of the most important were Ascope, located in the extreme northeast section of the valley, and the departmental capital, Trujillo. In the 1850's Ascope had been little more than a way station for mule trains bound for the central highlands of La Libertad and a notorious hideout for the region's bandits. However, its important geographical location on the main road leading from the coast to the highlands soon favored its development as a commercial center of considerable importance.[3] By the time Antonio Raimondi visited the town on another trip through the north in 1868 its commercial life had taken a sharp turn for the better. The Italian traveler noted that, commercially, Ascope was making gigantic strides almost daily and that a great many new stores were experiencing a booming trade with the coastal valleys and the highlands.[4]

A few years later in 1873 the burgeoning commercial activity of the town warranted the establishment of a bank (Banco de Ascope), one of only a handful in operation at that time in the nation's provinces.[5] While the effects of the War of the Pacific temporarily halted the economic progress of Ascope, the town apparently recovered its former prosperity with the recuperation of the valley's sugar industry in the 1890's.[6] By 1900 Ascope had been elevated to district capital and proclaimed officially a city by Congress.[7] The arrival of large numbers of Indian migrants to work on the valley's cane fields, coupled with a sharp increase in the amount of currency in circulation from the sugar industry, provided a strong stimulus to the area's commercial development. Not only did the *enganchadores* stock their plantation *bodegas* from stores located in Ascope and other valley towns, but also an increasing number of *ambulantes*, or itinerant vendors, began making the rounds of local plantations

[3] Julio Víctor Pacheco, "Historia nacional: Fragmentos de la obra inédita; historia de los valles de Chicama, Chimú y Virú," *La Industria*, 2 parts, March 18 and 25, 1922.

[4] Raimondi is quoted in Pedro Davalos y Lissón, *La primera centuria*, I, 190.

[5] Carlos Camprubí Alcazar, *Historia de los bancos en el Perú: 1860-1879*, p. 101.

[6] Raúl E. Haya, "Trujillo industrial de 1870 a 1920," *La Industria*, January 6, 1921.

[7] Pacheco, "Historia nacional."

to sell their wares purchased from area merchants. The planters, too, looked to local import houses to supply the material needed to operate their expanding operations as well as goods to maintain their country life styles.

Of greater commercial importance than Ascope, however, was Trujillo, which was located in the adjacent Santa Catalina Valley. Traditionally, Trujillo had been the cultural and commercial focal point for the region's three major valleys as well as the interior, highland provinces. With the rise of the sugar industry in the late 1860's the economic pulse and prestige of the departmental capital quickened considerably.

Through the nearby port of Salaverry, which by the 1870's had replaced the more northern port of Malabrigo as the department's major coastal docking facility,[8] came nearly all the manufactured goods consumed by the area's growing population. Domestic manufacturing was largely absent, and the tastes of Trujillo and the surrounding society, shaped as it was by its European-oriented planter aristocracy, tended toward the consumption of foreign goods. Then, as now, prestige and status, whether that of a humble mestiza servant emulating the lady of a planter town house or that of a plantation field foreman at Casa Grande, was reserved in the class hierarchy of the region for those who purchased and displayed all manner of European items on the streets of Trujillo or nearby villages and towns.

The major benefactor of such a psychology was the city's merchant class, which, by the turn of the century, had grown considerably in size and importance.[9] Finding ready markets for their imported goods, Trujillo's merchants readily resold their merchandise not only in the city itself, but also to eager merchants in the outlying towns and villages as well as to planters, *ambulantes*, and plantation *enganchadores*. So prosperous were many of the importers becoming that intermarriages with the older planter aristocracy apparently became common. One such case was the uniting of the Hoyle family, owners of a powerful Trujillo import house, and the Larco family, which by the early twentieth century had been accepted into Trujillo's social elite. Such liaisons were to have more than passing importance later when the planter and merchant classes were to join forces against the expansion of Casa Grande.

[8] *Memorial que presenta el sindicato de la "Empresa del Muelle y Ferrocarril del valle de Chicama" a la representación nacional*, p. 11; hereafter cited as *Memorial Ferrocarril*. In 1875 a railroad was built connecting Salaverry to the towns of Trujillo and Ascope (Alejandro Garland, *Las vías de comunicación en el Perú*, p. 24).
[9] *La Industria*, January 1, 1919.

The commercial progress of the region, tied as it was to the general prosperity of the sugar industry, continued throughout the years before World War I. Except for a brief recession around the turn of the century, the industry continued the steady growth that it had experienced during the 1890's.[10] Moreover, a growing population, stimulated by the continued strong migration from the sierra, produced a persistent increase in demand for goods throughout the region. Census figures in this regard are revealing. Reflecting the growing number of sugar workers on the area's plantations, districts like Chicama, Chocope, and Paiján, for example, between the official census of 1876 and estimates made in the year 1916 more than doubled in population, while the towns of Ascope, Chicama, and Trujillo exhibited a similar population rise.[11] This increase becomes quite spectacular if one considers that it occurred primarily between the years 1890 and 1916 when migration from the sierra was the heaviest[12] and not during the decade of the eighties when the war with Chile had ravaged and temporarily depopulated the region.

With the advent of World War I, the commercial activity of the region was given a sharp boost. A steep rise in the demand for Peruvian sugar abroad ushered in a new "golden age" for the region's planters.[13] Again, a renewed demand for braceros to work in the fast-expanding sugar industry occurred, further swelling the region's population and concomitantly stimulating commerce and trade throughout the department's coastal valleys.

During the war years Trujillo, in particular, experienced rapid commercial growth, further cementing its position as the most prosperous trade center in the region. Juan Armas, the son of a prosperous Trujillo mer-

[10] See Chapter 1.
[11] During these years the population of the district of Chicama jumped from 1,953 to 5,000, that of Chocope from 2,554 to 6,000 and that of Paiján from 2,944 to 6,000. The 1876 figures are taken from the official census of that year as recorded in Ministerio de Hacienda, *Censo general de la república del Perú, 1876*, V, 994-1000, 1001-1009, and 1030-1038, respectively. Since the next official national census was not taken until 1940, the population figures for 1916 are estimates reported in Germán Stiglich, *Diccionario geográfico peruano y almanaque de "La Crónica" para 1918*, pp. 149, 158-159, and 340, respectively. For the towns of Ascope and Chicama, see the appropriate pages in both these sources. Stiglich gives no estimates for Trujillo. However, Trujillo's estimated population for 1923 was 23,000, more than double the official 1876 figure of 10,436 (Juan L. E. Armas M., *Guía de Trujillo*, p. 84).
[12] See Chapter 2.
[13] See Chapter 1.

chant of that period, described the vibrant commercial activity of the
capital in those days:

The volume of business at that time was considerable. There were at least
twelve major retail stores that were experiencing great prosperity. Many of
these stores, as was the custom, also provided banking services, receiving
savings deposits and lending money. Trujillo during these years was an
entrepôt for a very large region, supplying, for example, most of the goods
for the area's large plantations. In addition, the city's merchants completely monopolized the commercial market of the interior provinces, including such distant areas as Cajabamba in the department of Cajamarca
and Pallasca in the department of Ancash. . . . The city's large commercial
houses also . . . had branch offices located throughout the region and
employed a great many employees who were well paid and received their
salaries punctually. The prosperity of these commercial houses thus contributed substantially to the economic well-being of the city and a large
portion of its middle class.[14]

Armas concluded by saying that Trujillo during this period "experienced
its best years of prosperity, a fact that led many visitors to comment that
this was the second most important city in the entire country."

This widespread prosperity, however, was soon seriously threatened by a
severe dislocation in the trading pattern of the region brought on in part
by the extension of the Gildemeister sugar interests at Casa Grande into
the realm of merchant activities. On July 21, 1915, an executive decree,
issued by the Benavides government, granted the German-Peruvian firm
the right to resurrect and renovate the long-inactive Chicama Valley port
of Malabrigo. Although purposely left somewhat vague, the decree further
granted the firm a franchise to import and export goods "relating to its
plantation operations" through the Malabrigo port. Finally, the concession
gave the company the right to construct and operate a railroad connecting
the port directly to Casa Grande.[15]

For several years the company, in its drive for vertical integration, had
been trying to obtain such a concession from the government. For one
thing, with its own railroad and port, Casa Grande would be able to export
its sugar far cheaper than by continuing the use of existing export facili-

---

[14] Armas, *Guía de Trujillo*, p. 83. Referring to the extensive business range of some
of Trujillo's import houses, Armas cited two such firms whose radius of activity
extended as far north as the department of Lambayeque and as far south as the
province of Santa located in the department of Ancash.

[15] Basadre, *Historia del Perú*, VIII, 3777.

ties. In the past the German-Peruvian company had, like other planters, transported its sugar via the only existing railroad connecting the valley with the port of Salaverry, some 150 kilometers away.[16] The new facilities would have the advantage not only of considerably shortening this distance, but also of being under the complete control of the company.

Furthermore, the concession would enable the firm to import, at substantially lower prices, consumer goods for a proposed company store, or bazaar, which was to replace the *bodegas* of the *enganchadores*. Company officials claimed that the purpose of the bazaar was to eliminate a common source of worker complaint against the *enganchadores*, long a symbol of hate among the braceros for their unscrupulous commercial practices.[17] However, despite such altruistic statements, the real purpose of the bazaar was more pragmatic. The company was simply seeking to maximize efficiency through further vertical integration, in this case devising ways of more profitably supplying the consumer needs of the plantation work force. Goods could be secured through the company's foreign or Lima commercial connections and imported at a cost far lower than from traditional local commercial sources.

It is also quite possible that the Gildemeisters may have had a secondary motive in pursuing the concession. The company was active in a number of other national and international activities, among them the importing business in Lima. Company officials may well have seen the concession as a first step in converting Casa Grande into a major trading center for the sale and distribution of goods throughout the region. Although such a design is difficult to verify, some clues as to its existence can be gleaned from a report published later by the company defending the concession from the attacks of its opponents. One of the points made by the tract's author was that the concession, and particularly the provision granting the construction of a railroad from Malabrigo to Casa Grande and eventually up into the nearby highlands, would create new commercial possibilities in the region by opening up a heretofore economically unexploited region.[18] Such a statement ignored the fact that Trujillo had traditionally main-

[16] It was widely claimed throughout the region that the English Peruvian Corporation, which operated the old railroad between Ascope and the Salaverry port under a government concession, charged excessively high rates. An editorial in *La Industria* on October 30, 1915, stated that Casa Grande sought the port and railroad concession in order to avoid the "excessive charges" of the Peruvian Corporation.

[17] *La Industria*, April 22, 1912.

[18] *Memorial Ferrocarril*, pp. 15-16 and 23.

tained trade hegemony in this "unexploited region" and that Casa Grande would in effect be moving to challenge this hegemony.

The opportunity to obtain the Malabrigo concession, after several previously vain attempts, had finally presented itself with the rise to the presidency of Colonel Oscar R. Benavides in 1914. The new president, having overthrown the previous Billinghurst government and thus temporarily unsettled the financial respectability of the government, soon found himself in economic difficulties. In February, 1915, the Gildemeisters, seeing the possible advantages to be gained from the government's predicament, offered the president a loan of some 44,000 pounds sterling.[19] The loan was promptly accepted, and the concession was granted to the Gildemeisters five months later.

Once the concession had been granted, Casa Grande lost no time rehabilitating the port. Soon temporary facilities had been constructed, and the company began to import directly from Germany and elsewhere large quantities of merchandise for the plantation's newly created "general bazaar." These goods were subsequently put on sale to Casa Grande's workers for prices considerably below the retail value of equivalent merchandise sold in stores throughout the region. Furthermore, it was not long before the surrounding population as well as merchants from the towns in the nearby highlands learned of the bargains to be had at the bazaar. Apparently, the company made no efforts to close the bazaar to outsiders, so that by the end of 1918 Casa Grande was bustling with crowds, and its bazaar was predictably doing a "land-office business." Substantially lower prices were made possible by the very fact that Casa Grande could count on the commercial power and organization of a corporation that reached far beyond the confines of Peru. Thus, the Chicama-based plantation was able to draw upon unlimited credit facilities, gain direct access to Lima and German wholesale markets, and import goods in large volume on its own transportation network—all of which was clearly far beyond the more limited commercial capabilities of local area merchants.

When the news of Casa Grande's proposed bazaar reached Trujillo, it produced immediate and widespread alarm among the city's merchant

[19]Ministerio de Hacienda, *Memoria del director del crédito público-anexo*, p. 38. See also the editorial in *La Prensa*, October 10, 1917, as well as Senator Durand's comments on the concession in Congreso Ordinario de 1917, *Diario de los debates de la H. Cámara de Senadores*, September 13, 1917, p. 285; hereafter cited as *Diario de los debates*.

class. Forced to pay high duty on goods imported through Salaverry as well as substantial transportation rates to the Peruvian Corporation, operators of the railroad from the port to the city,[20] Trujillo's merchants realized that they could not compete for any length of time with the commercial advantages of a company with the size and power of Casa Grande. They further recognized that unless the bazaar was effectively closed to outsiders the concession meant not only the elimination of the formerly lucrative trade with Casa Grande, but also the collective collapse of the city's traditional trade hegemony in the region. As a result, the city's merchants quickly mounted a fierce campaign to close down the bazaar.

This campaign, which began to unfold during the first few months of 1917, was spearheaded by the Cámara de Comercio, Agricultura e Industria del Departamento de La Libertad. Founded in 1902 by Eugenio Loyer, a prominent merchant, and Raúl E. Haya, the father of the founder of Aprismo, Víctor Raúl Haya de la Torre, the Chamber had played an active and important role in the political and economic life of the city and region throughout its fifteen-year history.[21] With main offices in Trujillo, the Chamber, despite its supposed departmental scope, drew its members from the power structure of the capital and was thus composed of the city's leading merchants as well as planters from the surrounding valleys.

The opening salvo in the Chamber's campaign against the Casa Grande bazaar occurred in early January, when a resolution was adopted by its membership expressing great concern over the concession of Malabrigo to Casa Grande and calling on organizations throughout the region to come to the defense of the area's vital economic interests. In part, the resolution, which was printed and widely circulated throughout the department, made the following indictment and appeal:

Trujillo already has a principal port at Salaverry and an auxiliary one at nearby Huanchaco, both of which adequately take care of imports and exports for the region. The creation of another port to serve only the private interests and convenience of a local agricultural company would be wholly prejudicial and harmful to other economic interests in the region.

---

[20] The Peruvian Corporation substantially hiked its carrying charges in subsequent years, a fact that weighed heavily upon Trujillo merchants. This rate increase was in part due to the fact that Casa Grande now exported its sugar directly through Malabrigo, thereby depriving the railroad of a traditionally lucrative source of business.

[21] Armas, *Guía de Trujillo*, pp. 88-89.

Such a port would considerably diminish the value of local stores and companies to the point where, economically, Trujillo and the surrounding countryside would enter into a period of complete decadence. The Chamber of Commerce is justifiably concerned for the future of our province should the commercial imports and agricultural exports of the region be detoured, as proposed, through the port of Malabrigo. We therefore call on all public officials, our representatives in Congress, and all concerned individuals to join with the Chamber in undertaking a tenacious campaign to prevent the construction of railroad and docking facilities at Malabrigo by the firm Casa Grande Zuckerplantagen.[22]

Response to the Chamber's resolution was not long in coming. During the next several months Alfredo Pinillos, another leading Trujillo merchant and long-time president of the Chamber, received numerous pledges of support from a variety of organizations throughout the department. The most notable of these came from groups whose direct economic interests were threatened by the concession. They included the Consejo Municipal de Salaverry, which represented the collective interests of the port; the Consejo Provincial de Trujillo; the Sociedad Ferrocarril de Protección Mutua de Trujillo, which spoke for the railroad workers of the Peruvian Corporation; and the newspaper *La Reforma*, which was owned by the planter Víctor Larco.[23] In addition, the area's planters, who had long been in conflict with Casa Grande and who probably saw their own interests threatened by the concession, almost unanimously lined up behind the position of the Chamber.[24]

Indicating the mounting concern of the area's merchants, the Chamber's attack on the Malabrigo concession grew in intensity over succeeding months. Pressure was brought to bear on the department's congressional delegation to present a bill in the forthcoming session that would rescind the concession, while Alfredo Pinillos also wrote personally to the president in an effort to have the grant cancelled.[25] Moreover, hoping to solicit

[22] Resolución General de la Cámara de Comercio, January 1, 1917, in Archivo de la Cámara.

[23] See the numerous letters from these and other organizations to the Chamber president over the period January-March, 1917, in Archivo de la Cámara. Also see various pledges of support in *Exposición de la cámara . . . en Malabrigo*.

[24] The planters' main objection to the concession was that Casa Grande, with its own railroad and dock facilities, would be able to reduce substantially its export costs, placing the region's planters at a further competitive disadvantage vis-à-vis the German-Peruvian firm.

[25] Alfredo Pinillos, Trujillo, to José Pardo, Lima, January 20, 1917, l.s., 2 pp., Archivo de la Cámara.

a favorable response to the proposed bill in Congress, the Chamber published an extensive tract outlining its position on the matter. An examination of this tract is revealing, for it illustrates not only the damage that the Chamber claimed the concession was causing the economy of the region, but also certain generally hostile attitudes prevalent in Trujillo toward the activities of Casa Grande.

The basic argument of the tract was that, by allowing Casa Grande to operate its own port for the purpose of importing goods at low cost to be sold at the plantation's bazaar, the government was unwittingly creating unfair competition, which would ultimately result in the destruction of the existing urban commercial life of the region. Its authors argued that towns like Ascope, Paiján, and Chocope were already in decline and that their eventual demise as urban trading centers was inevitable if a bazaar was allowed to operate at Casa Grande. Furthermore, they submitted that Trujillo, the traditional supplier of goods for these towns as well as for the surrounding plantations, would likewise suffer stagnation, since its former markets would surely be absorbed by Casa Grande's "widening field" of commercial endeavors.[26] Finally, indicating outright hostility to the German-Peruvian firm, which over the past decades had already absorbed much of the area's cultivable land, the authors accused the firm of attempting to monopolize the entire region from Trujillo to Pacasmayo.

Is it in the interest of this weak nation . . . to allow within its borders a *German* company of the economic power of Casa Grande Zuckerplantagen? Is it in the interest of our country to increase Casa Grande's power by granting it the exclusive property rights over a large area of national territory like the port of Malabrigo in order for it to build and operate its own railroad and docking facilities? What does the future offer us under these conditions and especially in view of the spirit of absorption and intransigency that characterizes the *German* colony [Casa Grande] here? If, enclosed in its present boundaries and limited to its agricultural business, Casa Grande now clashes and still tries and desires to absorb all its neighbors, what will it do tomorrow with an even wider radius of action and with greater and more diverse powers?[27]

What is particularly significant here is the tract's strongly worded nationalistic appeal, in which Casa Grande is identified as a wholly foreign operation despite the fact that the Gildemeisters, who managed the plantation, claimed, not without some justification, to be Peruvians.

[26] *Exposición de la cámara . . . en Malabrigo*, pp. 81-85.
[27] Ibid., p. 84, translation and italics mine.

While the Chamber's campaign against the Malabrigo concession continued to gather momentum, Casa Grande by no means remained silent. Using the columns of *La Industria*, which in recent years had begun to defend the interests of the German-Peruvian firm, Casa Grande countered the arguments of the Chamber. Like the Chamber, it too published an extensive tract defending its position in the matter. The crux of this position was that the new port and railroad facilities would serve to open up heretofore unexploited regions of the highlands of La Libertad, creating new commercial possibilities and that, contrary to the Chamber's charge, the traditional trade of Ascope and Trujillo would not be affected, since the area had never really been accessible for commercial exploitation.[28] Such an argument, however, was largely fallacious, for, as Armas stated, both Ascope and Trujillo had traditionally maintained trade hegemony in this region and now stood to lose this preeminence to Casa Grande.[29]

By mid-September the controversy had extended beyond the local confines of Trujillo to Lima with the introduction of the bill of annulment in Congress by the three senators from La Libertad—Agustín Ganoza, Víctor Larco, and José Ignacio Chopitea.[30] All three were prominent sugar planters in the Chicama-Santa Catalina region who had long been in hostile competition with Casa Grande. The senators summed up the Trujillo opposition to the Malabrigo concession in a parliamentary document published in *La Prensa* (Lima) on October 10, 1917. In it the senators declared that the concession was injurious both to the state, which would lose large amounts of customs revenue from the diminution of trade through Salaverry, and to the general commercial trade of Trujillo, which would be detoured to Casa Grande, via Malabrigo.

Additional controversy was injected into the question during a heated debate in Congress. The participants in the exchange were Senator Juan Durand, a major opponent of the concession, and Senator Miguel Echenique, an employee of Gildemeister and Co. in Lima,[31] who defended the concession.

[28] *Memorial Ferrocarril*, pp. 15-16 and 23. How Casa Grande reasoned that Ascope, in particular, would not be damaged by the Malabrigo concession is difficult to understand. Once the railroad from Malabrigo to Casa Grande was built (and the proposal was to extend it even farther into the highlands), merchants in the sierra would no longer buy their goods from Ascope but rather at the bazaar at Casa Grande.

[29] Armas, *Guía de Trujillo*, p. 83.

[30] *La Industria*, September 15, 1917.

[31] Juan Pedro Paz Soldán, *Diccionario biográfico de peruanos contemporaneos*, p. 155.

Durand. I have many arguments [against this concession], which I do not wish to present for fear of hurting the sensibilities of certain people. However, it seems clear to me that, in the final analysis, the effective customs supervision of Malabrigo by the government will be completely impossible. Can a government employee who is assigned the job of supervising and regulating the imports of such a port, on a salary of thirty or forty libras, resist the influence and demands of a powerful company like Gildemeister and Co.? Certainly, no such employee or employees, upon the arrival of ten thousand closed crates, will be able to check their contents to assess their legality. I am sure that, if he tried to do so, he would be dismissed from his job immediately.

Echenique [*interrupting*]. That statement is an afront to the government.

Durand [*continuing*]. It is nothing of the kind. I am simply referring to a fact of life. I know that in parts of that region [Chicama-Santa Catalina] there are goods circulating for less price than in Lima. With the unloading of only two ships at Malabrigo, the merchants of Ascope have already received large amounts of goods at half the price found in Trujillo for similar merchandise. This would certainly increase with the granting of this concession. Now if the port is in private hands and if the railroad is in private hands and the merchants of the region have to go to Casa Grande for their merchandise, the day that Casa Grande wants to ruin any native merchant or coerce him into submitting to its commercial monopoly, all the company would have to do is abandon his shipment on the docks or in transit to the plantation.

Echenique [*interrupting*]. Such a shipment would go through Salaverry.

Durand [*continuing*]. In Salaverry the port is government controlled and regulated so that the state and the nation receive their customs revenue, while in Malabrigo these taxes simply would not be paid. In Salaverry goods are taxed, while in Malabrigo they would enter the country duty free.

Echenique [*interrupting*]. The government will not permit that to happen.

Durand [*continuing*]. Whether or not the government permits it, it is a fact that this happens today and will happen more frequently once the concession is legalized. There exist in this country certain interests that are so powerful that even the government is incapable of acting to control their activities.

Echenique. But the government is obligated to prevent such contraband.

Durand. All I have to say is that the customs apparatus at the port of Malabrigo will not function nearly as effectively as in Trujillo and that this will be due to the fact that Malabrigo will be in the private hands of Casa Grande.[32]

Several points are worth noting in this exchange. First, Durand charged, not illogically, that government customs officials assigned to the port would not be able to police it adequately, given the powerful economic and political influence of the Gildemeisters in the region. This warning, together with his assertion, unchallenged by Echenique, that already contraband goods were circulating freely in the area, presumably from Casa Grande via Malabrigo, lend credence to the theory that Casa Grande's secondary objective may indeed have been to become the main commercial entrepôt for the region. Second, Durand raised the specter of nationalism when he argued that, once large stocks of merchandise were imported by Casa Grande and circulated in the area, the German-Peruvian company would be in the position to ruin any local merchant who came to rely on the bazaar as a regular source of cheaper goods by simply cutting off his supply. The implication was that Casa Grande, in his mind a wholly foreign firm, would then be able to step easily into the void left by a bankrupt national.

Significantly, Echenique's only reply to these charges was a weak one—that the government would strictly enforce the provisions of the concession, which limited the goods imported by Casa Grande to those essential to its operation and which assumed the usual collection of customs taxes on such items. In view of the "realities" of Peruvian politics, there is no reason to believe that the government had the power or inclination to enforce such a policy against such powerful interests as the Gildemeisters. Indeed, the mere fact that the company had opportunely loaned the government a large sum of money, and would do so again in the near future, casts serious doubts on the government's desire to enforce strictly the provisions of the concession.

Despite the arguments of the concession's opponents, as well as the pressure exerted by the department's power structure, the move to annul the Malabrigo concession failed when on October 16, 1917, the Senate defeated the measure by a vote of twenty-one to fourteen.[33] The way was now officially clear for Casa Grande to operate Malabrigo, although the implication of Durand's comments was that the company had been using

[32] *Diario de los debates*, October 11, 1917, pp. 579-580, my translation.
[33] *La Industria*, October 17, 1917.

the port ever since the executive decree had been issued in 1915 and perhaps even earlier. By April, 1918, the Chamber reported that the port was in full operation and that the damage already done to Trujillo's commercial interests was considerable.[34]

The records of the Ministerio de Hacienda y Comercio reveal that the quantity of goods that passed through Malabrigo during the immediate postwar years was indeed large. Between December, 1919, and March, 1921, some eleven permits were issued to unload cargo directly at Malabrigo. Of these, at least four were specifically listed as carrying general merchandise destined for resale at the Casa Grande bazaar. The *Ardover* out of Hamburg, for example, was issued a permit to unload two hundred tons of general merchandise on February 19, 1921.[35] Trujillo merchant and transport interests not only had lost a previously lucrative supply trade to Casa Grande, but also were now in the process of incurring further losses to the plantation bazaar acting as a retail outlet for the entire Chicama Valley.

Meanwhile, the continuation of a steady flow of commercial goods through Malabrigo to Casa Grande was further assured in June, 1920, when the German-Peruvian firm made a large loan to the then fledgling regime of Augusto B. Leguía. The loan, which amounted to 200,000 pounds sterling,[36] further cemented relations between the government and the Gildemeister firm.

While the opening of Malabrigo and the creation of the new bazaar at Casa Grande began to alter the traditional trade patterns of the region, to the commercial detriment of Ascope and Trujillo, new economic troubles descended upon the area. The region's sugar industry, which had been making huge profits during and immediately after the war, suddenly began to encounter serious difficulties. The root of the problem was the rapid postwar recovery of the European beet-sugar industry, which cut sharply into former Peruvian markets while also causing a glut on the world sugar market, which depressed prices.[37] Widespread paycuts as well as layoffs in the work force of the area's plantations soon followed. Since the economy of the northern coast was largely tied to the state of the sugar industry,

[34] "Memoria que presenta el consejo de . . . la cámara—1918," 8 pp., Archivo de la Cámara.
[35] See Ministerio de Hacienda y Comercio, *Memorias*, 1920 and 1921, first part, pp. 56-177 and 73-81, respectively.
[36] Terms of the contract can be found in the 1921 volume of ibid., pp. 1293-1294.
[37] See Chapter 1.

the latter's decline, which by 1924 had reached severe proportions, brought on a general commercial depression throughout the area.

During the next several years, as the sugar industry continued to decline, the commercial crisis of Trujillo deepened. By 1929, prior to the onset of the world depression, four major import houses had gone bankrupt. Furthermore, a large number of smaller retail stores (possibly as many as fifty) were forced to liquidate and close during this period.[38] While no exact figures are available, a sizeable number of small merchants and *empleados* were either thrown out of work or forced to take substantial salary cuts. Bankruptcy of some of the city's older and larger firms, which had traditionally served as savings banks,[39] caused further economic distress by wiping out the savings of a substantial portion of the area's middle class. The upshot of this situation was a growing expression of hostility on the part of many segments of the city's middle class toward Casa Grande, which, in view of its commercial policies of recent years, was largely blamed for the crisis.

This hostility was not a new phenomenon and had been ripening for a number of years. Perhaps its first open manifestations had been visible during the strikes of 1917 and 1921, when many *empleados* of the German-Peruvian firm had joined with workers in condemning the company's policies. On these occasions, it will be recalled, outbreaks of violence had erupted over instances of alleged maltreatment of Peruvian employees by their German superiors. Furthermore, during the bloody 1921 strike in the region, Antenor Orrego had to some extent succeeded in mobilizing support for the strikers among some elements of Trujillo's middle and working classes. This support not only included expressions of sympathy for the strikers' cause, but also involved some financial aid to their beleaguered forces.[40]

The longstanding conflict between the Gildemeisters and the Larcos, moreover, further contributed to this hostile sentiment.[41] Community sympathy generally lay with the Larcos, who were seen as the defenders of Peruvian sovereignty against the "invasion" of the Teutonic Gildemeisters.

[38] "Memoria de la cámara–1928," 4 pp., Archivo de la Cámara.

[39] Armas, *Guía de Trujillo*, p. 86. Commercial establishments acting as banking institutions were not uncommon in the provinces, where the number of banks was usually small.

[40] See Chapter 2.

[41] See Chapter 1.

The demise of the Larcos in 1927 was widely interpreted as one further, indeed decisive, step in the Gildemeister plan of monopolizing the entire area.[42]

Finally, as Trujillo's commerce felt the adverse effects of the competition from the German-Peruvian firm as well as the declining sugar industry, hostility grew more intense. It was particularly reflected in the pages of *El Norte*, which ever since its foundation in 1923 had tended to speak for the city's middle class.[43] In 1924, for example, the paper ran a series of articles analyzing the causes of the city's commercial crisis in which heavy blame was placed on the unfair commercial policies practiced by Casa Grande. The paper further attacked not only the commercial but also the land absorption activities of the German-Peruvian company and concluded that the firm would end up absorbing the entire commercial-agrarian life of the region.[44]

At the same time, the Chamber stepped up its longstanding campaign against Casa Grande. Shortly after receiving yet another rebuff in its efforts to get the German-Peruvian company to curtail voluntarily its ever widening commercial business,[45] the Chamber issued two reports analyzing the causes of the present commercial crisis. Both attributed the crisis to the unfair competition of the plantation's bazaar, charging that its operations had expanded so rapidly in recent years that the company was now virtually monopolizing the import trade of the entire region.[46]

A few months later, the new president of the Chamber and owner of one of the city's largest import houses, Rómulo Hoyle, estimated that the

[42] Interview with Leopoldo Pita Verdi, Lima, March 21, 1967. Carlos Manuel Cox, another Trujillano and early Aprista leader, confirmed this (interview, Lima [Miraflores], June 1, 1967).

[43] The paper defended the interests of employees in salary disputes with management, small landowners from the agrarian attacks of Casa Grande and Cartavio, and the merchants in conflict with the Gildemeister import policies. Its director was the youthful Antenor Orrego Espinoza, who, in 1930, was elected president of the Sociedad de Empleados de Trujillo.

[44] See particularly the paper between September 21 and 28, 1924.

[45] In a letter to Ganoza dated November 15, 1926, Hans Gildemeister politely agreed to meet personally with the directors of the Chamber, but adamantly refused to discuss any reduction in the level of the bazaar's commercial activities (Archivo de la Cámara).

[46] Informe de la Comisión por la Asamblea General de Comerciantes, Agricultures y Industriales, Trujillo, to president of the Chamber, Trujillo, November 29, 1926, l.s., 5 pp., Archivo de la Cámara, and "Memoria de la cámara de comercio: Datos sobre la situación económica de Trujillo," 4 pp., Archivo de la Cámara.

bazaar was costing Trujillo merchants some twenty thousand pounds sterling a month.[47] Such losses as well as Casa Grande's continued intransigence served to further harden the community's already resentful attitude toward the company. Indicative of this attitude was a letter directed to the Chamber in May, 1930, and signed by over one hundred local merchants, attacking the "blatantly ruinous" practices of Casa Grande. After reiterating these practices, the protesting merchants drew a direct parallel between the company's past policy of absorbing small landholdings in the region and its more recent attempts to monopolize the trade of the area. Finally, they warned that, unless something was done to stop Casa Grande, Trujillo would soon find itself in the same miserable state of decay and abandon as Ascope, Magdalena, and other towns in the region that had, over the past ten years, virtually ceased to function as vital urban centers because of the policies of Casa Grande.[48]

Paradoxically, by the 1930's the state of urban life in the Chicama and Santa Catalina valleys had virtually come full circle since the days of the early 1860's. At that time towns were small and insignificant, while life was centered, as in colonial times, on the region's numerous haciendas. Then, stimulated by the expansion and growth of the nascent sugar industry, urban life bloomed. Towns like Ascope and Trujillo became thriving commercial and staple-producing centers, supplying the nearby plantations with needed supplies.

Ironically, however, the sugar industry, which had earlier given life to these towns, began around the turn of the century to destroy them. At first, decline came in the form of sugar cane, which increasingly invaded the lands surrounding the region's towns, lands formerly devoted to staple production and which sustained a large number of small, independent farmers who populated these urban centers.[49] Subsequently, the area's towns, principally Ascope and Trujillo, were rocked by the commercial competition of the enormous sugar combine, Casa Grande. Finally, while the traditional trade pattern of the region was being altered, a sharp postwar drop in the price of sugar in the principal European capitals crippled the entire economy of the area.

The upshot of these events was a rising tide of discontent and resent-

---

[47] Rómulo Hoyle, Trujillo, to Cecilio Cox, Trujillo, January 18, 1927, l.s., 2 pp., Archivo de la Cámara.
[48] Signed letter to the president of the Cámara, Trujillo, May 28, 1930, 4 pp., Archivo de la Cámara.
[49] See Chapter 3.

ment among the formerly prosperous petite bourgeois of the region. As hard times intensified, this segment of the community increasingly identified and singled out as its enemy the foreign-owned sugar combine Casa Grande, which it blamed for the region's economic troubles. The alienation of yet another segment of society in the Chicama-Santa Catalina region further weakened the traditional modus vivendi and paved the way for future disorders and violence.

5. The Trujillo Bohemia and Víctor Raúl Haya de la Torre: The Rise of the Reformers

While the rise and consolidation of the sugar industry continued during the first decades of the century to dislocate the traditional patterns of life in the Trujillo region, causing in the process widespread discontent among the general population, the political response to these changes remained for some time largely ineffective. It is true that protests from time to time appeared in the local press, denouncing the concentration of land as well as the wretched working and living conditions of the region's sugar braceros. Occasionally, such protests found a hearing in Congress, as with the Malabrigo affair in 1917, but in no instance did the outcome result in any positive moves to alleviate or correct the abuses.

The reason for this general lack of a political response was twofold. First, those groups adversely affected by the process of modernization in the sugar industry were still largely unorganized and politically too inarticulate to press their demands effectively on the existing political structure. Some scattered attempts were made, for example, to organize the remaining small farmers in the region into a protective association capable of exerting political pressure to prevent the absorption of their lands by the larger plantations. However, the general level of political awareness among the region's *agricultores* was still too low for such a plan to succeed. Similarly, though achieving a greater measure of success, the incipient labor movement suffered, at least in its early stages, from the same problem. Not until 1921 was the political awareness of the average sugar bracero sufficient to enable the erection of a rudimentary labor organization capable of a modicum of united political action.

A second reason lay in the very nature of the established political structure of the region. On the local level the major political offices, as might have been expected, were either directly or indirectly controlled by the major sugar interests of the area. Although occasionally these interests would come into conflict over questions of individual concern, such as water rights, they generally acted in a concerted manner to defend the existing order.

On the national level the story was similar, though with some variation. The congressional delegation from Trujillo invariably came from the region's traditional sugar aristocracy.[1] For the most part, this group defended the broad interests of the area's sugar industry as well as the status quo in general. However, it is significant that when the interests of this traditional planter element diverged from the larger corporate entities in the area, particularly Casa Grande, the latter were generally able to carry the day. Perhaps the best example of this power was the celebrated Malabrigo affair, in which the traditional sugar interests, siding with the Trujillo merchant establishment against Casa Grande, attempted unsuccessfully to get Congress to annul the concession of the port of Malabrigo to the German-Peruvian company. Significantly, the Malabrigo affair indicated that local political power no longer resided with the traditional sugar planters or, for that matter, with the Trujillo merchant establishment. Rather, power now lay with the corporate interests of Casa Grande and the Gildemeister family, whose political influence, unlike their competitors', reached all the way to the Presidential Palace in Lima, where according to the rules of Peruvian politics most major local issues are usually decided.

This fact was not surprising given the traditionally preponderant influence of the nation's large exporters on the highest circles of government. During the "Aristocratic Republic" (1895-1919) the composition of virtually every regime was heavily dominated by representatives of this

---

[1] Two of the three senators from La Libertad from 1909 to 1921 were the powerful sugar planters Víctor Larco Herrera and José Ignacio Chopitea (see Víctor E. Ayarza, *Reseña histórica del senado del Perú*, pp. 28-147).

powerful economic group. The fact that the nation's foreign-exchange position and, indeed, the government's very financial standing largely hinged on the condition of the nation's exporters made this an inevitable aspect of high-level Peruvian politics. Consequently, the sugar exporters of the north coast had long occupied a foremost position within the ruling Civilist party. Indeed, several of the nation's most distinguished Civilist leaders, including two-time President José Pardo, came from the ranks of the major north-coast sugar planters.

Although the rise of Leguía to power in 1919 ended the Civilist party's monopoly on the presidency, it by no means signaled a complete end to the influence of the sugar exporters in the highest echelons of national policy making. For one thing, Leguía himself was tied to the sugar industry by virtue of his long association with the British Sugar Estates, whose holdings in Cañete and Nepeña he at one time had managed.[2] Furthermore, as Jorge Basadre has correctly stated, although Leguía broke the political power of the Civilists, he by no means moved to curtail their traditional economic and social position in the country. Indeed, they, along with other sectors of coastal society, tended to profit immensely from Leguía's economic policies.[3] Also, Leguía, like his Civilist predecessors, could not afford to move against the interests of the sugar exporters for fear of the adverse impact this might have on the overall stability of the national economy.[4] Finally, some of the foreign sugar companies established strong political ties with whatever political group or faction happened to be in control of the Presidential Palace. One need only point to the Gildemeisters, who, by the astute use of loans, established close relations with the Pardo and Leguía governments—both political enemies.

The upshot of these circumstances was that virtually every Peruvian government from 1895 through the *oncenio* was in one way or another vitally connected to the large sugar interests of the north coast. This fact explains to a large extent the general unresponsiveness of the central government to local pleas in that area to remedy the economic and social dislocations distressing much of the population in the face of rapid modernization of the sugar industry. The prosperity of the industry, no

[2] Basadre, *Historia del Perú*, VIII, 3554. Basadre suggests that Leguía continued the friendships he had made throughout the industry even after becoming president again (*Perú: Problema y posibilidad*, p. 183).

[3] Basadre, *Perú*, p. 183.

[4] Leguía's actions in intervening in Larco's financial troubles in 1927 indicated the continuing concern of any Peruvian government as to the state of the sugar industry (see footnote 51, Chapter 1).

matter what its cost to the local socioeconomic structure, was simply too important to the central government for it to consider tampering with its development.

Despite the general intransigence of both the local and the national power structure in the face of rising social pressures, there appeared in Trujillo in 1915 a small group of intellectually restless Liberteños, who, in questioning the general mores of Trujillo society, in time came to challenge the political dominance of the area's political elite. Dubbed the "Trujillo Bohemia" by the Limeño journalist and writer Juan Parra del Riego who visited Trujillo in 1916, the group was formed as a kind of avant-garde literary club. Its founders were José Eulogio Garrido, a local poet and writer, and Antenor Orrego Espinoza, a Trujillo journalist and later major ideologist for the Aprista movement. The group, which at its height probably numbered no more than ten or fifteen members, mostly students of middle-class background at the University of Trujillo, included, among others, the poet César Vallejo, the painter Macedonio de la Torre, and the later founder of Aprismo, Víctor Raúl Haya de la Torre. According to Garrido, the group met every Wednesday and Saturday in his house to discuss the latest literary news contained in the most recent Limeño journals, which arrived weekly by steamer from the capital. In addition, members recited their own poetic compositions as well as passages from their favorite poets like Darío, Nervo, and Whitman. The group also had its social aspects, its members frequently meeting to lunch together in an outdoor cafe on the Plaza de Armas or to undertake excursions to the nearby archeological ruins of Chanchan or to the beaches of Las Delicias.[5]

While espousing avant-garde literary views that often scandalized the more traditional Trujillo literati, the group also railed against other conservative aspects of Trujillo society and culture. Trujillo at the time still presented the picture of a static and closed aristocratic Peruvian city of past centuries. Juan Espejo Asturrizaga, a member of the *bohemia*, captured the spirit of Trujillo of that time when he wrote:

Trujillo still conserved the slow, undisturbed and conventlike atmosphere of its colonial past. The majority of its families lived a completely with-

---

[5] For a short but valuable discussion of the literary activities of the Trujillo *bohemia*, see Luis Monguió, *La poesia postmodernista peruana*, pp. 48-50. See also Antenor Orrego's prologue to César Vallejo, *Trilce*, pp. 15-17, for a more intimate account of the activities of the *bohemia*.

drawn and cloistered existence. The quiet solitude of its streets was scarcely disturbed by the flow of noonday traffic . . . and after seven o'clock in the evening the same streets were once again silent and deserted. Life slipped by gently within the confines of its aristocratic homes, protected by their heavy, iron gates and latice-worked colonial windows. Such was Trujillo, a haughty, egotistical and closed society whose citizens still retained a very medieval conception of class and who resisted change tenaciously.[6]

To the middle-class members of the *bohemia*, eager to experiment with new ideas and intellectual currents as well as establish their own identity, this aristocratic society seemed hopelessly narrow and restrictive. Restless and rebellious, they thus struck out individually and as a group against the seemingly vain and petty conventions that were the norms of Trujillo society.

Though politics was in general never the primary concern of the group, its members could not, by the very nature of their criticisms of Trujillo society, avoid becoming involved in political questions. Indeed, some of the group's members, particularly Orrego and to a lesser extent Haya, Alcides Spelucín, Espejo, and, later, Carlos Manuel Cox, took an active part in local politics. Orrego was the acknowledged leader of the more politically active element in the *bohemia* and perhaps best expressed the philosophy of the group regarding involvement in politics.

We did not want to resign ourselves to an "ivory tower" sort of existence, which seemed petty, egotistical, and sterile. It seemed necessary to burst out of our little world and we did. Since we were not and could not be conformists, because it would have been the negation of our very beings, we had to clash with everything and everybody. Trujillo's institutions, public powers, social conventions, university, an insolent and exploiting plutocracy, its sacred falsehoods, class customs, lack of honesty and honor, a humiliating servileness, its exploitation of the worker, its bureaucracy, professional politics, and general presumptuous ignorance—all had to suffer the ferocity of our attacks.[7]

Orrego, like most of the *bohemia*'s members, came from a modest middle class background. He had been born in 1892 on his family's

---

[6] Juan Espejo Asturrizaga, *César Vallejo: Itinerario del hombre, 1892-1923*, p. 31, my translation. Espejo's work is a valuable first-hand account of the *bohemia* by one of its first members.

[7] Antenor Orrego's prologue to Alcides Spelucín, *El libro de la nave dorada: Poemas*, pp. 17-20, my translation.

hacienda, Montán, in the province of Chota in the sierra of Cajamarca. At the age of eight he moved with his family to Trujillo, apparently because of the better opportunity for schooling in the departmental capital. He soon entered the Lazarist Seminario de San Carlos y San Marcelo, where he first met the Hayas, Agustín and Víctor Raúl, as well as the Spelucín brothers. Upon graduation he moved on to the University of Trujillo and shortly thereafter cofounded the *bohemia*.[8]

At about this time Parra del Riego described Orrego as a quiet and timid young man who, should he go to Lima, would surely be "eaten alive" by the more aggressive and boisterous Limeño intellectuals.[9] Be that as it may, the youthful reformer soon made a reputation for himself in Trujillo. Using the columns of, first, *La Reforma* and then *La Libertad*, Orrego increasingly began to speak out on local political issues. However, it was not until the 1918 labor strike in the Chicama Valley and its 1921 sequel that Orrego became directly involved in the social problems which were, by then, racking the sugar valleys of the region. During this time he strongly defended the demands of the strikers and in 1921 wholeheartedly threw the support of the daily *La Libertad*, which he edited, behind the efforts of the workers to organize into unions.[10]

While Orrego was beginning to do battle on the side of the sugar workers from the pages of *La Libertad*, another member of the *bohemia*, Víctor Raúl Haya de la Torre, was engaging in a different sort of political activity. Haya, three years younger than Orrego, was born in Trujillo in 1895. Though official biographers have made much of his supposed aristocratic background,[11] Haya's origins were actually considerably more modest. His father, Raúl Edmundo Haya who was born in Cajabamba in the adjoining department of Cajamarca, came from a family of schoolteachers who apparently had some difficulty making ends meet.[12] His mother, it is true,

---

[8] See the review of Antenor Orrego's *Pueblo Continente* in *América* 6, nos. 1-2 (April-May 1940): 6-7.

[9] Juan Parra del Riego, "La bohemia de Trujillo," *Balnearios* 7, no. 281 (October 22, 1916).

[10] Joaquín Díaz Ahumada, *Historia de las luchas sindicales en el valle de Chicama*, pp. 34-35. See Espejo, *César Vallejo*, p. 48. *La Libertad* was subsequently closed down in 1921 by the authorities for its activities in behalf of the strikers.

[11] See particularly Felipe Cossio del Pomar's two biographies, *Haya dela Torre: El indoamericano* and the lengthier *Víctor Raúl: Biografía de Haya de la Torre*.

[12] The most revealing treatment of Haya's early life can be found in Luis Alberto Sánchez's first biography of the Aprista leader, *Raúl Haya de la Torre o el político*; hereafter cited as *El político*. Regarding Haya's paternal grandparents, Sánchez wrote: "During their struggle for life, after the failure of a trip to the jungle in which

came from a prominent Trujillo landholding family, but this fact, in addition to Raúl Edmundo's later election to Congress,[13] was not sufficient for the family to be invited to join the exclusive Club Central, Trujillo's equivalent to the aristocratic Club Nacional in Lima. Despite objections to the proposed liaison with the socially inferior Cajabambino by members of the De la Torre family, the marriage took place in 1894 and Víctor Raúl was born a year later.

From a financial standpoint the Haya-De la Torre union was not particularly successful. Raúl Edmundo, who prior to 1895 had founded several short-lived magazines in Trujillo,[14] continued to pursue a career in journalism, founding, along with a business partner, Teófilo Verjel, the bi-weekly newspaper *La Industria* shortly after his marriage. Soon his father-in-law died, leaving the bulk of his estate to his eldest son. Thus, doña Zoila Victoria's inheritance was small, only one of the family houses in Trujillo, which soon became home for her growing family.[15] In 1900 Raúl Edmundo and his partner sold *La Industria*, but Haya stayed on as the paper's editor. Meanwhile, the two partners had formed a printing and stationery company, which, among other things, printed *La Industria*.[16] The business prospered until the death of Verjel in 1909, forcing Raúl Edmundo, who apparently lacked the business acumen of his former partner, to take over the company's sole direction. A year later the firm floundered and went bankrupt. As a result, Raúl Edmundo was compelled to seek new employment as an accountant for the wealthy sugar planter Víctor Larco in order to supplement his income as editor of *La Industria*.[17]

Though the family was forced, particularly after 1910, to live on a modest scale, Raúl Edmundo took care to provide a good education for his three sons, Víctor Raúl, Agustín, and Edmundo. All attended the Seminario de San Carlos y San Marcelo, where the youth of many of Trujillo's

---

all had high hopes, don Raúl and his parents established a school in Moyobamba, since don José Haya and his wife dona Jacoba Cárdenas had previously been school teachers in Cajabamba" (p. 15, my translation).

[13] He was a deputy from Trujillo from 1906 to 1912 (Cossio, *Víctor Raúl*, p. 135).

[14] *La Primavera* (1887-1890), the literary journal *El Album* (1888), and the weekly *El Correo del Norte* (1891).

[15] Luis Alberto Sánchez, *Haya de la Torre y el Apra*, p. 18; hereafter cited as *Haya y el Apra*.

[16] The name of the firm was Haya, Verjel, y Cia, Sociedad Industrial de Tipografía y Utiles de Escritorio.

[17] See Sánchez, *El político*, p. 34, and Espejo, *César Vallejo*, p. 29.

best families were educated.[18] After graduation in 1913 the young Víctor Raúl, then eighteen, entered the University of Trujillo, bent on pursuing a career in law, although he seems to have been more interested in a possible literary career.[19] Contrary to the claims of his Aprista biographers, there is little evidence that he took more than a passing interest in the social upheavals that were beginning to shatter the Trujillo calm.[20] Indeed, Haya later admitted that his social consciousness was not awakened until his first lengthy contact with conditions in the Peruvian sierra, in Cuzco, in 1917. Rather, his political abilities, already evident, began to manifest themselves within the confines of the university, where in 1916 he was elected secretary and then vice-president of the Centro Universitario. In the same year Haya was also chosen, along with Eulogio Garrido, to head a delegation representing the university to inaugurate a monument to José Gálvez in Cajamarca.[21]

While his activities in local university politics and the *bohemia* proved stimulating, Haya, like other *provincianos* of his age, no doubt yearned to leave the more restrictive and confining atmosphere of Trujillo for the

[18] Such schools, under the concept of noblesse oblige, often admitted the sons of promising rural and urban middle-sector families. This explains the presence of Orrego and the Spelucín brothers, while the De la Torre name sufficed to open its doors to the Hayas.

[19] He later wrote a play called *Triunfa Vanidad*, which was performed in Trujillo by a traveling group of Spanish actors and for which César Vallejo wrote a poem. The play, however, put an end to any literary aspirations Haya may have harbored, for even he recognized that it left something to be desired (see Cossio, *Víctor Raúl*, pp. 64-67).

[20] Both Sánchez and Cossio, in trying to validate Haya's early credentials as a social reformer, eagerly point out that during his high school days be became friends with the local anarcho-syndicalist leaders in Trujillo and often went to read radical literature in the modest library of their locale (Sánchez, *El político*, pp. 45-46, and Cossio, *Víctor Raúl*, pp. 52-53). Haya, however, in a later autobiographical article written in 1928, curiously never made mention of the social upheavals that were racking the plantations around Trujillo, and there exists little evidence that he was a champion of radical causes or the labor movement at this time. Interestingly, in an interview, Haya stated that, although he totally sympathized with the sugar workers during the bloody Chicama Valley strike of 1912 and indeed supported the anarcho-syndicalists in Trujillo, in retrospect, this was due more to a certain "romantic conception" he had of the workers' plight than to any developing notion of social justice (interview in Lima, July 20, 1971).

[21] According to Cossio, Haya ran on a reform list, anxious to displace the traditional, conservative student directorate. The members of the *bohemia*, including Vallejo, he says, militated on behalf of the reform list (*Víctor Raúl*, p. 62; see also Espejo, *César Vallejo*, pp. 41 and 47).

excitement of Lima. Moreover, the ambitious Trujillano, nicknamed revealingly "el principe de la gran ventura" (the prince of great fortune) by his *bohemia* colleagues,[22] probably already nurtured the idea of further honing his political skills on the more formidable stage of national student politics. So, when a wealthy relative died leaving him a small inheritance, Haya decided to embark, in the summer of 1917, for the capital in order to continue his studies at the University of San Marcos.[23]

The departure of Haya along with a few other members of the group for a time disrupted the activities of the *bohemia*. However, it was not long before new members were brought into the group and it showed renewed signs of life. During the next few years many members of the group became involved in the strikes that were now erupting regularly throughout the region. The violent suppression of the 1921 strike in the Chicama cane fields, which had gained the strong support of the progressive elements of Trujillo, temporarily stalled this drive for reform. Orrego, because of his outspoken support of the strikers from the pages of *La Libertad*, found himself out of a job, while the local authorities rooted out and jailed some of the strike leaders who had found refuge in the city and its environs. In general, an atmosphere of conservatism and repression greeted the return of Alcides Spelucín, an early member of the *bohemia*, from abroad in late 1922.

Spelucín was one of three sons of a prosperous Ascope merchant who, during the late war years, had seen his business, along with those of his colleagues, gradually ruined by the sharp competition of Casa Grande. Schooled at San Carlos, where he met Orrego and Haya, and later at the University of Trujillo, Spelucín had been an original member of the *bohemia*. Returning from abroad in November, 1922, the aspiring poet and writer, in need of regular employment, hit upon the idea of founding a new, "independent" newspaper in Trujillo to replace the now defunct *La Libertad* and *La Razón*. Along with his friend Orrego, Spelucín succeeded in convincing his uncle Juan A. Vega, a wealthy miner who owned several small mines in the sierra of Cajamarca, to back the project financially. Quickly, a staff, headed by Orrego and Spelucín and including Belisario Spelucín (a brother), Federico Esquerre, Juan Espejo Asturrizaga, and Carlos Manuel Cox, was brought together, and the first

[22] Espejo, *César Vallejo*, p. 54.
[23] Cossio, *Víctor Raúl*, p. 29.

edition of the newspaper *El Norte* appeared on the streets of Trujillo in February, 1923.[24]

In conservative Trujillo, *El Norte* soon gained the reputation as a liberal, reform-oriented newspaper generally attune to the interests of the area's lower and middle sectors. Articles and editorials frequently appeared defending such diverse interests as those of the sugar braceros, small landholders, *empleados*, and merchant community, all of whom, as has been seen, were engaged in one way of another in resisting the policies of the great sugar companies. Often the editorial tone of the paper was violently xenophobic, railing about the abuses ostensibly being perpetrated by the German-Peruvian plantation Casa Grande against the entire Trujillo community.[25]

While *El Norte* was getting established, news of Haya's triumphs in Lima was continually reaching Trujillo. Haya had arrived in Lima during the summer of 1917. Contrary to the claims of his biographers, who maintain that Haya's revolutionary zeal was already apparent,[26] there is no evidence that in 1917 the future *jefe máximo* of Aprismo was in the least bit radical or revolutionary. Indeed, a close examination of one of his few autobiographical writings reveals quite a different picture.

While residing in Europe in 1927 Haya wrote an article for the Costa Rican journal *Repertorio Americano* in which he reminisced about his early days in Lima and first meetings with the Peruvian *pensador* Manuel González Prada.[27] In this article Haya revealed the essentially conservative nature that characterized him at the time. For one thing, he readily admitted that upon his arrival in Lima he was no radical, but rather "un jovencito a la criolla, enfermo hasta los huesos de esa frivolidad epidémica—peste de gente 'decente' " (a flippant young man, afflicted to the quick with that epidemic frivolity characteristic of the upper class). Furthermore, he recalled that at that time he had no overwhelming drive to meet Manuel González Prada, who even then, despite his advanced years, was still the patriarch of Peruvian radicals.[28] Indeed, Haya recollected that only a certain "curi-

---

[24] Interviews with Sra. Carmela Spelucín viuda de Orrego, May 29 and 31, 1967, Lima (Miraflores). Carmela, the sister of Alcides Spelucín, married Antenor Orrego. Also see Espejo, *César Vallejo*, p. 135.

[25] See particularly *El Norte* for the year 1924.

[26] See the first chapters of Sanchez's biographies of Haya as well as those by Cossio.

[27] Víctor Raúl Haya de la Torre, "Mis recuerdos de González Prada," *Repertorio Americano* 15, no. 6 (August 13, 1927): 84-85.

[28] Manuel González Prada was one of a number of Peruvian men of letters who, outraged by Peru's catastrophic demise in the War of the Pacific, sought to determine

osity" whetted by the mysteriously cloistered life that González Prada then followed, led him to seek out the venerated author shortly after arriving in the capital. These were clearly not the thoughts of a young radical ostensibly instilled with the burning rhetoric found in the pages of *Horas de Lucha*. Finally, Haya, in tones mocking what he considered his youthful foolishness, admitted that the prominent figures of the day, mostly Civilistas, had held for him a certain fascination, bordering perhaps on hero worship. He wrote: "I arrived in Lima thinking about the great honor of being in the same classrooms with personages of whom the newspapers had said so many things. Sr. Smith, the teacher; Dr. Jones, the wise man; the witty Sr. So and So, all produced a certain fascination for me. And the first impression of our men of letters was really admirable. They were solemn, elegant, measured, and courteous men who spoke in high-pitched voices, making theatrical gestures as they conversed, and they seemed to me to be geniuses, absolute geniuses, indisputable geniuses, indeed universal geniuses!"

Haya's first excursion to Lima soon proved a short one, for in August, 1917, he was offered the post of secretary to the newly appointed prefect of Cuzco, which he quickly accepted.[29] The job, though it did not pay very much, gave him his first opportunity to travel to the old imperial city and view first-hand life in the Peruvian highlands. Haya spent the next seven months in Cuzco, attending to the duties of his office, studying at the university, and traveling whenever possible throughout the region. During these sojourns into the surrounding countryside, often in the company of the prefect, who was making his official rounds, Haya was able to view intimately the life of the mass of submerged Indians, who formed the bulk of the highland population. Apparently, what he saw greatly impressed him, for he later wrote, "I would never have felt such strong affection for the Indians, or love for highland Peru, or grief at the great social injustices, or rebellion against the barbarous political system, if I had not lived in Cuzco."[30]

_____
the reasons for the nation's seeming impotence. In carefully reexamining the nature of Peruvian society, González Prada concluded that the roots of Peru's society and body politic were thoroughly decayed and corrupt and that only through revolutionary change could a national regeneration be effected. See his numerous writings, including his most well known book, *Horas de Lucha*.

[29] The prefect, Colonel César González, had previously occupied the same post in La Libertad and at that time had become friendly with the Haya de la Torre family (Sánchez, *Haya y el Apra*, p. 39).

[30] Víctor Raúl Haya de la Torre, *Construyendo el aprismo: Artículos y cartas desde el exilio, 1924-1931*, p. 101, my translation. He continued: ". . . then and only then did I understand the magnitude of the problem and decided to become a soldier of

Though he had learned a great deal in his new position, including a very rudimentary knowledge of Quechua, which he would later employ advantageously for political ends, Haya soon grew restless for the political bustle of Lima and San Marcos. In late April, 1918, he undertook the arduous journey back to the capital via Arequipa and the port of Mollendo. Not long after arriving in Lima, the young Trujillano found it necessary to find employment, for the modest inheritance that had enabled him to come to Lima originally had now all but disappeared. In the traditional Peruvian manner, Haya sought out a prominent, though distant friend of the family, in this case the well-known Limeño lawyer Eleodoro Romero, who promptly hired Haya as a law clerk in his office at fifty soles a month. The new position, in addition to providing Haya with a means of livelihood while studying at San Marcos, also gave him access to a formidable private library, where, for the *first* time, he began reading widely the works of Renan, González Prada, Sarmiento, Marx, Einstein, and others. Haya later wrote that it was in this law office that all his rebelliousness was born.[31]

The Lima into which Haya now settled in mid-1918 was a city pulsating with activity and change. Since the advent of World War I the Peruvian economy, like its other Latin American counterparts, had been experiencing a remarkable surge. Between 1914 and 1919 the nation's exports more than tripled while light industry, moving to fill the void created by the decline of imports from the European belligerents, likewise boomed.[32] This economic expansion further accelerated the formation of a new urban proletariat and middle class, which had been underway since the turn of the century. By 1918 these two new segments of Peruvian society were beginning to make a substantial impact upon the traditional political and social life of the nation.

During the war years, for example, the pace of sindicalization within the ranks of the rapidly growing urban proletariat greatly accelerated. Led by the ubiquitous anarcho-sindicalists, a number of important industries had been unionized by the close of World War I. More importantly, organized

---

the cause which would fight for its solution." See also his 1925 letter to the Argentine educator Julio R. Barcos in Haya's *Por la emancipación de la América Latina*, pp. 99-100.

[31] Víctor Raúl Haya de la Torre, "Autobiográfica," *Repertorio Americano* 17, no. 4 (July 28, 1928): 50.

[32] For import-export statistics see Basadre, *Historia del Perú*, VIII, 3864-3865. Regarding the rise of light industry, Basadre reports that by the year 1923 a total of 29 million soles was invested in the manufacture of wool and cotton textiles, flour, soap, candles, matches, cigarettes, hats and similar items, with a total employment of thirty thousand (X, 4720).

labor, in the face of a ruinous price-wage squeeze occasioned by the war boom, was becoming increasingly militant. During the immediate years leading up to 1918, the nation witnessed no less than ten major strikes, most of which were accompanied by serious bloodshed. All these were minor outbreaks, however, compared to the general strike of 1919 in favor of the eight-hour day, which virtually paralyzed Lima. The strike was eventually broken by the then Pardo government (1915-1919), but not before the army was called out to restore order.[33]

While labor unrest became frequent toward the end of the war, the nation's emerging middle sectors were also growing restless. For one thing, Peru's middle income groups, like the urban proletariat, were caught up in the devastating upward spiral of living costs that had plagued the country ever since the early years of the war. In large measure this spiral was due to a sharp shift in agricultural production, which saw coastal lands previously devoted to food staples converted to the cultivation of more lucrative export crops. Acreage devoted to sugar production, for example, expanded 23 percent between 1913 and 1919, while land planted into cotton increased almost 60 percent from 1915 to 1919.[34] The ensuing scarcity of food staples more than doubled prices in the markets of Lima and other major cities during the war years, creating widespread discontent among the popular classes. Further adding to the economic plight of the middle class was a tax structure that, though modified to some extent during the war, still weighed most heavily upon the nation's middle and lower income groups.[35]

It was within this general framework of growing unrest that Haya, already cognizant of his bent for politics,[36] plunged into the political arena at San Marcos. And, fortunately for Haya, nowhere were the forces for change more clearly in operation than in the staid and venerable cloisters of the national university. Traditionally the exclusive domain and training ground for the nation's elite, San Marcos in recent years had experienced an enormous influx of students from predominantly middle-class back-

---

[33] Ibid., VIII, 3902-3908.

[34] Calculated from figures in Ministerio de Hacienda y Comercio, *Extracto estadístico del Perú, 1940*, pp. 201 and 209. For an excellent study of the effects of the war on Peru's economy, see Hernando Lavalle, *La gran guerra y el organismo económico nacional*. Less complete but also valuable is L. S. Rowe, *Early Effects of the War upon the Finance, Commerce and Industry of Peru*.

[35] Basadre, *Historia del Perú*, VIII, 3866-3869.

[36] It is not without significance that, after his return from Cuzco, a relative remarked that Haya had the potential to become "un gran político" provided that he did not attack the existing system (Sánchez, *Haya y el Apra*, p. 41).

grounds. From a student body of 789 in 1907, San Marcos had almost doubled its enrollment to 1,331 ten years later.[37] As this segment of the student population grew, the archaic structure of the university increasingly began to come under attack.

Manifestations of ferment within the university had indeed been visible in Peru for some time. As early as 1907 the students at San Augustín University in Arequipa had organized the first student strike in the nation's history. A year later a full-blown student organization, the Centro Universitario, had appeared on the campus of San Marcos University in Lima, and its leaders were calling for the organization of a university extension to extend the facilities and opportunities of the university to Lima's working-class barrios. Similarly, in 1909 a San Marcos medical student had issued a call for greater student participation in the operation of the university, in effect the first declaration for *cogobierno* within the Peruvian university. Changes within the university, therefore, were well afoot when Alfredo Palacios, the spokesman for the Córdoba reform movement, arrived in Lima in 1918. While it has traditionally been thought that his presence in Lima triggered university reform in Peru, in fact Palacios's activities at San Marcos simply further stimulated the already well developed reform impulse at that citadel of higher learning.[38]

Haya's role in this stage of the university reform movement was actually quite minimal. Still virtually unknown in university circles, he realized that he would have to work his way into the movement's leadership cadre before he would be in a position to establish a personal reputation. This posed the first major dilemma of Haya's political career, for the leadership of this phase of the movement was largely split into two opposing groups. Originally it had been initiated by a group of students in the Faculty of Letters.[39] It quickly spread to other faculties and by August, 1919, a Central Reform Committee (Comité Central de Reforma) had been formed

[37] Jesús Chavarría, "La desaparición del Perú colonial (1870-1919)," *Aportes*, no. 23 (January 1972), p. 149.

[38] A revisionist interpretation of the university reform movement in Peru can be found in Jesús Chavarría, "A Communication on University Reform," *Latin American Research Review* 3, no. 3 (Summer 1968): 192-195. See also Mark J. Van Alsen, "University Reform before Córdoba," *Hispanic American Historical Review* 51, no. 3 (August 1971): 451. For a more traditional treatment of the university reform movement, see Basadre, *Historia del Perú*, IX, 4330-4333. A more detailed account can be found in Enrique Cornejo Koster's chapter, "Crónica del movimiento estudiantil peruano, 1919-1926," in *La reforma universitaria*, ed. Gabriel del Mazo, pp. 87-181.

[39] Particularly, Raúl Porras Barrenechea, Guillermo Luna Cartland, and Humberto del Aguila.

to coordinate the movement. As the movement gained momentum, the Federación de Estudiantes del Perú (FEP), which had been controlled by conservative elements since its reorganization in 1917, also began to involve itself in the question of reform.[40] In effect, Haya therefore had to decide which group would not only gain control of the movement, but also afford him the best opportunity to rise to a position of influence and leadership.

Haya chose to work within the organizational structure of the FEP. For one thing, he already had a position or base from which to operate within the FEP, for he had come to Lima charged with the student representation from the University of Trujillo. Also, since his return from Cuzco, Haya had been active in FEP politics and indeed in the early months of 1919 had gained some attention as one of three FEP delegates charged with establishing liaison between the student organization and the workers who were striking for the eight-hour day.[41] Most importantly, he no doubt astutely saw that the FEP, a more well established and permanent student organization, would eventually displace the Reform Committee and take over leadership of the movement.

Thus, during the balance of 1919, Haya devoted his unceasing attentions to the question of university reform and politics within the FEP. His goals appeared to be twofold: to prepare the ground for his candidacy for the presidency of the FEP and to help the organization gain full control over the reform movement. The latter was achieved with surprisingly little difficulty when the Reform Committee collapsed, apparently because the university administration chose to negotiate with the FEP.[42] However, no sooner had the FEP gained full control over the movement than a sharp division appeared within its ranks over the question of tactics. Nevertheless, Haya, displaying the political skill for which he would later become famous, maneuvered among the various factions and succeeded in October in being elected as a compromise candidate to the presidency of the FEP.[43]

This office gave Haya the sounding board he had been seeking, and he did not hesitate to exploit it skillfully. Unable to play a significant role in the formulation and enactment of the reform program, which by the time he took office had been largely accepted by the Leguía government,[44] Haya

---

[40] Basadre, *Historia del Perú*, IX, 4330-4332.

[41] Ibid., VIII, 3907. For an exaggerated account of Haya's participation in the 1919 strike, see Cossio, *Víctor Raúl*, pp. 92-105.

[42] Basadre, *Historia del Perú*, IX, 4331.

[43] Cossio, *Víctor Raúl*, p. 122.

[44] Basadre, *Historia del Perú*, IX, 4332-4333.

adroitly conceived the idea of organizing a national student congress designed to record student views on both the university reform question and major national issues.[45] Though probably unnecessary in view of the recent success of the reform movement, the congress would give Haya the opportunity to gain considerable national publicity while at the same time allow him to solicit support for a pet project of his involving the establishment of student-operated night schools for the nation's workers. The idea of holding a congress was generally well received by the student sector as well as the Leguía government, which viewed it as a chance to further cement student support for the fledgling regime.[46] In early March, 1920, a score of student delegates representing the various national universities met in the imperial city of Cuzco to discuss the major issues of the day.

The Cuzco congress further revealed Haya's growing penchant for placing political expediency and personal aggrandizement above ideological conviction. From the outset of the congress the mood of the majority of delegates appeared to be largely conservative. They seemed content to debate the means for effecting the recently won university reforms rather than ways of extending the reform movement to other areas of society.[47] Well aware of this mood, Haya apparently decided to reserve all his political skill and influence as presiding officer to obtain passage of a resolution supporting his project for the creation of night schools for workers or, as they later came to be called, popular universities (*universidades populares*). When a resolution was presented stating that the FEP would always defend the postulates of social justice, Haya chose not to throw his full weight behind the proposal, and it was soundly defeated.[48] Later, however, Haya vigorously defended the resolution to create the popular universities, which proved to be the only progressive resolution passed by the congress.

The creation of the popular universities provided yet another vehicle for the enhancement of Haya's growing reputation in and out of reform circles. Designed to promote closer relations between students and the emerging urban proletariat, the UP's were established as student-operated extensions of the major national universities. The idea, which actually was

[45] Cornejo Koster, "Crónica del movimiento estudiantil," p. 93.

[46] The Leguía government actually provided travel funds for all delegates, including Haya.

[47] For a brief account of the congress, see "El congreso nacional de estudiantes del Cuzco," *Mercurio Peruano* año III, 4, no. 22 (April 1920): 311-312. See also *Primer Congreso Nacional de Estudiantes . . . del 11 al 20 de marzo de 1920.*

[48] Cornejo Koster, "Crónica del movimiento estudiantil," p. 94.

an old one,[49] was to have the students teach classes for the workers in order to advance their general level of education as well as social and class consciousness.[50] Presumably, the bonds established between the two groups would further the struggle for national reform and social justice. Though originally nonpartisan, the UP's (later dubbed the Universidades Populares González Prada—UPGP) would subsequently be converted by Haya into a major arm of the Partido Aprista Peruano.

After terminating his one-year term as president of the FEP in October, 1920, Haya turned his full energies to the organization of the UP's. The project was no mean task, considering the general skepticism that probably greeted the idea from student and worker alike. Haya, however, brought to the job several important attributes, not the least of which was a great oratorical skill as well as a remarkable ability to convince and persuade people. With respect to the latter, a political opponent, describing Haya several years later, wrote: "There flowed from him, from his bearing, from his words, the almost juvenile gayety, fresh, warm, contagious. . . . He was charming and brilliant; he made each person he talked with feel specially loved, apart from others."[51] Moreover, already his unusual skill as a slogan coiner, which later played such an important role in fashioning a political movement, was beginning to appear in speeches before worker groups. For example, at one meeting designed to stir worker enthusiasm for the UP's, Haya, in language characteristic of later Aprista speeches, pronounced: ". . . la universidad popular no pide nada sino voluntad, fe, deseo de superación" (the popular university asks of you all only determination, faith, and the will to overcome).[52]

By the end of 1921 Haya had largely accomplished his goal to organize the UP's. In Lima a score of student-professors were giving classes in several working-class *barrios*, while UP's were also springing up in the major provincial cities. In the meantime, Haya had been named by the FEP to travel to Montevideo, Buenos Aires, and Santiago in order to seek closer relations with the student federations in the southern part of the

[49] Basadre dates the immediate origins of the UP's to the Billinghurst government (1912-1914), which established a similar program among the working-class elements of Lima (*Historia del Perú*, VIII, 3707-3708).

[50] See Cornejo Koster, "Crónica del movimiento estudiantil," p. 96.

[51] Eudocio Ravines, *The Yenan Way*, p. 21.

[52] Cossío, *Víctor Raúl*, p. 141. For a description of the UP's, see Cornejo Koster, "Crónica del movimiento estudiantil," pp. 105-120.

hemisphere.[53] In order to finance his trip, Haya received an advance on his salary from the director of the Anglo-Peruvian school for whom he had gone to work after his departure from the law offices of Dr. Romero.[54] The trip lasted some five months and brought Haya into contact with several prominent student and political leaders in Uruguay, Argentina, and Chile.[55]

Soon after his return to Peru in June, 1922, Haya decided to visit his family in Trujillo. Some five years had elapsed since he had first left his native city for Lima, and he was now returning with a considerable reputation as one of Peru's leading student figures. Arriving in Trujillo in early July in the company of his brother Agustín, who had also been studying at San Marcos, Haya was enthusiastically received by family and friends alike. During the next few days Haya renewed old acquaintances from his *bohemia* days, including Antenor Orrego, who immediately arranged for Haya to give a series of speeches. Though Trujillo at this time was still largely in a state of shock from the recent violence in the Chicama cane fields, Haya was reluctantly granted a permit to speak by the prefect, who also happened to be a friend of the family. Nevertheless, when his first speech proved too "inflammatory" for local authorities, Haya was warned not to discuss in his subsequent talks the recent social disturbances in the region.[56]

While Haya was visiting Trujillo, the Lima political caldron once again began to heat up, largely because of the increasingly dictatorial stance of President Augusto Leguía. Leguía, it will be recalled, had come to power in 1919 on a reform program aimed at curtailing the influence and power of the traditional, aristocratic Civilist party while attempting to capture the support of the nation's emerging urban middle and lower sectors. For a period after his accession to the presidency, Leguía had moved to effect these aims by rooting out Civilists from the government and supporting the reform demands of the middle and lower classes.

However, the course of the Leguía regime soon took a new turn. Relying

[53] Actually, it appears that Haya more or less appointed himself to carry out a previous FEP agreement with Argentina to exchange representatives, for the FEP was in a complete state of anarchy in early 1922 (see Sánchez, *Haya y el Apra*, p. 92).

[54] The director of the school was a Presbyterian minister from Scotland by the name of John MacKay, who apparently helped Haya financially on a number of occasions.

[55] For more details on the trip, see Sánchez, *Haya y el Apra*, pp. 94-115.

[56] Cossio, *Víctor Raúl*, p. 170.

more and more upon large foreign investments and loans and the support
of a new rich class of entrepreneurs that had come into existence during
the profitable war years, Leguía saw no need to brook either opposition
from the dethroned Civilists or to continue to cater to the wishes of the
urban middle and lower sectors. By 1921, therefore, the campaign
against the Civilists had reached its zenith with the suppression of the
two prominent Lima dailies, *La Prensa* and *El Comercio*, and the subsequent jailing of many distinguished supporters of the old party. Moreover, much of the promised reform legislation either failed to materialize
or remained a dead letter, while at the same time Leguía grew hostile to
reform elements within the labor and student sectors.

It was to this general political climate that Haya returned from his
Trujillo trip to learn that Leguía, in a bizarre attempt to facilitate his
reelection, was planning to have the nation dedicated to the Sacred
Heart of Jesus.[57] Haya quickly realized that Leguía had created an
extremely volatile issue capable of galvanizing virtually all sectors of the
opposition from left to right into a formidable anti-Leguía coalition.
Without hesitation, Haya, who doubtless saw in such an issue the perfect
chance to further his political ambitions, plunged into the job of organizing these disparate forces for a mass protest demonstration against
Leguía's plan.

The demonstration, when it came in mid-May, 1923, proved far more
successful than even Haya probably had foreseen. Several thousand dem-
onstrators, including such strange bedfellows as Civilists and Anarchists,
massed on the morning of the twenty-third at San Marcos and, after
hearing Haya denounce the government, marched en masse to the Plaza
San Martín in the heart of downtown Lima. Before reaching their objective, however, the protestors were met by sword-wielding cavalrymen,
called out by Leguía to quell the "disturbance." By day's end the demonstration had its martyrs, as two protestors had been killed and many others
wounded.

Though exiled in the wave of repression unleashed by Leguía soon after
the demonstration, Haya had won a tremendous personal victory. For one
thing, he had dealt Leguía a stunning political defeat, further damaging the
president's popular image. Furthermore, the demonstration catapulted
Haya into national prominence and gave him a reputation that would serve

[57] For a good analysis of this whole episode, see Sánchez, *Haya y el Apra*,
pp. 118-128, as well as Basadre, *Historia del Perú*, IX, 4033-4034.

him well in future years.[58] Indeed, the events of May 23 and their aftermath have provided endless material for later Aprista propagandists bent upon building the political image of Haya. Finally, for the moment at least, Haya could claim sole leadership of reform forces throughout Peru.

Meanwhile, the 1923 demonstrations had also triggered disturbances at the University of Trujillo. Since its founding, the university had been the only major institution of higher learning north of Lima. Traditionally, its student body had been drawn from the prominent families of the main northern cities of Piura, Lambayeque, Cajamarca, and, of course, Trujillo. During the first decades of the twentieth century, however, the composition of the student population at the university, as at San Marcos, began to change, reflecting the slow rise of a provincial middle class throughout Peru. Increasingly, the university drew its student body from prosperous, middle-class families who lived not only in the region's major cities, but also in the smaller towns that dotted the northern sierra.[59]

As at San Marcos, the middle-class invasion of the university resulted in rising pressures to reform the antiquated university system. Though not as violent or successful as its Lima counterpart, the Trujillo university reform movement took much the same direction as San Marcos's. Generally, the demands of the reformers hinged on the widespread student desire to have a greater voice in the administration of the university. And, as in Lima, the Trujillo reformers moved early to establish a rapport with the city's laboring class in hopes that a united worker-student front would be sufficient to force changes in the university system.

One of the leaders of the Trujillo movement was Carlos Manuel Cox, later a founder of the Aprista party in Peru. Cox, who was born in Trujillo in 1902, came from a prominent, aristocratic background. While his grandfather, Cecilio Cox Doray, had served as mayor of Trujillo during the War of the Pacific and belonged to the exclusive Club Central, Carlos Manuel's father had begun his career rather modestly as a bank clerk, later becoming an accountant for a local import-export house and eventually manager of the Trujillo branch of the Banco Italiano.[60] His mother was the daughter of a successful Trujillo merchant of German origins. After

[58] Ravines stated that Haya became a national hero vitually overnight as a result of his actions in the demonstration (*The Yenan Way*, p. 15). Later, however, Haya's opponents claimed that his actions in 1923 had been anti-Catholic and used the issue somewhat effectively against him.

[59] Espejo, *César Vallejo*, p. 31.

[60] Raúl Garbín et al., *Diccionario biográfico del Perú 1943-1944*, pp. 175-176.

graduation from the Colegio Nacional San Juan in 1919, Cox entered the University of Trujillo to continue his studies in the Faculty of Letters. At the same time, his uncle Cecilio, a prominent lawyer and sometime politician who owned the newspaper *La Reforma*, introduced Carlos Manuel to Antenor Orrego, who was then the editor of the newspaper. Through his acquaintance with Orrego, Cox was soon drawn into the Trujillo *bohemia* and later its successor, *el grupo norte*.[61]

Contact with the politically minded Orrego, as well as work on the staff of *La Reforma*, quickly stimulated Cox's interest in politics. It was not long before the youthful Trujillano became active in university reform politics and was elected to the first of several positions within the university's student federation. By 1921 Cox was assisting Orrego in founding the first popular university in Trujillo. Later the same year, during the bloody Chicama strike, Cox, along with Manuel Barreto, a local auto mechanic and union organizer who was later killed in the Trujillo revolution of 1932, helped organize the Comité de Obreros y Estudiantes Pro Huelga sympathetic to the sugar workers.[62]

These and other reform activities at the university were cut short by the violent suppression of the Chicama Valley strike in early 1922 and the wave of government repression that followed. A year later Cox, along with a number of other student reformers of *el grupo norte*, including Manuel Vásquez Díaz, Alfredo Rebaza Acosta, Enrique Albrecht Arias, and Pedro Lizaraburu, all of whom later became prominent Aprista leaders in the region, organized a short-lived strike at the university in support of the May 23 student-worker demonstration in Lima against the regime of Leguía. After the Chicama strike, however, local authorities were in no mood to risk a further outbreak of unrest and possible violence and quickly moved to break the strike.[63] A number of students were expelled from the university, including Cox, Vásquez Díaz, and Haya's brother Agustín, all of whom left for Lima in hopes of continuing their studies and agitation at San Marcos.[64]

The events of 1922-1923, then, more or less marked the formal dissolution of the original Trujillo *bohemia*, or, as it had later come to be called,

---

[61] Interview with Carlos Manuel Cox, Lima (Miraflores), June 1, 1967.

[62] Ibid.

[63] Luciano Castillo, the Piurano who later founded the Socialist party in Peru, was also a student leader at the time in Trujillo (see Cornejo Koster, "Crónica del movimiento estudiantil," pp. 156-162).

[64] Cox, interview, June 1, 1967. Cox went on to become an official of the FEP at San Marcos.

el grupo norte. What had begun as a purely literary group of youthful, restless middle-class intellectuals had, at Orrego's prodding, steadily become politicized, with most of its members by 1923 actively drawn in one way or another into the arena of reform politics. While the expression of avant-garde literary modes had originally brought the group together, once organized, its members had come to recognize that not all was right in other realms of Trujillo society. Reaching out for an identity and a place in a highly traditional and class-conscious society, while at the same time finding avenues of economic and social mobility largely restricted or closed, the group became increasingly radicalized. This radicalization focused on some of the major social and economic problems that the modernization process had triggered in the area, problems that had in many instances directly affected the *bohemia*'s members and families. Although largely scattered in various directions as a result of Leguía's repressive actions in 1923, the group's members would retain their personal ties, and, subsequently, many would come together again to forge the Partido Aprista Peruano in 1930-1931.

6. Haya in Exile and the Genesis of
APRA: 1923-1930

When Haya left Peru in 1923, he carried with him very little in the way of a developed and organized political ideology, apart from a few vague notions about social justice and the need for "revolutionary change" in Peru. Indeed, the need to develop such a program had really seemed unnecessary during the pre-1923 period, when Haya was able to utilize easily his remarkable political skills to ride the crest of student and popular opposition to the dictatorial regime of Leguía. However, his sudden exile, though it momentarily boosted his prestige immensely throughout the country, brought home to him the necessity of formulating and effectively propagandizing a political program, lest his exalted position within the reform movement be completely undermined by his absence. After all, it would not be long before his May twenty-third exploits would be forgotten and others, like the returning José Carlos Mariátegui, would step in to fill the void created by his departure.[1]

---

[1] According to Eudocio Ravines, this is in fact what happened: ". . . four months later Haya de la Torre was exiled . . . and José Carlos Mariátegui took over the leadership of his followers and of others who had not belonged to the original group" (*The Yenan Way*, p. 15). Mariátegui had returned from Europe shortly before the May twenty-third demonstrations, fortified with Marxist ideas.

With this in mind, Haya, during his subsequent travels abroad,[2] began to formulate a political ideology that he no doubt hoped would both keep his name prominent among reform groups in Peru and provide the basis for the creation of his own movement.[3] Visiting Panama, Cuba, and Mexico— the latter at the invitation of Mexican Minister of Education José Vasconcelos, who, due to his interest in youth and reform, offered the Peruvian exile a minor post—Haya came into contact with a wide range of important intellectual and political figures, many of whom contributed substantially to the genesis of his political philosophy. It is important to note that Haya never seems to have been a particularly original thinker as some have claimed, but rather his genius lay in his ability to gather, adapt, and popularize the ideas of others.

For example, Haya was heavily influenced by the Indianista movement in both Peru and Mexico, as well as by Vasconcelos's concept of the "raza cósmica."[4] Already showing his genius for capsulizing and adapting the ideas of others, Haya, while in Mexico, coined the term Indoamerica, which he felt was a more appropriate designation for Latin America in view of the region's large Indian and mestizo population. Indeed, in many respects, Haya's Mexican experience reaffirmed his awareness of the well-spring of Indian nationalism, which Indianismo had tapped among a rising generation of Mexican and Peruvian mestizos. Certainly, the potential appeal of Indoamerica to the mestizo middle class, now emerging into political prominence in Peru and desperately in search of its own identity, was not lost on Haya. The young Peruvian exile soon began to employ it in his writings, and, when he returned to the political wars in Peru in 1931, the term had become a regular and much used part of his political lexicon.

By the time Haya presented to the Mexican Student Federation in May, 1924, the red-and-gold flag of Indoamerica as a gesture of friendship and simultaneously announced the creation of the Alianza Popular Revolu-

---

[2] A useful account of Haya's exile period can be found in Sánchez, *Haya y el Apra*, though the author's obvious bias must be discounted on controversial points.

[3] It is the purpose to deal here only with those portions of Haya's political ideology that pertained directly to the social and economic problems of the northern coast of Peru and that found a strong political response there. For the aspects of Haya's political ideas that concerned other continental or Peruvian problems considered peripheral to this study, the reader is directed to Harry Kantor's *The Ideology and Program of the Peruvian Aprista Movement* and to Haya's works themselves.

[4] Haya had arrived in Mexico at about the time that Vasconcelos was putting the final touches on a book entitled *La raza cósmica*, which was published in 1925. In it the Mexican philosopher predicted that a new race would emerge from the blending of the "treasury of all previous races" in Latin America.

cionaria Americana (APRA), his still rudimentary ideology was based almost entirely on the precept of anti-American imperialism. Considering the number of prominent Latin American intellectuals (most notably Manuel Ugarte)[5] who were espousing such an idea at the time, one wonders how Haya could have expected to create much of a stir with such a notion. However, this is to underestimate the deep-rooted resentment of North American imperialism that was sweeping the continent during the 1920's. Moreover, Haya realized not only the political potential of the doctrine, but also that, besides the Communists, few if any political movements in Latin America had been predicated solely on anti-American imperialism.[6]

What is important to emphasize here is that Haya, using the dialectic as a vehicle for analyzing Latin America, was in a sense trying to synthesize what he saw as both the positive and the negative aspects of the Latin American ethos. His widespread adoption of Indoamerica was, so to speak, his way of expressing the positive in the Latin American *ser* (essence of being), while antiimperialism was for him the negative side of the Latin American *estar* (daily existence). In later Aprista ideology he sought to reconcile, synthesize, and apply both these opposing concepts for analyzing the sociology of Latin America into viable political terms as expressed in a political movement. Always the adapter, he succeeded brilliantly in fitting political theory to the praxis of political reality.

It was not until the following December that Haya spelled out in somewhat more detail the aims of APRA and formulated his now famous five-point program. In general, the main objective of APRA, as outlined in an article published by Haya sometime later,[7] was to forge a broadly based political alliance composed of all segments of society that ostensibly

---

[5] Haya later admitted that Manuel Ugarte's book, *El destino de un continente*, had considerably influenced his thoughts on the subject. He also stated that his travels to Panama and the Caribbean brought home to him the great dangers of North American economic penetration into the area. See Haya's first book, *Por la emancipación de la América Latina: Artículos, mensajes, discursos 1923-1927*, pp. 23-24. Other prominent Latin Americans who were espousing similar antiimperialist views were José Ingenieros, Alfredo Palacios, Joaquín García Monge, and Jesús Silva Hertzog, to name a few.

[6] The guerilla movement of Sandino in Nicaragua, though it did not erupt until a few years later, was based almost exclusively on the same doctrine.

[7] The article entitled "What Is the APRA?" originally appeared in English in *The Labour Monthly* 8 (December 1926): 756-759. It can be found in a number of Haya and Aprista works under the title "¿Qué es el Apra?" For example, see Haya's *Por la emancipación*, pp. 187-195, which is used here.

suffered from the economic exploitation of North American imperialism. This alliance, or, as he called it, *frente único*, would include workers, students, and intellectuals as well as elements of the middle and peasant classes, all of whom would provide a united front against United States penetration into Latin America.[8] According to Haya, APRA cells would be established in each Latin American country and would adhere to the five general points of Haya's program:

1. Action against Yankee imperialism.
2. Political unity of Latin America.
3. Nationalization of lands and industry.
4. Internationalization of the Panama Canal.
5. Solidarity of all oppressed peoples and classes of the world.

Finally, each national APRA cell apparently would be free to add other points to the program, according to national conditions and circumstances.

Since he wanted to attract the widest possible popular following to the Alianza, Haya deliberately formulated the APRA program in the broadest and most general terms. Other than stating generally that "political power ought to be captured by the producing classes,"[9] nowhere did he indicate specifically how North American imperialism was to be eliminated from Latin America. It is interesting to note that shortly before the announcement of APRA's program a similar organization called the Liga Antiimperialista Panamericana, sponsored by the Communists, was founded in Mexico but was given short shrift by Haya, who later charged that it had no political program.[10] Whether or not this was true, it indicated Haya's unwillingness to join any political movement in which he was not the leading figure. Evidently, ever since his exile or perhaps even earlier, Haya had had his sights set upon creating his own political movement. An exchange between an acquaintance of Haya's, the Arequipeño poet Alberto Guillén, and the then minister of government in the Leguía regime, German Leguía y Martínez, is revealing in this regard. Asked by Guillén if Haya had ever been a Leguiista, Leguía y Martínez answered, "No, Guillén, Haya has never been anything else but 'hayista.'"[11]

By the time the article "¿Que es el Apra?" had appeared in 1926

---

[8] Haya probably modeled this *frente*, or *bloque antiimperialista*, as he sometimes called it, on the Kou Min Tang founded by Sun Yat Sen in China, for he frequently drew the analogy between APRA and the Chinese political movement.

[9] Haya, *Por la emancipación*, p. 192.

[10] Ibid., p. 189; see also his comments in *El antiimperialismo y el Apra*, pp. 53-54.

[11] Alberto Guillén, "Haya delatorre ha dicho verdad," *Repertorio Americano* 17, no. 10 (September 8, 1928): 151.

explaining the movement, Haya had left Mexico and traveled to Russia, where he had observed the new Communist system firsthand. Profoundly impressed by what he saw, though certainly not willing to abandon APRA for the Communist party,[12] Haya, after recuperating in Switzerland from an attack of tuberculosis diagnosed while in Russia, traveled to London, where he enrolled in the London School of Economics. Already, he had had some modest success in propagating APRA, for by early 1927 a few Aprista cells had been established in Latin America, most notably in Buenos Aires and Mexico City, and also in Paris by groups of exiled Peruvians.[13] Moreover, Haya, now writing incessantly, was doing his utmost to propagandize his movement. In numerous articles and letters he continually stressed the importance of APRA and, grossly exaggerating, claimed that the movement was rapidly gaining adherents throughout Latin America, including Peru. This claim, of course, was a blatant distortion, for the "party" during the period 1923 to 1931 consisted of only a handful of enthusiastic students and had virtually no popular following. It is a measure of Haya's publicity genius that the movement got as much attention as it did during his years in exile.

Haya remained in England for about a year, studying first in London and then at Oxford. In early 1927 he took advantage of his proximity to the continent to attend the International Anti-Imperialist Congress at Brussels, where he managed to gain some notoriety by verbally sparring with his Communist hosts over the question of Latin America's role in the world revolutionary movement. Back again at Oxford, Haya continued to study and develop his ideas about Latin America and APRA. Finally, in August, 1927, he departed for the United States, spending the following few months observing American life and debating at several New England universities.

By the time Haya arrived in Mexico from the United States, his conception of APRA had substantially matured. During his stay in Europe he had published a number of articles in various European and Latin American journals,[14] most of which dealt with what he considered his "bread-and-

---

[12] Haya flirted for a long time with the Communists, though only apparently for tactical reasons—for example, for the platform they could provide among leftist groups for APRA. For their part, the Communists until 1928 harbored the hope of luring Haya into the Party (see Ricardo Martínez de la Torre, *Apuntes para una interpretación marxista de historia social del Perú*, II, 281).

[13] Other cells had been founded in Central America and Cuba, areas of widespread resentment against United States imperialism.

[14] For those interested in tracing the evolution of Haya's thought, many of these early articles later appeared in several of his books, including *Por la emancipación* and *¿A donde va Indoamérica?*.

butter" political issue—that of the perils of North American economic imperialism in Latin America. However, it was not until the Cuban Communist Julio Antonio Mella published a scathing attack on APRA, sarcastically entitled "¿Que es el Arpa?" which appeared in early 1928 in Mexico,[15] that Haya decided to set down systematically in book form the major outlines of his emerging political philosophy. The result was *El antiimperialismo y el Apra*, which Haya finished in March of that year, though it was not published until several years later.[16]

In *El antiimperialismo y el Apra*, Haya set out to show how the Latin American Communist party was incapable of building an effective and viable antiimperialist, revolutionary movement in Latin America. Arguing that the Latin American environment was wholly different from that of industrial Europe, Haya first adamantly contended that the Communists were wrong in believing that Marxian theory could dogmatically be applied with success to Latin America.[17] This assertion did not mean, however, that Haya rejected outright Marx's ideas. On the contrary, he was strongly influenced by Marx but believed that his ideas had to be shaped and molded to fit the American experience.[18]

More importantly, Haya felt that it was folly to rely solely upon an urban proletariat to make the revolution in Latin America, for, unlike the Europeans, Latin American society was largely agrarian and preindustrial in the Marxian sense and thus lacking in a strong, well-defined working class.[19] Haya did not dispute that such a class was in the process of formation in Latin America. On the contrary, the rise of mining, export agricultural, and even light industrial enterprises ever since the turn of the century had brought about a widespread demand for cheap labor, and, as a result, a new proletariat class was gradually coming into being. Nevertheless, according to Haya, this emerging class still lacked the unity and strong class consciousness necessary to build a successful revolutionary movement. Indeed, he contended that in many respects this new proletariat was, temporarily at least, better off than it had formerly been in terms of wages and general living standards and that it would take some time for it

[15] For a reprint of this pamphlet, see Julio Antonio Mella, "La lucha revolucionaria contra el imperialismo: ¿Que es el Arpa?" *Amauta* 4, nos. 31-32 (June-July, August-September 1930): 41-49, 24-37.

[16] See Haya, *El antiimperialismo*, introduction, pp. 14-16.

[17] Haya would later develop this concept into his famous Time-Space theory, which he elaborated in *Espacio-tiempo histórico*.

[18] See Haya, *El antiimperialismo*, pp. 117-118.

[19] Ibid., pp. 54-55.

to develop a genuine revolutionary consciousness based on the realization that it was being exploited by foreign capitalism.[20] Thus, Haya correctly concluded that "a political party composed only of the proletariat is a party without any possibilities of success in Latin America."[21]

Since the Latin American proletariat was not strong enough to lead the struggle against foreign imperialism alone, Haya proposed that it form an alliance (*frente único*) with the middle classes of the continent in order to accomplish this goal.[22] It was Haya's belief that the Latin American middle classes were generally suffering far more from the pernicious effects of imperialism than the proletariat. He wrote: ". . . the monopoly that imperialism imposes cannot avoid leading to the destruction, stagnation, or regression of what we generically call the middle class. Thus, just as industrial capitalism, upon appearing in the economically highly developed countries, reduces, absorbs, and proletarizes [*proletariza*] the petite bourgeoisie . . . imperialism subjugates or destroys economically the middle classes of the backward countries that it penetrates. The small capitalist, the small industrialist, the small urban or rural proprietor, the small miner, the small merchant, the intellectual, and the white-collar worker, etc. form the middle class whose interests imperialism attacks."[23]

Moreover, trying to counter the idea that the petite bourgeoisie was essentially conservative, Haya reasoned that the middle classes in Latin America had a greater aptitude for the revolutionary struggle than their European counterparts. In Europe the middle classes had already long since defeated the old, feudal landed class and had won political power. In Latin America this had not yet occurred, and the feudal class, allied with foreign imperialism, was now threatening the very existence of the middle

[20] Throughout this work Haya seems to be drawing heavily upon the Peruvian experience, particularly in the following passage, which is not applicable to the more industrialized Latin American countries like Argentina. He wrote: "The skilled worker in the small workshop and the independent artisan, upon being attracted to a new form of production that has large amounts of capital, receives a regular and higher salary, becomes for the moment better off, and is incorporated with certain advantages to the category of the industrial proletariat. The same thing also happens to the poor *campesino*, peon, and indigenous serf. Once he becomes a member of the proletariat within a large manufacturing, agricultural, or mining company, he almost always enjoys a temporary period of well-being" (ibid., pp. 63-64, my translation).

[21] Ibid., p. 54, my translation.

[22] Ibid., pp. 148-149. Haya first suggested the important role of the middle classes in the antiimperialist struggle in an article in *Amauta* 2, no. 9 (May 1927): 6-7.

[23] Haya, *El antiimperialismo*, p. 65, my translation.

classes.[24] As Haya saw it, the Latin American middle classes were, therefore, more than ready to spearhead a drive to oust foreign imperialism and its oligarchical allies.

Once Haya had identified the component parts of what he hoped would become the clientele of APRA, namely, the discontented sectors of the middle classes along with the emerging proletariat, he turned to the question of how to achieve the main goal of the movement—regulation of foreign imperialism. Earlier he had stated that the key to this objective lay in the seizure of political power, for it was here, he maintained, that foreign economic interests gained and maintained—in collusion with the ruling class—access to the Latin American economic structure. Paraphrasing Lenin, he wrote, ". . . the fundamental question in the antiimperialist struggle in Indoamerica is the question of power."[25] For this reason, Haya felt that it was absolutely necessary to organize the movement in Peru into a political party rather than remain, as the Communists and, later, Mariátegui maintained, a loosely constructed alliance of the discontented and oppressed segments of the population.[26]

Although in *El antiimperialismo y el Apra* Haya did not specify how APRA was going to defeat the ruling class and achieve political power, he did indicate what it would do once in power. Advocating a policy of socialism coupled with economic nationalism, Haya stated that imperialism would be controlled through the widespread nationalization and eventual "cooperativization" of foreign enterprises. He wrote: ". . . the first defensive act of our peoples has to be the nationalization of our wealth, snatching it from the claws of imperialism. Then, it is necessary to

---

[24] Ibid., pp. 150-151.

[25] Ibid., p. 53, my translation.

[26] The fact that Haya was set upon establishing a political party in Peru eventually contributed to the ideological schism with Mariátegui. For some time, Mariátegui had been willing to cooperate with Haya within the broad confines of an alliance in which, despite some differences, the two men could agree on certain general precepts, such as opposition to American imperialism. However, Mariátegui could not agree to the formation of a party, as Haya proposed, precisely because he disagreed with many of the specific ideas voiced by Haya, which would become part of the party program (see Martínez de la Torre, *Apuntes*, II, 295-296). Furthermore, Mariátegui felt that the formation of a revolutionary party in Peru at the time was premature, for as yet there existed no "revolutionary consciousness" among the oppressed sectors of the society. He believed that only through a long and concerted educational effort could these sectors be brought to this consciousness and only then was the creation of a successful political party possible.

hand over this wealth to those who work it and to also increase it generally for the collective good of society, in other words, the progressive socialization of society's wealth by the state, which will then institute a vast program of cooperativism."[27] Furthermore, since he was certain that after its initial defeat foreign imperialism would regroup its forces for another assault on the national economy, Haya proposed the creation of what he called the antiimperialist state (*el estado antiimperialista*). Such a state, he argued, would limit private initiative; control production, commerce, and the circulation of national wealth; and deny, when necessary, individual and collective economic rights for the national good—in short state regulation of the imperialist, capitalist system.[28]

Once this antiimperialist state was constructed and the proletariat and middle classes were freed from the yoke of imperialist domination, Haya believed that a second stage of revolutionary development might be possible. This stage would be characterized by the eventual seizure of power by the working classes, which would then make a "socialist revolution" according to the Marxist blueprint of the "dictatorship of the proletariat."[29] However, Haya said that this stage would come much later and he was deliberately vague on specific details. The main purpose of the APRA revolution, he reemphasized, was the liberation of Latin America from foreign imperialism.

While Haya had been formulating and finally recording the broad outlines of his political ideology for Latin America, he had also seen to it that these ideas were publicized as widely as possible in Peru, where he hoped to convert APRA into a viable political party. This had been difficult in recent months because of a general crackdown on "leftist activities" in Peru by the Leguía government, which, among other things, temporarily closed *Amauta* and arrested a large number of "suspected Communists." Nevertheless, prior to the 1927 repression, Haya had succeeded in making considerable headway in spreading his ideas, particularly in and around his home town of Trujillo.

This success was in part explicable by the fact that Haya had developed strong personal and ideological ties with the Trujillo reform group, which

---

[27] Haya, *El antiimperialismo*, pp. 74, 121, 124, my translation.
[28] Ibid., pp. 138-141. Nevertheless, this did not mean that the state would reject outright foreign capital, for Haya recognized that Latin America could not progress and modernize its archaic economic structure without the aid of foreign capital. Thus, Haya was proposing to control, not eliminate, foreign capital for the good of the nation (ibid., pp. 154-159).
[29] Ibid., p. 122.

centered around the figure of Orrego and the newspaper *El Norte*. However, much of Haya's political message regarding the perils of imperialism struck home in a region where the giant, foreign-owned sugar combines had been disrupting the traditional agrarian and commercial patterns of the area for years. Indeed, even before Haya had begun to formulate his ideas on the subject, *El Norte*, it will be recalled, had constantly spoken out against the commercial- and land-absorbing tendencies of the German-Peruvian plantation, Casa Grande.[30]

Thus, when Orrego and others on the staff of *El Norte* began to receive word of Haya's five-point APRA program and other antiimperialist pronouncements, they did not hesitate to report them in blazing headlines in the pages of their newspaper. This became particularly true as the commercial crisis, generally attributed to the monopolistic policies of Casa Grande, deepened in and around Trujillo during the years 1926 and 1927. The following report of a letter Haya had written to a Trujillano was typical of the content of *El Norte* articles about Haya and APRA that appeared during this period. Under the headline "The Founder of APRA or the American Antiimperialist Party Insists that the Program of His Party for Peru Implies Nationalization of Wealth and Defense of the National Sovereignty Threatened by Yankee Imperialism," the article stated:

. . . the letter [from Haya] then explains the dangers of the present economic situation in Peru. It goes on to say that imperialism invariably produces monopoly, the great trust and ultimately the destruction of small capital, small property, and small commerce. It is precisely because of imperialism that in Peru today bankruptcies are occurring regularly and national commerce is going through a profound crisis. The trust, the powerful monopolistic child of imperialism, is destroying all competition. For this reason, imperialism is primarily a threat to the middle classes—to the small capitalists and merchants. It is for this reason that imperialism is an enemy of the nation and the nation ought to revolt against it.[31]

Such articles, though cut short by Leguía's closing of *El Norte* in late June, 1927, struck home to a population that had long experienced the turbulent effects of modernization and succeeded in sowing the seeds of Aprismo throughout the Trujillo region.

Another major vehicle for the propagation of Haya's ideas in Peru during

[30] See Chapter 5.
[31] *El Norte*, June 5, 1927, my translation.

these years was the leftist journal *Amauta*, directed by Mariátegui. Ever since founding *Amauta* in 1926, Mariátegui had generously provided Haya with a sounding board for APRA, even though signs of ideological discord between the two would-be revolutionaries were already becoming apparent. Haya, for one, probably regarded Mariátegui as a potential threat to his own plans for leading the Peruvian left and sought to stake out a position different from that of a potential rival.[32] More importantly, Eudocio Ravines was undoubtedly correct when he wrote some years later that a break between Mariátegui and Haya was inevitable. He stated that, "although on the surface they maintained friendly relations, they were not really congenial. Mariátegui was an intellectual, a theoretician; while Haya demanded action, and was impatient of the other's thoughtful approach to the questions of the day."[33]

Ravines has put his finger on a very important point, one that goes far toward explaining not only the rupture with Mariátegui, but also the seeming paradoxical duality in Haya's political behavior. Despite his obvious penchant for political activism, Haya has always perceived himself primarily as a political theorist, constantly portraying himself as a true Latin American *pensador*. His many books and personal acquaintantships with intellectuals throughout the world have led many of his followers and sympathizers to accept, not without some reason, the view that Haya is indeed an important political thinker. One need only point out his work *Espacio-tiempo histórico*, in which he gives Einstein's theory of relativity a unique political twist to confirm the view of Haya the *pensador*. Yet, no one will deny the strong, if not overriding, political activism in Haya's character. It is precisely these seemingly complimentary yet in fact often clashing roles of theoretician and activist that produced a conflict and tension in Haya's public behavior. Haya the activist has all too often had to compromise the high-sounding theories expounded by Haya the *pensador*, and the result in the public mind has often been confusion and indeed disappointment. Indeed, many ideological followers of Haya have, at times, felt disillusioned and betrayed by his actions and have subsequently turned violently against him.

Although Mariátegui could certainly not be classified as a follower of

---

[32] Luis Eduardo Enríquez suggests this and in support quotes a letter he received from Haya in 1930 that accuses Mariátegui of wresting away many of his former working-class supporters (see *Haya de la Torre: La estafa política mas grande de América*, pp. 45-46).

[33] Ravines, *The Yenan Way*, pp. 14-15.

Haya, he, too, was clearly puzzled and irritated by Haya's seeming obsession to use virtually any pretext to effect Lenin's exhortation for revolutionaries to seize power. The so-called Plan de México of 1928, in which Haya announced the formation of the Partido Nacionalista Libertador Peruano (PNL),[34] was a case in point, and, eventually, the episode led to a final rupture between the two leaders of the Peruvian left. Although very little is known about the plan, it seems clear that the impatient Haya was arming a plot to overthrow the Leguía government. Apparently, Haya believed that, with the approach of the 1929 elections in Peru, Leguía, who had been in power for nine long years, was politically vulnerable. While declaring his own presidential candidacy under the newly formed banners of the PNL (an affiliation of APRA), perhaps in hopes of stirring the populace into open opposition to Leguía, Haya also moved to organize an armed uprising of workers in the oil region of Talara, under the leadership of a Captain Felipe Iparraguirre.[35]

Whatever the chances for success, and in retrospect they seem to have been very meager indeed given the extent of Leguía's strong hold over the country, the plan never really got off the ground. There was virtually no popular response to Haya's announced candidacy, and Iparraguirre was arrested by the authorities several months after his surreptitious arrival in Talara. Moreover, Haya, who was making his way south to Peru should the plan show signs of succeeding, was detained by the authorities in Panama, specifically at the behest of United States officials who had had him under diplomatic surveillance since 1923 as a suspected Communist and avowed anti-American. He was promptly placed on the next ship to Europe.[36]

When the entire episode and its failure came to light, it quickly became a source of serious embarrassment to Haya and caused a severe rift among the Peruvian reformers. Mariátegui, for one, was appalled at the unilateral and seemingly frivolous way Haya had proceeded in the serious matter of

[34] A copy of the manifesto can be found in Martínez de la Torre, *Apuntes*, II, 290-293.

[35] Sánchez, *Haya y el Apra*, pp. 203-231. The fact that Haya was organizing an armed revolt against the government indicates that his declaration of candidacy was merely a diversionary move to distract the government from the Talara plan. This interpretation seems to be confirmed by his explanation of the plan in the famous letter to César Mendoza dated Berlin, September 22, 1929, which is reproduced in Partido Aprista Peruano, *El proceso de Haya de la Torre*, pp. 5-9.

[36] J. G. South, U.S. Legation, Panama City, to secretary of state, December 20, 1928, a.l.s., 2 pp., General Records of the Department of State Relating to the Internal Affairs of Peru, 1910-1937, Decimal File, No. 810/43 A.P.R.A./6, NA, RG 59.

making a revolution and implied that his tactics were reminiscent of those traditionally used in the very same corrupt Peruvian political system that he ostensibly was committed to change. When Haya replied to Mariátegui in less than courteous tones, charging the Limeño, among other things, with excessive "tropicalism and Europeanism," formal relations between the two abruptly ended.[37] Considerable discontent with Haya's high-handed tactics was later voiced in other reform circles, including several Aprista cells. An important figure in the movement, writing some years later, referred to the general dismay Haya's candidacy in 1928 had caused among his followers, most of whom believed it to be a futile and an "absurd" tactic. Indeed Haya, himself, while not admitting any tactical error, did later acknowledge that the move had caused widespread dissension among his followers. For a time it appeared that Haya would be left with few supporters.[38]

During the uproar and subsequent splintering of the reform movement, Haya, through no design of his own, found himself in Germany. He had arrived in Bremen in December, 1928, after having been arbitrarily placed on board a German freighter in Panama by the local authorities. Once in Germany, Haya made his way to Berlin, where, thanks to a number of contacts made during his first European trip, he obtained work in the Wirtschaft Institut Latein Amerika. For the next few years Haya lived in Berlin, writing, studying, and attempting to revive the now practically defunct organizational structure of APRA, which had suffered a number of defections after the failure of the Plan de México. Indeed, as a former Aprista later so colorfully put it, "there were hardly enough of us at that time to take up all the space on a single bench in a public park."[39] Not until after the fall of Leguía in August, 1930, would APRA be revived and transformed by Haya into a major political force in Peru.

[37] See the exchange of letters between the two, which are reproduced in Martínez de la Torre, *Apuntes*, II, 296-299. Haya later accused Mariátegui of causing the failure of the plan by not supporting his supposed diversionary candidacy for the presidency (see the previously cited Mendoza letter, Partido Aprista Peruano, *El proceso*, pp. 5-9). However, apparently, Mariátegui knew nothing about the proposed Talara revolt, though the Apristas later claimed that Haya informed him of the entire plan in a letter sent by special courier from Mexico (see particularly, Sánchez, *Haya y el Apra*, p. 205).

[38] Enríquez, *Haya: La estafa*, pp. 82 and 88. For a detailed discussion of this debate, which includes several important documents, see Martínez de la Torre, *Apuntes*, II, 295-375.

[39] "...apenas llenábamos un banco de parque publico" (Enríquez, *Haya: La estafa*, p. 80).

7. The Political Response: From Elections
to Revolution, 1931-1932

On August 22, 1930, an obscure army lieutenant colonel named Luis M. Sánchez Cerro ushered in a new era in Peruvian politics when, in command of the notoriously coup-conscious Arequipa garrison, he revolted against the long tottering Leguía regime.[1] In a matter of days the once-powerful Leguía, who had ruled Peru dictatorially for most of his eleven-year political reign, found himself painfully ill in a dingy cell on a naval cruiser in Callao harbor, and Lima's ubiquitous creole politicians were once again busily conspiring to guide the nation's political destinies. Little did many of them then realize that, despite the seemingly traditional pattern of political events leading up to the August coup, the rules of the political game would never again be quite the same. The unknown Sánchez Cerro— significantly, a mestizo of modest origins—had, in toppling the Leguía

---

[1] Sánchez Cerro's Arequipa manifesto, which was ostensibly composed by the prominent local lawyer José Luis Bustamante y Rivera, included the following points: no presidential reelection, the holding of municipal elections, renovation of the judicial system, decentralization, and revocation of the mandatory *conscripción vial* (see "Manifiesto de Arequipa a la nación," reproduced in Luis Alayza y Paz Soldán et al., *Homenaje a Sánchez Cerro 1933-1953*, pp. 93-99).

government, unwittingly inaugurated the beginnings of mass participation in the Peruvian political process.

The coup against Leguía had not been altogether unexpected. The onslaught of the world depression and the subsequent rash of barrack revolts throughout Latin America had made the fall of the loan-dependent Peruvian government practically a foregone conclusion. Indeed, Leguía had been forced to devalue the sole 18 percent as its foreign exchange value had dropped from $4.00 in October, 1929, to $3.68 in August, 1930. Soon, the political gossip in Lima immediately prior to the coup was not so much whether a government takeover was imminent, but who would lead such a move.[2]

The news of the political demise of Leguía was greeted with jubilance by Haya, who, from his exile in Bremen, immediately set in motion plans for organizing an Aprista party in Peru. Actually, like others, he had earlier anticipated that the fall of Leguía was near and had alerted his followers, who were scattered about Latin America and Europe, to be prepared to leave for Peru the moment the fateful day arrived. Thus, soon after Sánchez Cerro took control of the government palace in Lima, a dozen or so exiled Apristas began to converge on Peru. By September a party executive committee had been established in Lima under the leadership of Luis Enríquez, a confidant of Haya, and moves were under way to organize the party throughout the country.[3] As for Haya, he cautiously remained in Bremen, awaiting the new government's reaction to the organizational efforts of APRA and appraising his chances of running for the presidency should new elections be called.

Haya's reluctance to return immediately to Peru was soon justified, for the "democratic springtime" that had followed the overthrow of Leguía quickly disappeared as the government began to crack down on all political activity. Several factors seem to have motivated the renewed government repression. For one thing, an alarming number of disturbances were erupting regularly

---

[2] What was surprising about the whole episode was the extent to which the once politically astute Leguía miscalculated his chances of forestalling a coup. Clinging right up to the end to the hope of being able to negotiate with the rebels, Leguía, in one of the few errors of his long political career, lost all chance of living out his remaining years in the relatively peaceful confines of Paris or New York. A year later he died miserably in prison from a painful urinary infection, unattended except at the very end by a physician—a bleak testimony to the sometimes brutal character of the Peruvian political system.

[3] Sánchez, *Haya y el Apra*, p. 258. The job of party organization was an extensive one, for apparently only a few if any Aprista cells existed in the country prior to 1930 (Luis Eduardo Enríquez, *Haya de la Torre: La estafa política mas grande de América*, p. 72).

throughout the country, threatening what little stability the new Sánchez Cerro regime had been able to establish. Pressed by the simultaneous outbreak of a rash of labor strikes, university disorders, and armed clashes between Apristas and Communists, and at the same time fending off a series of attempted countercoups led by disgruntled Leguiistas, Sánchez Cerro seemed to have little choice other than to resort to repressive measures to restore order.[4] However, the fact that the government chose to move most heavily against the Apristas indicated that more than the restoration of order may have motivated the actions of the mestizo colonel. It became increasingly clear that Sánchez Cerro, supported by elements of the old Civilist party, which had been ousted from power by Leguía in 1919, had more permanent designs on the presidential chair and was preparing his own "autoelection" to the office.

Sánchez Cerro's decision to hold "elections" in which he would be the principal candidate provoked a strong negative response not only from the Apristas, who by now were struggling to stay out of prison, but also from the recently organized Acción Republicana. A moderate party that occupied the center of the political spectrum,[5] Acción Republicana openly advocated the holding of free elections in which only civilians could run for the presidency. This demand was supported by a wide range of political groups that opposed the election of Sánchez Cerro. As economic conditions continued to deteriorate and amid rising opposition, Sánchez Cerro resigned, turning over the government to a junta of notables, headed by Monseñor Holguín, apostolic administrator of the archdioceses of Lima. The junta, however, was unable to deal effectively with the crisis, and, again, the army proved to be the deciding factor. In January, 1931, the Arequipa garrison once more revolted, this time against Sánchez Cerro, and, after a series of complicated political maneuvers, the lieutenant colonel was forced into exile, soon embarking for Europe to await political events. A new junta, headed by a respected old Pierolista named David Samanez Ocampo, was installed in the government palace in early March, 1931. The junta had the strong military backing of Gustavo Jiménez, commander of the powerful Lima garrison, which had played a key role in bringing about the resignation of Sánchez Cerro.[6]

---

[4] See Carlos Miro-Quesada Laos, *Sánchez Cerro y su tiempo*, pp. 67-119.

[5] The party was organized in January, 1931, by a group of prominent lawyers, including Ernesto and José María de la Jara y Ureta, Alberto Ulloa Sotomayer, and Jorge Basadre.

[6] Jorge Basadre, *Chile, Perú y Bolivia independientes*, pp. 647-648.

Representing a broad cross-section of national opinion,[7] the new junta soon announced its intention of holding nationwide elections in which all political factions except the Communists would be allowed to participate. In addition to a new president, the junta declared that the nation's voters would also be called upon to select representatives to a new constituent congress. The details of a new electoral law that would satisfy the nation's diverse political groupings proved to be the most thorny problem the junta had to resolve in carrying out these new elections. In a generally moderate compromise between the more radical Aprista forces and the conservative supporters of Sánchez Cerro, the junta removed property qualifications for voting, instituted the secret vote, and guaranteed minority representation in Congress, while rejecting the institution of complete universal suffrage.[8]

With the advent of the new Samanez junta in March and the subsequent relaxation of political controls, the activities of the Aprista forces throughout the country accelerated rapidly. Aprista leaders who had been jailed or forced into hiding by the Sánchez Cerro government were freed by the new junta and immediately dispatched to the provinces by the party to direct organizational efforts for the upcoming campaign. In Lima the party was officially registered as the Partido Aprista Peruano and a new executive committee, headed by the Trujillano Carlos Manuel Cox, was constituted. In the charged atmosphere of the capital, where the effects of the depression had radicalized much of the middle and working classes, it was not long before the newly organized PAP began to attract a large following. By May the party had founded several newspapers throughout the country, including *La Tribuna* in the capital, while Haya, still in Germany, prepared to return home to open his campaign for the presidency. Finally, the executive committee of PAP announced that the first of a series of regional Aprista congresses would meet in Trujillo to hammer out the party's platform and program for the forthcoming electoral campaign.

In Trujillo the incipient PAP organization had been sporadically operating since the fall of Leguía. Again, it was Antenor Orrego who spearheaded the activities of the movement in and around the northern capital city. Having been forced to curtail his political activities since the closing of *El Norte* by Leguía in 1927, Orrego had apparently remained in Trujillo

---

[7] For example, all major regions of the country were represented on the junta.

[8] APRA had called for the institution of all these provisions, but considered the compromise a major victory, considering the strength of the opposition forces (see *La Tribuna*, May 27, 1931). The party had, however, also demanded complete universal suffrage, including the right to vote for eighteen-year-olds and women.

during the Leguía dictatorship. With the fall of Leguía, Orrego once again began to publish *El Norte*, resuming the paper's long-standing policy of defending the interests of the region's small merchants, farmers, white-collar workers, and sugar braceros. Now a staunch follower of Haya, Orrego gradually converted the newspaper into an official organ of the Aprista movement in the region. In the pages of *El Norte*, Orrego, as before, focused particular attention on the social ills created by the foreign sugar plantations in the area, while gradually beginning to develop the Aprista approach to remedying these ills.[9]

By May, 1931, Orrego had painstakingly succeeded in forging the first links of a grass-roots political coalition that was to ensure Aprista domination of politics in the region for the next several decades. The coalition, patterned essentially on Haya's long-standing antiimperialist model, was composed of the area's disaffected intellectuals, small farmers, merchants, artisans, and white-collar workers and the braceros of the major sugar plantations. Victims of the social and economic dislocations resulting from the modernization of the sugar industry in the region, these alienated sectors, now further affected by the depression, became the stuff of the new Aprista party. Nowhere was the coalition better reflected than in the composition of the first executive committees of PAP in Trujillo and the surrounding towns.

In Trujillo the party committee counted among its membership four persons who could be classified as intellectuals, three who had close ties with the area's sugar braceros, three who were involved in local commerce, and Orrego, who, as president of the local Sociedad Union Empleados, represented the city's white-collar workers.[10] Moreover, significantly, several of these PAP officials came from families like the Spelucíns, which had suffered directly from the abrupt economic dislocations occasioned by the rise of the sugar cartels.[11] For example, Francisco Dañino Rebatto,

---

[9] See *El Norte* for the period.

[10] A list of the members of the PAP executive committee for Trujillo can be found in *La Tribuna*, May 24, 1931. Information on the occupations and backgrounds of these officials was provided from conversations with Leopoldo Pita Verdi, Luis Cáceres Aguilar, Carlos Manuel Cox, and Sra. Carmela Spelucín de Orrego—all Trujillanos of the period.

[11] To cite a few examples: Dr. Enrique Albrecht Arias was the son of the pioneer sugar planter of Casa Grande who had been forced to sell out to the Gildemeisters; Alejandro Spelucín, whose brothers were also Apristas, came from a family of once prosperous merchants in Ascope whose business had been ruined by the competition from Casa Grande's bazaar; Luis Cáceres Aguilar's family were small farmers in Santiago de Cao, an area of constant struggle with the Grace plantation Cartavio.

secretario del interior, came from a family of small merchants whose business had been severely affected by the bazaar at Casa Grande. As one traveled from Trujillo to the surrounding towns, the composition of PAP committees changed somewhat with small, independent farmers predominating. For example, in the town of Virú in a neighboring valley, the PAP committee was dominated by three members of a family of small farmers.[12]

In early May, Orrego, moving swiftly in the new climate of political freedom, called these newly formed provincial committees together and convened the first regional Aprista Congress in Trujillo. Composed of the newly selected PAP officials from La Libertad and adjacent departments, the congress was the first attempt of the party to formulate a specific program acceptable to the diverse elements of the coalition. The result of the congress was the drafting of an extensive eighty-nine-provision program, which dealt dramatically with the major social and economic problems affecting the region.[13]

Of the specific sectors of the coalition, the sugar workers received by far the most attention from the congress's seventy-some delegates. Provisions were passed calling for the elimination of the *tareaje*, or piece-work system, establishment of a minimum wage, prohibition of the hated *enganche* system, institution of the right to organize and strike, obligatory unionization, creation of adequate sanitary and health facilities on the region's plantations, and equal treatment and payment of foreign and national employees engaged in similar work. Most of these provisions went far to correct many of the grievances voiced by the sugar workers in the violent strikes of 1917 and 1921.[14] In addition, the congress called for the "cooperativization" of the coastal plantations, a move aimed at the foreign-owned sugar companies that would further accrue to the benefit of the workers.

Specific remedies for the grievances of the area's small farmers and merchants were also high on the congress's agenda. In the case of the former, provisions were drafted calling for extensive irrigation projects, the creation of regional small-farm loan banks, and a thorough reform and

[12] See, for example, *APRA*, May 7, 1931, for the Virú committee (interview with Leopoldo Pita Verdi, Lima, March 30, 1967). According to Pita, it was from this sector that APRA drew much of its rural strength.

[13] The program is reproduced in both *APRA*, June 5, 1931, and *La Tribuna*, June 3, 1931.

[14] See Chapter 2.

overhaul of the water distribution system. The latter, it will be recalled, was the main instrument used by the planters to despoil the landholdings of the region's small farmers and as such had long been a source of tremendous resentment to them.[15] As for the merchants, the Apristas promised to eliminate the single most distressing grievance to *comerciantes* of the Trujillo region—the revocation of the government concession of Malabrigo to Casa Grande, which had resulted in the introduction of large quantities of lower cost merchandise throughout the area. This issue had reached such a high degree of emotional intensity that, despite the world-wide depression, it was widely seen as the major factor preventing the return of commercial prosperity to the region.[16] In addition, a further sop to the area's merchants called for nationalization of the foreign-operated railroad system. High rail rates had long been criticized by this sector of the population, and nationalization was seen as the only major remedy to the problem.

The remaining provisions of the platform dealt with larger questions affecting all elements of the departmental coalition. For example, rent control, price ceilings on certain basic food staples, provisions concerning the extension of education, and a mandatory increase in the percentage of cultivable land devoted to staple production were all written into the party document. Having finished their work, the seventy-eight delegates, armed with the new platform and the writings of Haya and other Apristas, which were hurriedly being assembled by the Lima executive committee, left Trujillo prepared to embark on a new period of proselytizing for the party.

As indicated in the party platform, one of the major aims of PAP was to penetrate the huge industrial centers of the region's plantations and gain the party allegiance of the sugar workers. With some 25,000 of these workers located on three main plantations throughout the area, the electoral advantages of attracting this sector to the party were obvious. However, the task in many respects would be a difficult one. The majority of workers were ignorant, illiterate Indian peasants from the highlands who were still only partially acculturated into the creole, coastal society. In order to politicize and recruit this entire group, let alone qualify it to vote by increasing its literacy, a herculean effort by PAP would be needed, particularly since the elections were to be held in October, only a few months away. Clearly, this was not feasible, though the party undoubtedly

[15] See Chapter 3.
[16] See Chapter 4.

took a longer-term view of the problem, hoping at least to set the process in motion and plant the seeds of eventual PAP control of this sector. On the other hand, the temporary success of the 1921 strike indicated that a certain degree of politicization was possible among a substantial sector of the work force and that, therefore, PAP efforts in this direction could expect some short-term results.

Another problem was the perennial opposition of the planters to any effort to organize the workers into unions. Perhaps for this reason no real effort was made by PAP in 1931 to embark on a sindicalization program among the workers; activity was limited to the establishment of a party organization among their ranks. In this way PAP could avoid the outright hostility of the planters toward any unionization attempts, which could lead to the armed intervention of local authorities. Furthermore, PAP officials evidently further reasoned that, once the party was organized, it could only be a short step to unionization. Such a plan had the obvious advantage of assuring Aprista control of unions when they were finally organized.[17]

Party efforts to penetrate the sugar workers in the region were headed by Manuel Arévalo Cáceres.[18] The son of a Santiago de Cao small farmer who had lost his lands to Cartavio, Arévalo was born in 1903 and at an early age went to work as a mechanic's apprentice on the nearby Grace-owned plantation. He was actively involved in the sindicalization movement in the valley during the 1921 strike and, along with other organizers, was arrested and jailed when Leguía suppressed the movement. During the next decade Arévalo worked briefly in the Northern Peru Mining Company copper mines in Quirivilca and for the Peruvian Corporation, which operated the railroad between Salaverry and Trujillo, losing both jobs because of his efforts to organize the workers into unions. The fall of Leguía in 1930 found him operating his own auto repair shop in Trujillo and still active in union activities as secretary general of the local Sindicato de Choferes.

Over the next year Arévalo, now an avowed Aprista, made considerable headway in organizing the party on the region's various plantations. Aiding

[17] Interview with Luis Cáceres Aguilar, formerly a PAP deputy to Congress from Trujillo province, Lima, June 10, 1967. Cáceres helped organize the plantation Cartavio for the party in 1931 and worked closely with his cousin, Manuel Arévalo Cáceres, the leading PAP organizer in the region among the sugar workers.

[18] These and subsequent data on the organization of PAP on the sugar plantations were provided from conversations with Luis Cáceres Aguilar, who is preparing a short book on the life of Arévalo.

the long-time organizer in these efforts were Haya's brother Agustín and Dr. Carlos C. Godoy, both of whom were highly respected among the area's sugar workers for their aid to the labor movements during the 1921 strike. Godoy, a local lawyer, had defended many of the strikers who had been arrested during the strike, while Agustín, acting for a time as the Leguía government's principal negotiator in the dispute, had generally treated the demands of the workers favorably.[19] In addition, Arévalo counted on the *campesino* Remigio Esquivel, who by his own efforts organized the plantation Laredo, and Manuel "Búfalo" Barreto, a burly, bearded, sometime auto mechanic and chauffeur for the Pinillos family who later became an Aprista legend for his actions during the Trujillo Revolution.

Again, as in 1921, the movement was organized by and made the greatest progress among the white-collar workers and skilled workers, who were more politicized than their bracero colleagues. APRA organizations sprang up rapidly at Cartavio, Laredo, and Chiclín, but predictably encountered more difficulty at Casa Grande, where company officials hired special police to root out "agitators and troublemakers." In spite of such tactics, the party was able to establish clandestinely a number of cells on the German-Peruvian plantation.

The party was equally successful in penetrating the small towns and villages of the region. Aprista leaders from Trujillo made regular campaign forays to towns like Chicama, Ascope, Paiján, and Santiago.[20] Addressing themselves to the long-standing problems of the region in party meetings and manifestations, they constantly stressed the theme that PAP was the defender of the small farmer, the merchant, and peon against the "usurping encroachments of the imperialist sugar companies." At every stop they pointedly attacked the companies for monopolizing commerce, stealing land, usurping water rights, buying local officials, twisting the laws to their own ends, and generally exploiting, in one form or another, the entire population of the region.[21] A convenient symbol of oppression, the sugar companies became the main target for Aprista rhetoric, for there was not a single person in the region who did not harbor some grievance or resentment, real or imaginary, against the likes of Casa Grande or Cartavio.

Local as well as national party literature also contributed to the unfold-

[19] See Chapter 2.

[20] See, for example, *APRA*, March 18, 1931, and *La Tribuna*, June 6, 1931.

[21] Interviews with Cáceres and Cox. See also the text of a speech given by Américo Pérez Treviño, a local PAP official, entitled "Azucar," in Pedro Ernesto Muñiz and Carlos Showing, *Lo que es el aprismo*, pp. 65-68.

ing party campaign in the region. For example, one of the earliest Aprista documents issued by the party executive committee in Lima made a direct appeal to the population of the region and the north coast in general by focusing on the same issues. Entitled *Llamamiento a la nación*,[22] the document in part read:

A calm and conscientious appraisal of the economic situation in Peru brings us to the disturbing conclusion that our country, unfortunately, is a semicolony. Our ground wealth, the land principally in the industrial region of the coast, has passed in great part to the hands of foreign companies, and properties that are still Peruvian are in imminent danger of falling into the clutches of foreign capitalists. As a clear example of this, we can cite the case of the Chicama Valley, which belongs, in almost its entirety to the German Gildemeister company. The unbridled economic power of this company has resulted in the virtual ruin of the province of Trujillo, crushing the national commerce that once flourished there and generally injuring, in the process, the vital interests of the nation.

The PAP document went on to attack foreign companies like Casa Grande for discriminatory hiring practices, miserable salaries, and failure to pay taxes.

More fuel to the growing Aprista campaign along the north coast was soon provided by the return of Haya, who by now was a declared candidate for the presidency. Carefully selecting his port of disembarkation for maximum propaganda impact, Haya landed in mid-August in the northern city of Talara, which was located in the heart of Peru's oil-producing country.[23] No sooner off the ship, Haya ceremoniously kissed Peruvian soil and declared to the assembled throng that Talara—dominated as it was by the International Petroleum Company—was another "Canal Zone of imperialism," which must be revindicated by nationalization.[24]

During the next six weeks Haya campaigned vigorously throughout the north-coast region. He visited virtually all the important coastal towns and villages from Piura to Lima, inaugurating a new style in Peruvian politics.

[22] Partido Aprista Peruano, *Llamamiento a la nación*, pp. 4-6, my translation. Another document that was apparently given wide distribution throughout the region by the party was a detailed study by the Trujillano Alcides Spelucín of the social and economic problems of the area (see his "El departamento de La Libertad, fecundo campo de ensenañzas respecto a la acción imperialista de nuestro país," *APRA*, October 20, 1930). Spelucín attributed these problems entirely to the policies of Casa Grande.
[23] *La Tribuna*, July 13, 1931.
[24] Enríquez, *Haya: La estafa*, p. 75.

For the first time in the nation's history, a major candidate for the presidency systematically campaigned in the provinces, bringing his person and ideas directly to the people. In the department of Lambayeque, which had many of the same social and economic problems as the Trujillo region, Haya visited Chiclayo, Pimentel, Ferreñafe, Lambayeque, Eten, Motupe, and Monsefú—towns that had never seen the likes of a presidential candidate. Appearing before hastily assembled crowds, Haya spoke generally of the need to renovate Peru; to abolish the abuses of foreign imperialism; to protect the interests of the small farmer, merchant, *campesino*, and bracero; and, finally, to institute a program of social justice throughout the nation. In addition, he was careful to discuss local problems, promising, for example, in places like Chongoyape to solve the problems of the small farmers and Indian communities.[25]

The same procedure was repeated in La Libertad, with the exception that he traveled into the sierra. Arriving in Trujillo on the twenty-eighth, he spent the next several days campaigning in the Chicama Valley, visiting Paiján, Ascope, Chocope, and Santiago de Cao, as well as the plantations Cartavio and Roma. Prevented from speaking at Casa Grande by company officials, he stopped in nearby Chicama, where he was heard by most of Casa Grande's several thousand sugar workers. Throughout the region he stressed the main theme that the foreign-owned sugar companies were destroying the economic and social life of the area.

While he was successfully appealing to the discontented legions of the northern coastal region, Haya was also astutely broadening his political umbrella elsewhere to include, among others, the former supporters of ex-President Leguía. Leaderless and with their own political apparatus in disarray, many Leguiistas had already begun to gravitate toward the newly formed PAP. Some saw the middle-class-oriented party as a ready-made vehicle to continue their struggle against the hated Civilistas and perhaps even regain power. Others, radicalized by the deepening effects of the depression, did not find the Aprista ideology as alien and incompatible as they had a few years earlier.

Politically sensitive to the possibilities of attracting this numerically

[25] See *La Tribuna* and *El Norte* for the months of July and August, 1931. Both these papers followed Haya's activities closely during the entire campaign. Traveling with Haya throughout most of this trip were his brother Agustín; Ingeniero Alfredo Saco, the party's agrarian specialist; Manuel Seoane, a close confidant and high party official; Manuel Arévalo, the union organizer; and Juan José Lora, the Chiclayano poet.

important group to his cause, Haya, for his part, increasingly tried to make
the ex-Leguiistas feel more at home within PAP. One way of accom-
plishing this without laying himself too blatantly open to criticism from
his opponents, who were already charging the Aprista leader with being
"soft on Leguiismo," was to voice concern over the health and well-being
of the deposed president. This Haya did on numerous occasions prior to
Leguía's death, signaling the latter's supporters that they would indeed be
welcome political allies.

Furthermore, it appears that the Aprista leader, as he continued his
campaigning outside the more radical north, subtly toned down some of
his earlier radical statements and positions, in a calculated effort not only
to attract former Leguiistas to PAP but also to broaden generally his
political base outside the north among moderates and even conservatives.
For one, the political analyst in the American embassy in Lima sensed a
change in Haya's tone outside the north when he reported that "the
party . . . has somewhat modified its original very radical and lurid denun-
ciation of foreigners and capital," although he was quick to add that
"enough remains to cause consternation should the Party eventually control Congress."[26]

In some respects this strategem of Haya's outside the north was a politically natural move to make. Haya had always felt that the growing middle
class represented the best avenue to political power. While Leguía had
occupied the presidency, however, Haya had been forced by the latter's
general popularity among this sector to seek support from its discontented
fringes. This he skillfully did by staking out a position on the left, a policy
that paid large dividends in the north, where Leguía's policies, if anything,
had worsened the status of the middle sectors. Once Leguía was gone from
the political arena and Haya needed to broaden his northern base of
support, the Aprista leader could afford to step back somewhat from his
earlier radical stance and occupy some of the center of the political spectrum formerly taken up by Leguía. Of course, such a moderating shift was
fraught with dangers, since it risked alienating some of his early followers.
But for the most part Haya succeeded in this policy, so that, as election
day approached, the American ambassador could quite accurately report

[26] H. P. Starrett, U.S. Embassy, Lima, to secretary of state, June 10, 1931, a.l.s., 5
pp., General Records of the Department of State Relating to the Internal Affairs of
Peru, 1910-1937, Decimal File, No. 823.00/709, NA, RG 59.

to Washington that "there seems to be no doubt that the old Leguiistas are throwing their fortunes in with Haya de la Torre."[2][7]

While Haya was broadening PAP's political appeal to more moderate elements of the Peruvian electorate, his main opponent in the election, Lieutenant Colonel Sánchez Cerro, was also busily conducting his electoral campaign, mainly in the south. The son of a modest *escribano* from Piura who had made a good marriage into the distinguished Rosa Cerro family, Sánchez Cerro had had quite a stormy political career ever since graduating from the Escuela Militar in Chorrillos in 1910. In 1914, for example, he was involved in the plot to overthrow the government of Guillermo Billinghurst. The new president, José Pardo, promptly rewarded him with a promotion to captain and an appointment as military adjunct to the Peruvian embassy in Washington. Returning to Peru in 1918, he again dabbled in politics, this time taking part in an abortive plot against Leguía. "Exiled" to Europe as part of the Peruvian military mission, the young mestizo officer returned to Peru in 1929 and within a year had skillfully engineered the downfall of the once powerful Leguía. However, unable to stay atop the topsy-turvy political panorama of 1930, Sánchez Cerro had been forced temporarily into exile. The plucky army colonel, apparently against the wishes of some members of the junta, returned to Peru in early July of the following year to campaign for the presidency. Upon his arrival in Callao, he was enthusiastically greeted by members of his recently organized Partido Unión Revolucionaria. Heavily bankrolled by the conservative Civilista party, which saw in him their last chance to regain power,[2][8] Sánchez Cerro, like Haya, quickly hurried off to the provinces to solicit votes.

During the next several weeks, Sánchez Cerro, capitalizing on his modest, mestizo background and reputation as the "slayer" of the unpopular Leguía, garnered considerable popular support in the southern provinces. However, his program to meet the economic and political crisis that faced the nation left a good deal to be desired. A rehash of old and empty political clichés, it stressed decentralization, balanced budgets, sound currency policies, continued foreign investment, and utopian projects to colonize the jungle. Not one to leave out the usual demagogic

[2][7]Fred Deering, U.S. Embassy, Lima, to secretary of state, September 16, 1931, a.l.s., 7 pp., State Department Decimal File, No. 823.00/747, NA, RG 59.
[2][8]G. G. Ackerson, Jr., U.S. Embassy, Lima, to secretary of state, April 28, 1932, State Department Decimal File, No. 823.00/876 and 877, NA, RG 59.

appeals, the conservative Sánchez Cerro, recognizing the tenor of the times, also interjected promises for land distribution and vindication of the submerged Indian masses, both of which, however, he emphasized would be long-term projects.[29]

In marked contrast to the conservative and largely unimaginative program of the Unión Revolucionaria, which had been dictated by a few of Sánchez Cerro's Civilist confidants, stood the platform of PAP. Hammered out by Aprista representatives from all regions of the country,[30] but with considerable guidance from Haya, the party program presented an extensive and detailed analysis of the economic and social problems confronting the country. More importantly, the platform was highly responsive to the changes that had occurred along the northern coast during the past several decades. Indeed, in one form or another, the major provisions of the earlier Trujillo congress were included in the national party program.[31]

It was, however, Haya's classic August twenty-third speech before an overflow Sunday-afternoon crowd in the Plaza de Acho in Lima that best expressed the Aprista vision of Peru.[32] Drawing upon ideas he had first developed in *El antiimperialismo y el Apra*, Haya brilliantly posed what has become the crucial dilemma of traditional societies in a rapidly modernizing world—namely, how could Peru reconcile its more "primitive" economic order with the process of accelerating modernization? For Haya, the driving force behind this change was the mechanism of foreign economic imperialism and its twin vehicles, foreign capital and the foreign corporation. Equipped with unlimited amounts of investment capital, new technology, and modern systems of organization, the foreign company seriously threatened, in Haya's view, to destroy the nation's traditional economic structure and in the process those social groups like the middle classes that were tied to the old system. It was the middle classes—"the small land owner, miner, and merchant"—who formed the essence of the nation and who were most threatened by the absorbing forces of foreign imperialism. "We must," Haya declared, "free [*liberar*] the small land

[29] Miro-Quesada, *Sánchez Cerro*, pp. 147-179.

[30] Luis Enríquez, who later broke from the party, maintained that during this period the PAP was largely democratic, with the *bases* playing an important role in the decision-making process (*Haya: La estafa*, p. 94).

[31] Compare the Trujillo document with Partido Aprista Peruano, *Programa mínimo o plan de acción immediata del Partido Aprista Peruano*.

[32] A complete text of the speech can be found in Víctor Raúl Haya de la Torre, *Pensamiento político*, IV, 17-67. For an interesting analysis of this speech, see François Bourricaud, *Poder y sociedad en el Perú contemporáneo*, pp. 141-156.

owner and miner who is forced to sell his property to 'la gran empresa.' "
Peru, he felt, had already gone far down this dangerous road, particularly
in the agricultural and mining sectors—clear allusions to the serious social
dislocations triggered by the foreign-dominated sugar industry on the
north coast and to United States mining operations in the central and
northern highlands. To oppose this process of economic "denationaliza-
tion" and to challenge the political dominance of the foreign oligarchy and
its domestic allies, Haya proposed the formation of his by now famous
tripartite political alliance, consisting of the middle class, the emerging
proletariat, and the submerged peasants (*campesinos*), all of whom he
perceived as victims of the imperialist process.

However, while he recognized the serious dangers inherent in economic
modernization, which in his words were producing both "dependence"
and an economic "disequilibrium" (*desequilibrio*) in favor of the foreign
sector at the expense of the national, Haya at the same time recognized
that Peru needed to adopt many of the techniques and systems practiced
by modern capitalism in order to survive. The solution was to construct
what he called here the "Aprista state," and on other occasions the "antiimperialist state," whose guiding philosophy would be to reconcile the old
with the new, to protect and guard, on the one hand, against the dangers
of national "absorption" (*absorpción*), while, on the other, accepting
needed innovations brought to Peru by foreign capitalism. Thus, foreign
capital would be welcomed into Peru as a force for constructive change
and modernization, but the state would devise control mechanisms to
ensure that such an outside element would not produce the undesirable
side effects of absorption so harmful to the national body politic. "We are
not," he declared, "enemies of foreign capital; however, we do consider it
absolutely necessary that the state control foreign capital so that its role
within the national economy may be one of cooperation and not of absorption."

Turning to more concrete proposals, Haya, pulled increasingly toward
the center by the exigencies of pragmatic electoral politics, considerably
moderated his earlier shrill calls for "revolution" and the construction of a
socialist society. While insisting upon guarantees for the besieged *comunidades indígenas* and small farmers in general, he moderately proposed the
creation of an Agricultural Credit Bank designed to spearhead his agrarian
reform program. Such an institution, however, not only would provide
loan funds to small farmers in danger of losing their lands, but also would
serve as the organizational focus for creating agricultural cooperatives—a

key element in Haya's agrarian program. In addition, Haya called for the convening of a National Economic Congress charged with the formidable task of formulating a national policy for economic reform and development. Composed of representatives from all economic sectors of the nation, including foreign entrepreneurs, *hacendados*, small farmers, peasants, professionals, technicians, businessmen, and merchants, the congress would first endeavor to survey the entire spectrum of the nation's economic structure, gathering for the first time statistical data on all aspects of "our economic reality" (*nuestra realidad económica*). Once the congress had formulated a more precise picture of the nation's economy, then, according to the technocratically oriented Haya,[33] it could rationally and scientifically proceed to map out a specific, long-range plan for development and reform. Indeed, Haya envisioned organizing the entire body politic around the corporativist principles expressed in the congress itself, with popular political participation and representation according to occupation—something he called "functional democracy" (*democracia funcional*). Such a reform, however, he assured, would seek to decentralize and regionalize the Peruvian economy—an appeal to the long-standing hostility of the provinces to the central power of Lima—and would also guarantee the position of the small merchant, artisan, and businessman, who were confronted with the spectre of the emerging corporation. At the same time Haya sought in the speech to placate the armed forces in the face of heavy criticism from the right that his proposals for reform threatened the basic integrity and vital interests of this important national institution.[34] And, finally, in a plethora of other proposals he called for greater efforts in the area of worker rights, broader educational opportunities, revindication of the Indian masses, a general "moralization" of public offices, and abandonment of the gold standard. In sum, the speech

[33] Haya strongly emphasized the need to infuse the government with *técnicos*, people who had the special technical training to deal with Peru's problems on a more national and scientific level than had heretofore been the case. While influenced by what he saw as the attributes of the highly trained English bureaucracy, Haya's plan contained an obvious appeal to the middle class, who would stand to benefit most from the creation of such a bureaucracy in Peru.

[34] At one time Haya had sharply criticized the politization of the Peruvian army and its tendency to support the status quo and the oligarchy. This was interpreted by his enemies on the right as an indication that he would move to curb the traditional power and authority of the military establishment, should he ever attain the presidency. Actually, as indicated in this speech, Haya sought only to "marginalize" the political role of the army and to turn its mission toward what today has come to be known as civic action programs.

crystalized Haya's conception of the future of Peruvian society as he envisioned it and reaffirmed in a moderate way his determination to set Peru on a new, dynamic, and reformist course.

Though clearly a reflection of the desire of a large segment of the country's population for reform, Haya's speech, despite its moderate tone, still proved too radical for the existing political reality of the nation. For one thing, Haya's allusions to the need for a complete renovation of national institutions and his earlier attacks on the upper classes, although largely rhetorical, thoroughly frightened the powerful conservative forces that still dominated the country politically and economically. Viewed by elements of the church, the military, and the coastal oligarchy, APRA was likened to the onslaught of the popular hordes bent on the destruction of the entire fabric of national life.[35] As a result, these forces threw their financial and political weight behind the candidacy of Sánchez Cerro and unleashed a violent attack against the party from the pulpit and the national press. It was therefore not long before both sides were engaged in a campaign of violent invective, which grew steadily more intense as election day approached.[36]

A last-ditch effort to heal what by now was a thoroughly polarized political situation that some saw as seeds for a potential civil war was made late in the campaign by a group calling itself the Concentración Nacional (CN). Promoted by such old-line political figures as Rafael Belaúnde, Augusto Pérez Araníbar, and Juan Manuel Polar, all prominent aristocrats, the CN called for both Haya and Sánchez Cerro, in the name of national unity, to withdraw from the contest. In their stead they proposed that the nation rally around the figure of Amadeo de Pierola, son of the former caudillo-president, whom they saw as a compromise, national-unity candidate. However, the gentlemanly and aristocratic times when such a solution might have been possible were long gone from Peruvian politics, and neither Haya nor Sánchez Cerro ever seriously entertained the idea.

Despite the tense, polarized atmosphere that ultimately prevailed on election day throughout the country, voting proceeded without any major incidents. Some 300,000 voters cast their ballots for four presidential and a host of congressional candidates. The final returns gave Sánchez Cerro 150,000; Haya 106,000; José María de la Jara, the candidate of Acción

---

[35] Bourricaud, *Poder y sociedad*, p. 166.

[36] It should also be pointed out that the steadily worsening economic situation no doubt further contributed to the rising political passions during the latter stages of the campaign.

Republicana, 22,000; and Arturo Osores, a splinter candidate, 19,600.[37] Although the usual charges of fraud were subsequently made by the Apristas, the elections from all indications seem to have been among the fairest in Peruvian history.

An examination of the Aprista vote profile in the presidential election reveals the decidedly regional character of the party appeal. Haya polled approximately 44 percent of his total vote from the five northern departments. Of the remaining 56 percent, 30 percent came from the populous department of Lima (including Callao), while the remaining sixteen departments in the nation contributed a total of only 26 percent. A further breakdown reveals that well over half of Haya's 44 percent in the north came from the departments of Lambayeque and La Libertad, where the nation's sugar industry was concentrated.[38] Finally, in the province of Trujillo, which included the Chicama and Santa Catalina valleys, APRA's vote was overwhelming, as Haya received nine out of every ten votes cast.

In many respects Haya's and APRA's showing in the election was impressive. When Haya had arrived in Talara a few short months before the election, he was a relative unknown in a country where communications were for the most part backward. Eight long years of exile had substantially dimmed the public memory of his triumphant student days, when he had brought the Leguía government to a virtual standstill. Furthermore, although he had opposed Leguía from exile, he could not hope to match the fame or popularity of his opponent, who had overthrown the unpopular dictator. Indeed, the humblest shepherd had probably heard of the exploits of the *macho*, mestizo lieutenant colonel who had brought down the once powerful Leguía. To have garnered 35 percent of the vote under such circumstances was no small achievement.

Likewise, APRA, the first mass, institutional party in the history of the country, had succeeded in a very short time in establishing itself as a major power in Peruvian politics. While Haya was going down to defeat, the party had elected 23 of 145 delegates (16%) to the forthcoming constituent congress. To a large extent the success of both Haya and the party

[37] Miro-Quesada, *Sánchez Cerro*, p. 174.

[38] These percentages were calculated from the departmental electoral totals, which were published in *El Comercio*, November 5, 1931. At this time *El Comercio*, which was strongly anti-Aprista, gave Sánchez Cerro approximately 150,000 votes and Haya only 97,000. Final government figures, however, published some time later, gave Haya an additional 9,000 votes, while Sánchez Cerro's total remained constant. Since APRA claimed fraud in the department of Cajamarca, it is possible that these additional 9,000 votes might have increased Haya's percentage somewhat in the north.

was based on the skillful manner in which both had tapped the longstanding dissatisfaction of the north coast. Carefully tailoring its appeal to the various middle and lower sectors of the coastal population, whose lives had been rudely disrupted by the dislocations caused by the modernizing sugar industry, APRA had succeeded in forging a viable coalition of the discontented. A subsequent bulwark of the party, this coalition remained intact for the next several decades, and only recently has it shown signs of breaking up.

The election of Sánchez Cerro to the presidency in early October was a bitter blow to the Aprista legions in and around Trujillo. For months the party had been promising to get at the root of the deep-seated economic and social problems that had for so long plagued the region. Indeed, a vast segment of the population had come to believe, during the highly charged electoral campaign, that Haya and the party represented the last real hope that these problems could be solved. Thus, when defeat came, for many, violence seemed to offer the only alternative to a status quo that had become increasingly intolerable.

Soon after the election, party officials, aware of a growing mood of anger and frustration throughout the region's population, moved quickly to channel such sentiment into the sphere of political action. For example, PAP officials called a general strike in early December to protest the allegedly fraudulent manner in which the National Electoral Commission had supervised the election count. In the Chicama Valley such political action coincided with a smoldering dispute between local *regantes* and officials of Casa Grande over the longstanding question of water rights in the area. The upshot was a bloody confrontation between small farmers and the rural police at Paiján, Chocope, and Ascope, which left a score of dead and injured. Characteristic of the polarization that continued to pervade the political scene, the government accused APRA of "inflaming" and "agitating" the public, while the party countered be decrying what it considered wanton acts of repression on the part of Sánchez Cerro. Confrontations such as these, here and elsewhere, only further accentuated the growing mood of militancy among the party's rank and file, and probably explain the initiation of a policy on the national level of confronting the new government with uncompromising opposition at virtually every turn. This tactic was particularly evident when APRA representatives, breaching the usual political etiquette, refused to attend Sánchez Cerro's inauguration on December 8.

Under such circumstances and in view of numerous well-founded rumors that PAP was conspiring with sympathetic military officers, the new minister of government, Luis A. Flores, ordered authorities to crack down hard on Aprista activities. On Christmas Eve police, in a vain attempt to capture Haya, invaded party headquarters in Trujillo, wounding several holiday celebrants and arresting a host of party officials, including Antenor Orrego. A few days later the government introduced into Congress a proposed law (*ley de emergencia*) suspending personal liberties and virtually declaring martial law to meet what was seen as growing Aprista intransigence. Using extralegal parliamentary means, the government coalition in Congress had little difficulty obtaining the necessary votes to pass the new law, and by mid-February a widespread crackdown on PAP was in full swing, with the arrest and exile of the party's twenty-three congressional delegates.[39] When a few weeks later an attempt was made by a young Aprista on the life of the president, who was attending mass in the church of Miraflores, the government redoubled its efforts to cripple the party. Finally, in early May, the authorities managed to capture the elusive Haya, who had gone into hiding in Lima at the home of a close family friend by the name of Plenge. Erroneously believing that the imprisonment of its leader would finally break the movement, the government organized a courtmartial and, in the wake of a short-lived naval revolt in Callao, charged the Aprista leader with plotting against the regime and alleged "Communist activities."[40]

Meanwhile, for some time now party officials in Trujillo and elsewhere had been laying plans for a civilian-military uprising originally designed to prevent Sánchez Cerro from assuming the presidency on December 8.[41] The plan called for a series of coordinated revolts that would gain control

[39] Among the exiled PAP representatives were the Liberteños Alcides Spelucín, Carlos M. Cox, Carlos C. Godoy, Américo Pérez Treviño, and Manuel Arévalo. Ever since the opening of Congress the newly elected PAP representatives had tried to block all attempts of the government to deal with the worsening economic crisis (see *Congreso Constituyente de 1931, Diario de los debates del Congreso Constituyente de 1931*, vol. I).

[40] For a summary of these events, see Sánchez, *Haya y el Apra*, pp. 279-302.

[41] The following account of the Trujillo revolution was culled from several sources, including Ciro Alegría, "Interpretación de la revolución de Trujillo," *Acción Aprista*, July 28, 1934, pp. 18-22; José Agustín Haya de la Torre, "Apuntes para la historia de la revolución de Trujillo," *Acción Aprista*, July 7 and 28, 1934, pp. 5-19, 8-13; Félix Echague, *Lo que ví y lo que se de la revolución de Trujillo*; *La Industria*, July 1931; Rogger Mercado, *La revolución de Trujillo*; Guillermo Thorndike, *El año de la barbarie, Perú, 1932*; and interviews with Sra. Carmela Spelucín de Orrego and Luis Cáceres Aguilar.

of key military and urban centers throughout the north, thus paralyzing the nation and forcing the capitulation of the president-elect. A number of army officers were involved in the plot, including Commandant Julio Silva Cácedo, a close friend of Haya's and army commander of the Trujillo region, and later General Gustavo Jiménez, ex-member of the Samanez junta and avowed anti-Sánchez Cerrista.

In Trujillo, which was to be the main focus of the revolt in the north, plans for the movement had been under way ever since the outcome of the elections. Its organizers included Haya, himself, until his imprisonment; his brother Augustín; Luis Cáceres Aguilar; a dentist named Baldwin; Alfredo Tello, a twenty-three-year-old schoolteacher and son of a local *agricultor*; Manuel "Búfalo" Barreto, the hot-tempered, charismatic union organizer; and Remigio Esquivel, head of the recently organized union on the plantation Laredo. Early in the new year quasi-military cells were being organized on the region's main plantations, staffed for the most part by ex-army veterans, who brought at least a modicum of experience in tactics and firearms to the movement. The revolt was to be touched off by an attack on the local O'Donovan army garrison by a group of 150 rebels from the hacienda Laredo under the command of Barreto. Coordinated attacks were to be launched simultaneously throughout the north, including such places as Cajabamba, Chimbote, Chiclayo, and Huaraz, while at the same time APRA followers were to take to the streets in Lima. At this point, General Jiménez, who was in exile in Arica, was to return to Chimbote by ship in order to assume military command of the movement.

Scheduled originally for early December, the revolt was postponed, apparently because of a security leak, and rescheduled for July 15. Meanwhile, the arrest and the trial of Haya, coinciding as they did with the intensified persecution of party members, had brought on a sense of increasing desperation among Aprista supporters throughout the region. Rumors that Haya was being tortured and was about to be executed circulated almost daily in and around Trujillo, further exacerbating tensions and contributing to the general feeling that something drastic had to be done immediately to alleviate the situation. With each successive postponement of the revolt, it thus became more difficult for PAP officials to restrain the civilian elements involved in the movement. Finally, apparently unable to hold back his overanxious followers, Manuel Barreto, against the orders of the PAP executive committee in Trujillo, prematurely launched the fateful attack on O'Donovan on the morning of July 7, 1932, a full eight days prior to schedule.[42]

After a fierce five-hour pitched battle between the surprised army defenders and the rebels, the Trujillo garrison fell, and the victors marched triumphantly into Trujillo. Within hours, streams of braceros, brandishing machetes and the red flag of APRA, poured into the city to join the uprising, while the leaders of the revolt hastily dispatched rebel contingents to assist in the seizure of nearby towns and plantations. The premature launching of the movement, however, not only caught most Aprista cells and cadres in the north by surprise, causing considerable confusion, but also prevented General Jiménez from successfully sailing from Tacna on his way to Chimbote to assume command of the uprising.

In Trujillo, meanwhile, the rebels, under the leadership of Agustín Haya de la Torre, who had assumed the position of prefect, symbolically established headquarters in the aristocratic Club Central and prepared to defend the city. Bolstered by the arrival of large contingents of sugar workers from throughout the region, which swelled rebel ranks to over six hundred men, and the captured arms from the O'Donovan garrison, which included a dozen Krupp cannons, the rebels feverishly set about constructing defenses to meet the government forces that had already been dispatched by ship from Lima and by land from Piura. By the end of the second day, it became increasingly clear that the expected companion revolts throughout the country had largely fizzled and that Trujillo was to stand virtually alone against the overwhelming power of the national government. No doubt indicative of the highly charged emotional mood of many rebels, all suggestions from the leadership to undertake a strategic withdrawal to the sierra to engage in guerrilla actions were rejected, and the main rebel force chose to remain and fight to the end.

---

[42] According to Thorndike, the PAP hierarchy in Trujillo had long been divided on the strategy of the revolt. Agustín Haya and most of the party executive committee favored a cautious, "go-slow" attitude with careful planning and emphasis on the military character of the movement. For them, the keystone of the uprising was General Jiménez, whom they hoped would rally the younger officer corps behind the movement. Barreto and Esquivel, on the other hand, reflecting the growing impatience of their union clientele on the plantations, favored immediate action, with civilian elements assuming the major responsibility of the movement. Barreto, like most of the rank and file, feared for Haya's safety and distrusted Jiménez, whom he believed in the end would betray the revolt. A compromise was reached by setting the revolt's date back several weeks to July 15, which apparently satisfied Barreto while retaining the plan to have Jiménez take command of the movement (*El año de la barbarie*, pp. 186-187).

Such a decision ultimately proved disastrous to the rebel cause. Government troops, advancing from both north and south, soon surrounded the city, while for the first time in Peruvian history hydroplanes bombed Trujillo, preparing the way for the final ground assault. Finally, on the fourth day of the revolt the city was recaptured and order restored. Although some of the rebel leaders managed to escape to the interior, including Agustín Haya de la Torre, others were quickly captured and summarily shot. During the next few weeks, over fifteen hundred civilians were executed by order of the military for their alleged participation in the revolt.

While the Trujillo revolt had to a large extent been planned and organized by the PAP as a purely political move, it nevertheless took on many of the attributes of the social upheavals that had, over the past decades, become characteristic of the region. As during the violent strikes of 1917 and 1921, the ranks of the rebels were largely composed of the region's sugar workers, who for some time had been a serious source of instability to the existing order. Although the revolt's middle-class leadership tried to establish order within the ranks of the rebels, a number of acts of terror and violence were committed by the desperate lower sectors. Thus, ten officers of the O'Donovan garrison, together with fifteen policemen and twenty-five civilians, were shot down in their cells during the final stages of the revolt, after the leadership had retreated to the sierra. It was rumored, moreover, that the leaders of the Laredo group that had stormed the garrison had marked a number of prominent Trujillo aristocrats and foreigners for execution. Apparently, only the death of several of these leaders in the attack, including Barreto, and the restraining influence of Agustín Haya de la Torre forestalled such actions.

Thus, the Aprista electoral campaign, which for the people of Trujillo and its adjoining valleys had begun so auspiciously in 1931, ended some sixteen months later in the blood of an aborted revolution. As they saw their sons executed at the ancient walls of Chan-chan outside the city, the collective spirits of the population sank to new depths of despair. Perhaps they had looked to Haya and APRA, as human nature is wont to do, as the last chance for salvation from wrongs that had for too long been ignored. Yet, both the man and the party, despite the long period of repression that followed, would not be forgotten. After all, the Trujillo revolution and its martyrs were the stuff of which party legends were made. And, more importantly, in a very real sense, APRA had championed the popular cause, a fact that was not to be forgotten in the region for decades to come.

8. APRA and the Politics of Sugar

The profound changes in north-coast society that led to the rise of APRA in the early 1930's and indeed triggered the bloody Trujillo revolution of 1932 were to a large extent related to the general impact on Peru of the industrial revolution of the late nineteenth and early twentieth centuries. Peru, not unlike its other Latin American counterparts, saw part of its economic structure during this period converted into a modern, export-oriented industrial complex, designed to fill the raw-material needs of Europe and the United States. If Peru did not have its Porfirio Díaz during this period to help speed the process along, it nevertheless did have a development-minded Civilist party in control of the nation's political apparatus. Thus, by the turn of the century, Peru's political leaders, with the aid of foreign capitalists, were actively pushing the nation along the road of export modernization, a task that was perhaps made easier by the total economic breakdown occasioned earlier by the destruction of the War of the Pacific.

During the first decades of the twentieth century, a substantial sector of the Peruvian economy was modernized and integrated into the world economy. The motor force behind this process of economic change proved to be foreign investment capital, which flowed into Peru in ever increasing amounts between 1890 and 1930. By 1925, for example, British investments in Peru stood at a high-water mark of some 125 million dollars, a figure that was soon surpassed by American capital, which rose from a modest 6 million dollars in 1897 to 63 million in 1914 and again to 200 million in 1930.[1] Carving out the export enclaves in sugar, cotton, copper, oil, and other raw materials that are dominant features of today's Peruvian economic landscape, this multinational investment capital was funneled into Peru by several major foreign companies, including W. R. Grace and Company, Cerro de Pasco Mining Company, British Sugar Estates, Gildemeister and Company, and International Petroleum Company. Moreover, as the export complex grew and provided capital for reinvestment, other sectors of the economy also spurted ahead. Banks, factories, and commercial houses proliferated, particularly in Lima, during the early regimes of the "Aristocratic Republic," while at the same time funds became available to undertake needed urban improvements, such as electrification, sewage disposal, and transportation.

While the impact of this economic development, stimulated as it was by foreign forces, tended to buoy the general economy of the nation, it also caused serious social and economic changes and dislocations in the process. In the cotton-growing department of Ica, for example, the introduction of modern methods and machinery set in motion a process of land consolidation that displaced many formerly small, independent farmers.[2] Likewise, in the mining areas of the central and northern sierra, foreign companies, abundantly wealthy in technological skill and capital, absorbed the enterprises of many small and medium-sized miners.[3] Moreover, in both these areas a new rural, wage proletariat emerged to provide the needed labor for these export industries.

[1] According to Max Winkler (*Investments of United States Capital in Latin America*, p. 904), total foreign investments in Peru in 1925 amounted to 298 million dollars. For figures on American investments, see U.S. Congress, Senate Committee on Foreign Relations, *United States-Latin American Relations*, p. 296.

[2] For a glimpse into this process, see Eugene A. Hammel, *Wealth, Authority, and Prestige in the Ica Valley, Peru*.

[3] A short, though suggestive, discussion of economic dislocation in the mining areas of Cerro de Pasco during the first few decades of the century can be found in Liisa North, "Orígenes y crecimiento del Partido Aprista y el cambio socioeconómico en el Perú," *Desarrollo Económico* 38, no. 10 (July-September 1970): 191-194. For the political ramifications of these dislocations in the mining areas, see Pedro Ernesto Muñiz, *Penetración imperialista: Minería y aprismo*. James C. Carey describes a particularly salient early example of the dislocative impact of American investment on native capitalists in the mining sector. "The Cerro Corporation had gotten its start in 1901 and 1902 when J. P. Morgan the elder, Phoebe Apperson Hearst (mother of

Nowhere was this process of dislocation and change more evident, however, than in the case of the emerging sugar industry along the north coast around the turn of the century. Due to a series of reasons, not the least of which were the effects of the War of the Pacific as well as the changing nature of the industry itself, the cultivation of sugar cane in areas like the Chicama and Santa Catalina valleys, which had traditionally been in the hands of medium and small producers, gradually began to concentrate into large, modern units. By 1930 this process of modernization and consolidation had reached such proportions that only two giant sugar companies, both foreign owned, dominated the landholding structure of the two valleys.

These developments had a far-reaching effect on the traditional economic and social structure of the region. For one thing, a large rural proletariat, for the most part composed of Indian migrants from the nearby sierra, gradually concentrated on the large plantations of the area. By World War I their numbers reached into the thousands, and the two valleys had literally been transformed over the course of three decades into one of the major industrial centers of the nation. An important consequence of this demographic explosion was the periodic outbreak, beginning around 1910, of serious labor disturbances that threatened the social equilibrium of the entire region.

Equally significant was the widespread disappearance of small, independent farmers from the region. Traditionally, these farmers, part of a rural middle class, had cultivated small plots of land in and around the region's urban centers. However, as the sugar industry developed, they increasingly became the victims of the inexorable drive of the sugar companies to gain access to both water rights and land throughout the valleys for the expansion of their cane crops. Because of the overwhelming economic and political power of the companies, the small farmers were simply powerless to defend their property. Aside from causing a widespread scarcity of food staples in the area, the process of expansion decimated this class of once

---

William Randolph), D. O. Mills (grandfather of Ogden Mills), James Ben Ali Higgins and several others risked nearly $10,000,000 in the sulphide ores near the two mining centers of Oroya and Cerro de Pasco. The corporation soon found itself in conflict with the Empresa Socavonera del Cerro de Pasco, usually referred to in English as the 'Cerro de Pasco Tunnel Company.' Matters were complicated by the fact that all the capital stock in the United States concern was owned by United States citizens, whereas Peruvian citizens owned almost all the stock in the Tunnel Company" (*Peru and the United States, 1900-1962*, pp. 21-22).

independent *agricultores*, forcing many of them to seek work on the area's plantations.

The effect of this process of dislocation, moreover, did not confine itself solely to the rural middle class. On the contrary, it reached up into the ranks of the traditional planter aristocracy, loosening and ultimately breaking, as the Malabrigo affair illustrated, its grip on the economical and political structure of the region. Unable to compete with the emerging corporate estates, the older planters sold out most or all of their lands and gradually sank into a more modest existence in their once resplendent Trujillo town houses, desperately in search of ways to reconcile a deeply rooted seignorial life style to the hard realities of a rapidly eroding income. For some, this adjustment meant taking refuge in local and sometimes national political and administrative posts, using their familial connections to serve the new corporate interests. For others, it signaled the moment to resort to the time-honored practice of marrying off their children to new wealth, perhaps in Trujillo but more likely in Lima. By the end of World War I, this once proud and powerful class was fragmented and in a total state of economical and political eclipse, reduced in all but lineage to middle-class status.

The traditional commercial pattern of the region and, consequently, the old merchant class was likewise significantly altered by the rise of the giant sugar companies. Under a concession from the national government, Casa Grande began in 1915 to import large quantities of commercial goods, ostensibly for resale to the plantation work force. Many of these goods, over the loud and persistent protests of Trujillo merchants, found their way outside the confines of the plantation, where they competed unfairly with goods from the departmental capital. Increasingly, Casa Grande became the commercial focal point of the Chicama Valley and nearby sierra, capturing much of the formerly lucrative trade of the area, which had long been considered the prerogative of Trujillo. Coinciding as it did with a marked downturn in the general economy of the region in the 1920's as a result of the depressed price of sugar on the postwar world market, this dislocation in trading patterns produced widespread repercussions throughout the area. By 1929, significantly before the onset of the world depression, some thirty commercial import houses throughout the region had gone bankrupt, throwing hundreds of middle-class families on to the jobless rolls. Moreover, towns like Ascope, Chicama, and Santiago de Cao virtually ceased to function as commercial centers, while Trujillo itself entered into a long period of depression. Blame for this troubled situation was, rightly or wrongly, placed squarely on the shoulders of Casa Grande by the area's merchant population, which saw the German-Peruvian company as the symbol of all that had gone wrong with the region's economy.

The general urban decline in the area was also the work of other factors. As the plantations grew, they tended to become urban centers themselves, providing the resident work force with all the services previously found in the nearby towns. It was perhaps natural, then, that, as the plantations consolidated, they tended to compete with and eventually replace the traditional towns of the area. Moreover, the disappearance of the small farmer, who composed a large part of the urban population of the region, further crippled these towns.

To a large extent these dislocations and alterations in *norteño* society were simply the logical results of the impact of economic development on a traditional agrarian society. Certainly, it could not be disputed that the rise and modernization of the sugar industry had, in spite of its cyclical nature, generally enriched the Chicama and Santa Catalina valleys. In converting the valleys almost entirely to cane cultivation, the foreign sugar companies were maximizing the agricultural potential of the region. It is doubtful that any other use of the land could have yielded the profits that sugar cane afforded during this period. Nevertheless, despite the general modernization of the agrarian economy of the region, the alteration of the traditional caste of society that resulted caused considerable distress to the existing population. Often adversely affected by this development, *norteños* became increasingly angry and resentful at what they believed to be the unjust exploitation of the region by foreign interests.

It was within this general milieu that the Aprista movement was born. Its founder and principal leader, Víctor Raúl Haya de la Torre, was himself a product of the Trujillo environment. He had grown up in a family bisected by lineage—his mother scion of an old, landed Trujillo family, his father the son of provincial schoolteachers. Early acquiring a taste for the aristocratic life of the old days from his mother (the family still lived in one of the old De la Torre town houses), Haya apparently became resentful that he could not achieve what he considered to be his rightful place in Trujillo society. On visits as a boy to the opulent home of the De la Torres, he was on more than one occasion humiliated by the deprecatory treatment he received from his cousin Macedonio, who relegated the youthful Haya to the poverty-stricken and thus socially inferior branch of the family. Further, as he reached maturity, Haya found the economic avenues to wealth and status, which he so desperately sought, closed to him, despite his good education, by the restricted ambience of Trujillo, dominated as it was by the sugar monoculture that provided limited upper-level job opportunities. In such circumstances, Haya became psychologically speaking a typical example of the Hispanic *resentido social*, intensely desirous of entering the ranks of the upper class while simultaneously frustrated and angered by his inability to achieve this goal.

As a youth, Haya had doubtless seen the process of social and economic change unfold throughout the Chicama-Santa Catalina region, although, deeply enveloped in his own personal feelings, he did not seem to react visibly to it. Years later, however, his self-awareness, sharpened by an increasingly acute political sense, would overflow the boundaries of his own situation as he realized that others, including many of his friends, felt equally discontented—if perhaps in some cases for differing reasons. The sources of this discontent seemed to derive precisely from the economic climate of Trujillo, the nature of which now became more sharply crystalized in Haya's political thinking as he read Marx, Lenin, and other revolutionaries. Despite the obvious difficulties in ascertaining accurately how the social and economic changes in the region may have directly influenced and interacted with Haya's later thought, there would nevertheless appear to be at least some causal relationship. Certainly the antiimperialist tenor of his ideas, as well as his concept of constructing a broad coalition of the oppressed classes, seemed to fit perfectly the general socioeconomic environment of the Chicama-Santa Catalina region.

This relationship seems equally clear-cut in the case of many of the movement's leaders, who, for the most part, were drawn from families that had suffered serious difficulties from the economic dislocations that had buffeted the area. The best example of these was the Spelucín brothers, who came from a family of Ascope merchants that had seen its business ruined by the rise of the Casa Grande commercial bazaar. All three brothers became militant Apristas and served for a number of years in positions of leadership within the movement.

In other instances the leadership tended to come from the ranks of dispossessed farmers, who had undergone a process of "proletarization." Such was the case, for example, of Manuel Arévalo, whose family had lost its lands to the plantation Cartavio. Both of these families were to a large extent representative of the general impoverishment and downward mobility that had affected the traditional middle sectors of the region.

Conceiving of themselves as innocent victims, they angrily turned to radical politics in hopes of changing their situation.

Other early party leaders were drawn from a group of young, disenchanted students of middle-class background at the University of Trujillo. This group, which came to be known as *el grupo norte*, plunged into radical politics at the university, largely because of discontent with the declining social and economic circumstances of their families and class. However, their political radicalization was also no doubt related to the rather meager professional possibilities they faced after graduation from the university. Certainly, the local economy, including the sugar industry, was so unsettled by the mid-1920's that it could hardly have accommodated the Hayas, Orregos, Coxes, and Spelucíns, and a growing number of other qualified and ambitious graduates from the university. Many tried to solve this dilemma by leaving Trujillo for seemingly greener pastures in Lima, but there, with the competition often fiercer, their professional expectations were also generally frustrated. Unable to take what they believed to be their rightful place in Peruvian society, they increasingly vented their frustrations with the existing system by involving themselves in radical and sometimes revolutionary politics.[4]

The party program that these leaders composed was in part a reflection of their own personal despair with society and a gloomy assessment of the future—a situation fraught with revolutionary implications. In a broader sense, however, the program was also designed to forge a coalition of the region's discontented—the impoverished merchants, the white-collar workers, the dispossessed farmers, and the new mass of sugar workers. Thus, while the foreign-owned sugar companies were blamed for virtually all the ills of society, specific measures to remedy the grievances of the disparate elements of the coalition were written into the party documents. Indicative of the success of the program was the fact that the party in its first national election polled approximately nine out of every ten votes cast in the region.

In that national election and, indeed, for the next several decades, Aprista voter appeal was largely confined to areas like the north coast, where the forces for economic change had for some time been altering and continued to alter the traditional fabric of society. Even in the northern highlands, aside from the mining centers, where one might have expected

----

[4] On the general phenomenon of the alienation of students and revolutionary leadership, see James Coleman (ed.), *Education and Political Development*.

party strength, APRA made strong inroads, particularly in the more traditional agricultural areas. This success was apparently directly related to the operations of the coastal sugar companies, which had begun sometime in the 1920's to purchase haciendas in the nearby sierra for the purpose of securing a more stable supply of both labor and food staples for their coastal plantations. The latter had increasingly become a problem on the coast as the steady expansion of sugar cane and other export products during the war had markedly curtailed the cultivatable land devoted to food staples. In expanding their operations into the sierra, the sugar companies saw the possibilities of not only securing a cheap supply of food for their plantation work force, but also commercially tapping the lucrative urban markets, where food prices had skyrocketed.

With the introduction of modern agricultural methods onto the old-styled sierra haciendas, the sugar companies once again set in motion a process of change that disturbed the life style of the native peasantry of the area. Tenant farmers, for example, who for decades had worked their small plots according to the traditional man-land relationships on the area's haciendas, were apparently uprooted from the best hacienda lands, which the sugar companies needed for additional pasturage or new crops. Either evicted altogether from the hacienda or relocated onto less desirable lands, these peasant farmers in either case found their traditional world shattered.[5] There seems little doubt that Aprista propaganda, reaching into the highlands of Cajamarca and La Libertad, made good use of these developments in building popular support for the party in the region. Indeed, the spread of APRA into these more remote areas was considerably facilitated by the constant flow of migrant labor between coastal plantation and mountain village. The periodic return of the partially acculturated and politicized bracero to his native community provided the party, in a day of poorly developed communications, with the ideal vehicle for transmitting and extending its ideas into the hinterland.[6]

Generally, however, APRA's popular appeal in the nation's highland

---

[5] For an excellent description of this process as it related to the case of the sugar plantation Laredo near Trujillo, see Solomon Miller, "Hacienda to Plantation in Northern Peru: The Process of Proletarianization of a Tenant Farmer Society," in *Contemporary Change in Traditional Societies*, ed. Julian H. Steward, pp. 147-175.

[6] Aprista penetration of this area was aided by the constant migrant-labor flow to and from the highlands, which increased contact between the more politicized population of the coast and the sierra. Laborers on the plantations, returning to visit their families in the highlands, no doubt played a large role in propagating Aprista ideas in the interior.

agricultural regions was an exception rather than the rule. In these more economically static and archaic areas, the southern highlands, for example, the party ever since 1931 consistently failed to elicit much of a popular response. Here, the traditional hacienda, unaffected by the changes occurring on the coast,[7] continued to dominate local life much as it had for centuries. Tailored as it was to express the widespread popular discontent with the rude economic dislocations brought on by modernization, APRA was simply unable to make much impact in areas untouched by these same forces of change.

Looking at the broader implications of this case, the relationship between the dislocative, modernizing process in the sugar industry and the radical Aprista political response seems to fit into a similar general sociopolitical pattern found in other parts of Latin America. Perhaps the most striking parallel can be found during the late Díaz period in southern Mexico, where an expanding and modernizing sugar industry spilled over onto the traditional *ejido* lands, displacing and proletarizing large numbers of Indian peasant farmers, who had worked their communal lands for centuries. As both McNeely and Womach have shown, the discontent resulting from this phenomenon directly fueled the peasant movement of 1910, which found its spokesman and leader in the figure of Emiliano Zapata.[8]

It should be noted, however, that the Morelos revolt was largely a rural phenomenon involving for the most part only dislocated *campesinos*. In Peru the Aprista movement was considerably broader in that it attracted support directly not only from dislocated small farmers, but also from the sugar workers (largely absent from Zapata's early activities)[9] and particularly the urban merchant class, adversely affected by trade dislocations. Moreover, the Morelos sugar industry was in the hands of native Mexican entrepreneurs and not foreign corporations—a fact that added a strong xenophobic character to the political explosiveness along the sugar belt of Peru's north coast.

In the same vein, Cuba provides a similar analogy during the early twentieth century. The classic study of Guerra y Sánchez on the effects of

[7] Indeed, the south coast, except for Ica, was not agriculturally comparable with its northern counterpart, in terms of modernization.

[8] See John H. McNeely, "Origins of the Zapata Revolt in Morelos," *Hispanic American Historical Review* 46 (May 1966): 153-169, as well as John Womach's masterful *Zapata and the Mexican Revolution*, particularly pp. 42-54.

[9] Womach, *Zapata and the Mexican Revolution*, p. 87. Only later were the sugar braceros brought into the movement (see p. 122).

the sugar industry on Cuban agrarian society is again suggestive of the Peruvian case.[10] Here, however, if anything, the rise of the *central* system and subsequent concentration in the industry seems to have produced even greater dislocation than in Peru. A corresponding political response can be found in the Grau reform movement that occurred in the year 1933 and drew much of its strength from the widespread rural discontent resulting from sugar modernization. Furthermore, the long-run effects of the expanding Cuban sugar industry cannot be divorced from the political rise of Fidel Castro in 1959.[11]

Other examples of this same phenomenon seem to have occurred in Argentina, as well as in other parts of the Caribbean (particularly Puerto Rico) and, possibly, even Brazil.[12] All tend to reinforce the idea that the rise of APRA along the Peruvian north coast was not an isolated case within the general framework of what might generally be called the reform politics of sugar in Latin America. Wherever the sugar industry entered its modern, corporate stage during the early twentieth century, the resulting disturbance of traditional society seemed to trigger widespread local discontent. This discontent ran so deep in some areas that it directly fueled the rise of a variety of political protest movements, some of a reform and others of a revolutionary hue.

The Aprista case would also seem to give credence to a more general theory on the political effects of modernization in Latin America advanced by the Argentine sociologist Torcuato di Tella.[13] Di Tella theorizes that the impact of modern economic development on a traditional society, in dislocating the existing socioeconomic order, tends to radicalize a sub-

[10] Ramiro Guerra y Sánchez, *Sugar and Society in the Caribbean: An Economic History of Cuban Agriculture.*

[11] See Ramón Eduardo Ruiz, *Cuba: The Making of a Revolution.*

[12] On the political repercussions of sugar modernization in the province of Tucumán, Argentina, see Torcuato S. di Tella, *La teoría del primer impacto del crecimiento económico.* In Puerto Rico the Partido Popular Democrático drew much of its initial support from the emerging sugar proletariat on the island's south coast, beginning in 1938 (Sidney Mintz, "The Culture History of a Puerto Rican Cane Plantation, 1876-1949," *Hispanic American Historical Review* 33 [May 1953] : 250). As for northeastern Brazil, a sugar-producing center since early colonial times, one would expect to find the same pattern reoccurring. However, although Harry William Hutchinson's study suggests some of the wider social and economic implications of the introduction of the *usina* system, no attempt is made to correlate these changes with political developments in the area. Interestingly, Hutchinson briefly describes the phenomenon of urban decline resulting from the introduction of the factory system, a process very similar in broad outlines to what happened in the Trujillo region (see particularly *Village and Plantation Life in Northeastern Brazil*, pp. 43-44).

[13] See Tella, *La teoría del primer impacto.*

stantial element of the populace. This effect is particularly true, he maintains, when the stimulus for this development comes from foreign sources in the form of large amounts of capital and extensive corporate organization. Using this analytical approach, it would be particularly significant to examine other so-called Aprista-type parties, such as Acción Democrática in Venezuela and the Movimiento Nacional Revolucionario in Bolivia, whose programs, ideologies, and general formation were very similar to those of the Peruvian party. It may well be that, like PAP, these Aprista-type parties also emerged as a direct response to the dislocative impact of economic modernization.

In addition to fitting into a general continental pattern involving the political effects of sugar modernization, the Aprista movement reveals certain traits about the political dynamics of the Latin American middle classes. The long-accepted interpretation of middle-class politics in Latin America in the twentieth century, drawn largely from urban Argentine, Chilean, and Mexican models, has been that this group represented a rising or emerging sector of the Latin American body politic, which, in contrast to the traditional oligarchy, was progressive, modern looking, and politically ambitious.[14]

The Aprista movement of the Peruvian north coast would tend to add another dimension to this thesis. The movement rather seemed to garner broad support from a traditional, displaced middle class of peasant farmers, merchants, and artisans whose economic and, indeed, social position was deteriorating in the face of rapid modernization. This traditional group—from which, significantly, most Aprista leaders were to come—was to a large extent conservative and at times backward looking, nostalgically hoping to roll back or at least stem the tide of change. Their response to the Aprista calls for reforms that would protect the small-property owner and restore the old competitive balance between the merchant class and the "intruding" sugar companies was also perhaps at times more firmly rooted in an emotional need to regain control of events and their lives rather than in the full intellectual realization of the consequences of APRA's platform. Thus, they paradoxically embraced Haya's strong attacks on the capitalist system and even indulged vicariously in the glories of socialism and collectivism.[15]

[14] See John J. Johnson, *Political Change in Latin America: The Emergence of the Middle Sectors*.

[15] All this is reminiscent of the Progressive movement in the United States, which exhibited a strong strain of inherent conservatism in protesting against certain trends in American society.

Of course, such radical talk was also tailored to appeal to the emerging working classes, without whose support the petite bourgoisie could not hope to achieve political power. And it was not without its effects. Largely by means of the consumate political skill of Haya, who brilliantly formulated and verbalized the desires of both groups, a strong working-middle class alliance was forged in the north.[16] Yet, dominated as it was by leaders from the traditional middle class, the APRA alliance never strayed very far onto the path of true revolutionary politics. Indeed, when times changed and conditions seemed to improve along the north coast, APRA, reflecting the middle-group predominance in the alliance, grew increasingly conservative.

This rightward tendency[17] was reflected in both the party's program and Haya's writings, as well as in the fact that many of its early leaders later left the party in disgust at what they considered Haya's "sell out" of his supposed revolutionary ideals.[18] Since the 1940's, for example, Haya has softened his position regarding capitalism and the role of foreign investment in Peru's economy. From his decidedly militant, antiimperialist, quasi-socialist stance in the 1920's and early 1930's, the *jefe máximo* of Aprismo became increasingly more tolerant of both the capitalist system and foreign investment. No longer, except in the usual context of Latin American politics, did he blatantly attack United States economic imperialism.[19]

Likewise, the party's political strategem underwent a gradual alteration during succeeding decades. Following the Trujillo revolution, the Aprista leadership began to move cautiously toward a rapproachement with the nation's governing elite, although, due to mutual distrust and fear, this policy took more than fifteen years to work itself out and even then proved rather fragile. Although cooperation was initiated during the

[16] Because of the inherent antagonism within the coalition, Haya had to tread a very fine line between often opposing group interests, a task which, for the most part, he has always performed brilliantly.

[17] Although he did not wholly explain why APRA had become increasingly conservative over the years, Fredrick B. Pike, in his article "The Old and the New APRA in Peru" (*Inter-American Economic Affairs* 18, no. 2 [Autumn 1964]: 3-45), did ably document this turn to the right.

[18] See particularly Enríquez, *Haya: La estafa*, and César Guardia Mayorga, *Reconstruyendo el aprismo*.

[19] A comparison of Haya's early writings, such as *El antiimperialismo y el Apra*, which, incidently, the party has seen fit not to reedit, and the recently published collection of his writings, *Pensamiento político*, throws into sharp focus the Aprista leader's recent moderation.

regime of General Oscar Benavides in the 1930's, it was not until 1945 that both parties were able to reach a major understanding, one that gave APRA for the first time a considerable measure of participation in the postwar government of José Luis Bustamante y Rivero. Three years later a military coup cut short this agreement, but, subsequently, the party hammered out another arrangement, the so-called Convivencia pact, with the regime of Manuel Prado in the 1950's. By the 1960's APRA had succeeded in gaining a relatively strong position within the existing political framework of the country, although this achievement inevitably meant compromising many of the party's former reformist positions.

While the inherently conservative nature of the traditional north-coast middle sectors that have dominated the coalition would suggest one possible explanation for the rightward drift of APRA in recent years, another fundamental reason can be found in the changing position of APRA's working-class constituency in the north. During the 1930's and 1940's the Aprista movement, although forced underground on numerous occasions by the government, was enormously successful in penetrating the sugar plantations in the north, where the mass of recently migrated Indian braceros made an ideal target for recruitment. Although decidedly a long-term proposition, the work of raising the political consciousness of this group and organizing it into Aprista labor unions began to show marked progress by 1945, when the party succeeded in organizing the Federación de Trabajadores Azucareros (FTA) and in electing a president, José Luis Bustamante y Rivero, who was committed, at least in part, to the realization of its program.

As the power of APRA deepened on the plantations and throughout the north, the party, through its unions, stepped up pressure on the sugar companies, which had long been intransigently resisting labor's demands. Throughout the postwar years APRA-controlled unions made significant gains for the mass of sugar workers of the north. Indeed, during this period most of the prolabor planks of the early Aprista program—including elimination of the hated *enganche* system, establishment of a minimum wage, institution of a union shop, and improvement in the living and working conditions on the plantations—were finally achieved. By the 1960's the Aprista working-class clientele, not only on the plantations but also in the mining and manufacturing sectors, had clearly become a select elite within the broad spectrum of the nation's laboring population. This fact, together with the achievement of a greater measure of political representation and power within the Peruvian polity as a whole, tended, among other things, to lessen Aprista militancy in behalf of reformist causes and to produce a general conservative drift in the party's political program. On the laboring front, as in the general political sphere, the party became increasingly concerned with protecting the hard-fought gains it had made over the years. Unwilling to risk these achievements in any serious confrontation with the existing power structure, of which they had become a part, APRA leaders worked instead to conserve and extend the position of their working-class clientele. Such a policy naturally had the effect of alienating many of those who not only had supported the revolutionary aspects of APRA in the 1930's, but also now saw the need to extend the party's conquests to other sectors of Peruvian society. But to the party leadership and to most of its working- and middle-class clientele, weaned in the bloody struggles of the 1930's, the risks of taking a more militant stand were clearly too great.

This conservative tendency within APRA during the 1950's and 1960's was clearly evident on the issue of agrarian reform. While, earlier, the party had fiercely attacked the sugar companies, proposing the nationalization and cooperativization of all coastal plantations as part of a general agrarian reform program, in recent years it became less anxious to effect such a policy. Generally, this turnabout was due to two main factors: First, nationalization was now seen as a distinct threat to the improved economic position of the APRA clientele on the plantations, the argument being that profits and, thereby, wages would suffer under government management. More importantly, the party's power monopoly as the main spokesman and bargaining agent for the sugar workers would conceivably be endangered by any nationalization program carried out by a non-Aprista government. In short, nationalization now ran counter to the vital interests of the party, and for this reason APRA leaders joined forces, in something of an unholy alliance, with the sugar companies to strenuously oppose any moves toward nationalization. Judging from the 1964 Agrarian Reform law passed during the Belaunde regime, which totally exempted the large, industrial plantations of the coast, the results of this policy from the Aprista point of view were totally successful.

Finally, the insurgent character of APRA was, in a sense, bound to diminish as a new generation, less affected by the modernizing process that had pushed their parents and grandparents off the land and out of commerce, emerged in the area. Raised in an environment that had now largely settled into the pattern of large-scale, industrial and corporate sugar planting, this new generation more easily adapted to life in the region. The radical Aprista rhetoric of yesterday simply no longer moved, as it once did, the north-coast population, which had become more thoroughly integrated into the new corporate economy of the area. By altering and reshaping the party program along new and more conservative lines, Aprista leaders simply brought it into harmony with the new mood and situation of its rank and file.

This is not to say that all the old tensions have disappeared and memories of the past have been totally erased from the popular mind. On the contrary, Aprista leaders, until recently, often found it politically convenient to allude to past injustices, particularly around election time, when the sugar companies were always easy targets for attack. Moreover, the remarkable reception accorded in Trujillo on October 6, 1969, to President Juan Velasco—the first president to visit the Aprista stronghold since the revolution—amply attests to the fact that old grievances still persist in the collective memory of the region. Velasco's measure nationalizing the foreign-owned sugar plantations, something the aging Aprista leaders were reluctant to press for fear of jeopardizing the political respectability and power that the party over the past decades had painfully achieved within the existing order, represents the fulfillment of long-held regional aspirations. Indeed, the popular enthusiasm for this measure can be interpreted essentially as symbolic behavior in recognition of the final materialization of generational goals and longings. Ironically, Velasco, a military figure, appears in the popular belief to have finally vindicated the bloody struggles of previous generations.

GLOSSARY

Acción Republicana: Republican Action party; founded briefly in 1931.
agricultor: small, independent farmer.
alianza: political alliance.
Alianza Popular Revolucionaria Americana (APRA): Popular Revolutionary Alliance of America; a continental political movement founded in 1924 by Víctor Raúl Haya de la Torre.
almacén: plantation general store.
Amauta: prominent journal devoted to literature, the arts, and politics; edited by José Carlos Mariátegui in the 1920's.
ambulante: itinerant peddler or vendor.
APRA. *See* Alianza Popular Revolucionaria Americana.
Aprista: pertaining to, or follower of, the Partido Aprista Peruano (Peruvian Aprista party), founded in 1930 as the Peruvian branch of the Alianza Popular Revolucionaria Americana.
Arequipeño: pertaining to, or native of, Arequipa.
archivo: archive or record file.
Aristocratic Republic: term used by the historian Jorge Basadre to describe the Peruvian political system between 1895 and 1919.
barrio: neighborhood.
bodega: plantation general store.
bodeguero: storekeeper.
bracero: plantation field worker.
brigada de agitación y propaganda: group of union organizers.
cacique: political boss.
Cámara de Comercio, Agricultura e Industria del Departamento de La

Libertad: Chamber of Commerce, Agriculture, and Industry of the department of La Libertad.

Cámara de Senadores: Peruvian Senate.

campesino: small, peasant farmer.

cañazo: popular, undistilled alcoholic beverage made from sugar cane.

Cartavio: Grace & Co.-owned sugar plantation located in the Chicama Valley.

Casa Grande: Gildemeister-owned sugar plantation located in the Chicama Valley.

casa hacienda: plantation manor house.

caudillo: political boss or leader.

central system: Cuban sugar-milling system by which a centrally located sugar mill processed the cane of surrounding small farms and plantations.

chicha: popular, homemade brew made from germinated corn.

Chiclín: sugar plantation owned by Rafael Larco Herrera located in the Chicama Valley.

cholo: Peruvian mestizo. *See also* Chapter 2, note 4.

Civilista: pertaining to, or a follower of, the Partido Civil, the dominant political party in Peru during the period 1895-1919.

Club Central de Trujillo: exclusive social club in Trujillo.

cogobierno: refers to student as well as faculty participation in the administrative affairs of the university.

comunero: inhabitant of an Indian community.

comunidad de regantes: district board composed of local landowners charged with the administration of water rights.

comunidad indígena: Indian community.

Concentración Nacional (CN): National Concentration party; formed briefly as an alternative to APRA and Sánchez Cerro in the 1931 election.

Conscripción vial: a law decreed by President Leguía in the 1920's drafting all able-bodied Peruvians to work on the nation's expanding road network. In practice the law affected mainly *comuneros*, or the members of Indian communities.

Consejo Municipal de Salaverry: municipal government of Salaverry, the port city for Trujillo.

Consejo Provincial de Trujillo: government of the province of Trujillo.

contratista: labor contractor.

ejido: Mexican term for Indian community.

el grupo norte. *See* Trujillo Bohemia.

El Norte: Trujillo newspaper.

el sólido norte aprista (the solidly Aprista north): refers to the traditional electoral strength of APRA in the northern departments of La Libertad, Lambayeque, and Cajamarca.

empleado: office worker of white-collar worker.

enganchador (literally, hooker): labor contractor employed by the sugar planters to recruit field workers for the coastal plantations.

enganche: (literally, hook): system of labor contracting commonly used on the coastal plantations as well as at mines in the highlands around the turn of the century.

escribano: notary public or legal assistant.

Escuela Militar de Chorillos: Peruvian equivalent to West Point.

fanegada: unit of land comprising approximately 1.59 acres.

Federación de Estudiantes del Perú (FEP): Federation of University Students of Peru.

Federación de Trabajadores Azucareros (FTA): Federation of Sugar Workers; a labor union.

Feria del Señor de los Milagros: a week-long religious celebration held in Lima every October honoring a miraculous and legendary Black Christ figure.

frente único: united front.

fundo: landed estate; usually smaller in size than a hacienda.

gamonal: large landowner, or *hacendado*, who behaves like a feudal lord.

golpe de estado: coup d'ètat.

gremio: labor guild or trade union.

hacendado: large landowner.

hacienda: large, landed estate or plantation.

huelga: labor strike.

Humboldt Current: cold-water ocean current off the Peruvian coast which partly determines mainland climate, particularly rainfall. It was discovered by the nineteenth-century German scientist and traveler Baron Alexander von Humboldt.

Indigenista: pertaining to, or partisan of, the revindication of the Indian and his culture.

informe: report.

ingenio: plantation sugar mill.

jefe máximo: head, or principal, leader.

juez: judge.

juez privativo de aguas: special judge charged with adjudicating laws pertaining to water rights.

La Industria: Trujillo newspaper.

La Patria Nueva (the New Fatherland): political slogan coined by Leguía expressing his vision for Peru during the presidential campaign of 1919.

latifundio: large, landed estate.

Laredo: sugar plantation located in the Santa Catalina Valley.

Leguiismo: pertaining to the regime and program of President Augusto B. Leguía, 1919-1930.

Leguiista: pertaining to, or follower of, President Augusto B. Leguía, 1919-1930.

Liberteño: pertaining to, or native of, the department of La Libertad.

libra: unit of currency equivalent to ten soles.

Limeño: pertaining to, or native of, the city of Lima.

macho: virile, manly.

mayordomo: plantation overseer or foreman.

mestizaje: process of racial or cultural mixing.

Ministerio de Fomento: Ministry of Economic Development.

Ministerio de Hacienda y Comercio: Department of the Treasury and Commerce.

municipio: town government or town hall.

oncenio: refers to the eleven-year rule of President Augusto B. Leguía, 1919-1930.

PAP. *See* Partido Aprista Peruano.

Partido Aprista Peruano (PAP): Peruvian Aprista party.

Partido Nacionalista Libertador Peruano (PNL): Peruvian National Liberation party; conceived by Haya de la Torre to challenge the reelection of President Leguía in 1928.

Partido Unión Revolucionario (PUR): Revolutionary Union party of President Luis M. Sánchez Cerro, 1931-1933.

patrón: term of respect used by braceros, peons, and other farm workers when addressing or refering to their planter or *hacendado* employer.

Patronato de la Raza Indígena: Foundation for the Protection of Indians; founded in 1922.

pensador: intellectual.

Pierolista: follower of the late nineteenth-century caudillo Nicolás de Pierola, who served as president from 1895 to 1899.

provinciano: pertaining to, or native of, the provinces; any Peruvian not from Lima.

serrano: pertaining to, or native of, the highland, or sierra, region.

sierra: highland region of the Peruvian interior comprising the Andes mountains.

sindicato: labor union.

Sindicato Regional del Trabajo (Trujillo): Regional Labor Union encompassing the Trujillo region.

sistema de riego: system of water distribution and rationing employed in arid agricultural regions.

Sociedad Ferrocarril de Protección Mutua de Trujillo: Railway Mutual Protection Society of Trujillo.

sol: Peruvian unit of currency.

taller: metal or machine shop.

tarea: fixed amount of work assigned to plantation braceros for which they are paid on completion; a piece-work system of labor.

técnico: technician.

Trujillo Bohemia (also *el grupo norte*): refers to a group of young, rebellious Trujillo students, artists, and writers who met regularly from 1915-1921 to discuss literature, the arts, and politics. Many of its members, such as Antenor Orrego, Víctor Raúl Haya de la Torre, César Vallejo, and Macedonio de la Torre, later became prominent figures in the world of Peruvian arts and politics.

universidades populares (UP): so-called popular universities organized in 1918 by Haya de la Torre and other students to promote education and political awareness among Lima's working classes.

usina system: Brazilian sugar-milling system equivalent to the Cuban *central* system; see above.

viceroy: highest administrative representative of the Spanish crown in the New World during the colonial period.

War of the Pacific: war between Chile and Peru-Bolivia, which lasted from 1879 to 1883 and was won by Chile.

yanacona: tenant farm or farmer.

yanaconaje: system of tenant farming.

BIBLIOGRAPHY

Manuscript Collections

Archivo de la Cámara de Comercio, Agricultura e Industria del Departamento de La Libertad. Trujillo.

Sala de Investigaciones de la Biblioteca Nacional del Perú. Lima.

United States, Department of State. General Records of the Department of State Relating to the Internal Affairs of Peru, 1910-1937. Decimal File. National Archives. Record Group 59.

Theses and Dissertations

Alcantara Mostacero, Roger. "El yanaconaje en los valles de Chicama y de Santa Catalina." Doctoral dissertation, Universidad de Trujillo, 1949.

Atoche, Carlos A. "El problema de una escasez de brazos que se nota en la agricultura de la costa, se resuelve con el elemento nacional, variando el régimen que impera en nuestros campos." Doctoral dissertation, Universidad de Trujillo, 1909.

Fitchett, Delbert Arthur. "Defects in the Agrarian Structure as Obstacles to Economic Development: A Study of the Northern Coast of Peru." Doctoral dissertation, University of California, Berkeley, 1962.

Karno, Howard L. "Augusto B. Leguía: The Oligarchy and the Modernization of Peru, 1870-1930." Doctoral dissertation, University of California at Los Angeles, 1970.

Kus, James S. "An Historical Geography of Irrigated Agriculture in the Chicama Valley, Peru." Master's thesis, Michigan State University, 1967.

Plank, John. "Peru: A Study in the Problems of Nation-Forming." Doctoral dissertation, Harvard University, 1958.

Books and Articles

Ache, R. *Enendemos rumbos: Articulos publicados en los diarios de Lima con motivo de los últimos movimientos obreros en el Perú.* Lima: San Martí y Cía, 1916.

Adams, Geo. I. *Caudal, procedencia y distribución de aquas de los departamentos de La Libertad y Ancash.* Lima: Imp. El Lucero, 1906.

Alayza y Paz Soldán, Luis, et al. *Homenaje a Sánchez Cerro 1933-1953.* Lima: Huascarán, 1953.

Aldrich, Earl M., Jr. *The Modern Short Story in Peru.* Madison: University of Wisconsin Press, 1966.

Alegría, Ciro. "Interpretación de la revolución de Trujillo." *Acción Aprista* (Trujillo), July 28, 1934, pp. 18-22.

Alexander, Robert J. "The Latin American Aprista Parties." *Political Quarterly* 20 (1949): 236-247.

Alvarado Z., Elías. *Episodios de la revolución aprista de Trujillo.* Lima: El Sol, 1933.

Alvarez Beltrán, Carlos M. *El problema social-económico en el valle de Chicama.* Trujillo: Universidad de Trujillo, 1949.

Apter, David. *The Politics of Modernization.* Chicago: University of Chicago Press, 1965.

Arguedas, José María. *Yawar Fiesta.* Lima: CIP, 1941.

Armas M., Juan L. E. *Guía de Trujillo.* Trujillo: Olaya, 1935.

Aspillaga, Antero, et al. *La crisis del azúcar: Informe de la comisión oficial.* Lima: Torres Aguirre, 1902.

Aspillaga Anderson, Ismael. *La industria azucarera peruana.* Lima: F. E. Rosay, 1926.

Astiz, Carlos. *Pressure Groups and Power Elites in Peruvian Politics.* Ithaca: Cornell University Press, 1969.

Ayarza, Víctor E. *Reseña histórica del senado del Perú.* Lima: Torres Aguirre, 1921.

Backmann, Carlos J. *Departamento de Lambayeque.* Lima: Torres Aguirre, 1921.

Basadre, Jorge. *Chile, Perú y Bolivia independientes.* Buenos Aires: Salvat Eds., 1948.

———. *Historia de la república del Perú.* 5th ed., 10 vols. Lima: Peruamérica, 1964.

———. *Perú: Problema y posibilidad.* Lima: Rosay, 1931.

Bermúdez, Oscar, *Historia del salitre desde sus orígines hasta la guerra del Pacífico.* Santiago: Universidad de Chile, 1963.

Black, C. E. *The Dynamics of Modernization: A Study in Comparative History.* New York: Harper and Row, 1966.

Bourricaud, François. *Poder y sociedad en el Perú contemporáneo*. Buenos Aires: Sur, 1967.

Burgess, Eugene Williard, and Frederich H. Harbison. *Casa Grace in Peru*. Washington, D.C.: National Planning Association, 1954.

Camino Calderón, Carlos. *Tradiciones de Trujillo*. Trujillo: Moderna, 1944.

Camprubí Alcazar, Carlos. *Historia de los bancos en el Perú: 1860-1879*. Lima, 1957.

Cárdenas Alegría, G. *La protección a la agricultura es la salvación nacional*. Trujillo: El Progreso, 1917.

Carey, James C. *Peru and the United States, 1900-1962*. Notre Dame, Ind.: University of Notre Dame Press, 1964.

"Casa Grace." *Fortune* 12 (December 1935): 95-101, 157-164.

Castañeda Rangel, Alfonso. "La industria azucarera en el departamento de La Libertad." *Revista de la Facultad de Ciencias Económicas* (San Marcos), no. 20 (April 1940), pp. 104-158.

Castro Pozo, Hildebrando. *Del ayllu al cooperativismo socialista*. Lima, 1936.

———. *Nuestro comunidad indígena*. Lima: El Lucero, 1924.

Centurión Herrera, Enrique. *El Perú actual y las colonias extranjeras: La realidad actual y el extranjero en el Perú a través de cien años, 1821-1921*. Bergamo, 1924.

———. *El Perú en el mundo*. Brussels, 1939.

Centurión Vallejo, Héctor. "Esclavitud y manumisión de negros en Trujillo." *Revista Universitaria* (Trujillo), nos. 3-4 (1953), pp. 31-69.

———. *La independencia de Trujillo: Apuntes para la historia de Trujillo, 1820-1821*. Trujillo: Universidad de Trujillo, 1962.

Chang-Rodríquez, Eugenio. *La literatura política de González Prada, Mariátegui y Haya de la Torre*. Mexico City: Studium, 1957.

Chaplin, David. *The Peruvian Industrial Labor Force*. Princeton: Princeton University Press, 1967.

Chavarria, Jesús. "A Communication on University Reform." *Latin American Research Review* 3, no. 3 (Summer 1968): 192-195.

———. "La desaparición del Perú colonial (1870-1919)." *Aportes* (Paris), no. 23 (January 1972), pp. 120-153.

Chávez Romero, Otilio, and Germán Muñoz Puglisevich. *Crónicas de la revolución de Trujillo*. Lima, 1934.

Chevalier, François. "L'expansion de la grande propriété dans le Haut-Pérou au XXe siècle." *Annales: Economies, Sociétés, Civilisations* 21 (1966): 815-831.

———. "Official Indigenismo in Peru in 1920: Origins, Significance, and Socioeconomic Scope." In *Race and Class in Latin America*, edited by Magnus Mörner. New York: Columbia University Press, 1970.

Cisneros, Carlos B., and Rómulo E. García. *Departamento de La Libertad.* Lima: San Pedro, 1899.

Coleman, James, ed. *Education and Political Development.* Princeton: Princeton University Press, 1965.

Collin-Delavaud, Claude. "Consecuencias de la modernización de la agricultura en las haciendas de la costa norte del Perú." *Revista del Museo Nacional* 33 (1964): 259-281.

Comité Interamericano de Desarrollo Agrícolo (CIDA). *Tenencia de la tierra y desarrollo socio-económico del sector agrícola: Perú.* Washington, D.C.: Pan American Union, 1966.

Congreso Constituyente de 1931. *Diario de los debates del Congreso Constituyente de 1931.* 4 vols. Lima, 1932.

Congreso Ordinario de 1917. *Diario de los debates de la H. Cámara de Senadores.* Lima: El Comercio, 1917.

Cornejo Koster, Enrique. "Crónica del movimiento estudiantil Peruano, 1919-1926." In *La Reforma Universitaria,* edited by Gabriel del Mazo. Buenos Aires: Ferrari-Bme Mitre, 1927.

Cossio del Pomar, Felipe. *Haya de la Torre: El indoamericano.* 2d ed. Lima: Nuevo Día, 1946.

——. *Víctor Raúl: Biografía de Haya de la Torre.* Mexico City: Cultura, 1961.

Costa Villavicencio, Lázaro. *Monografía del departamento de La Libertad.* Trujillo, 1956.

Cotler, Julio. "Crisis política y populismo militar." In *Peru: Hoy,* edited by José Matos Mar et al., pp. 87-174. Mexico City: Siglo Veintiuno, 1971.

Cox, Carlos Manuel. *En torno al imperialismo.* Lima: Atahualpa, 1933.

Cuneo Vidal, Rómulo. *La huelga de Chicama: Informe aprobada por la Sociedad Pro Indígena sobre los sucesos de Chicama y las medias que deben ponerles repara.* Lima, 1912. [Also appeared in *La Prensa* (Lima), October 10, 1912.]

Curletti, Lauro A. *El problema industrial en el valle de Chicama: Informe del Ministro de Fomento.* Lima: Imp. del Estado, 1921.

Davalos y Lissón, Pedro. *La primera centuria.* 4 vols. Lima: Gil, 1919-1926.

Davies, Thomas M. "The Indigenismo of the Peruvian Aprista Party: A Reinterpretation." *Hispanic American Historical Review* 51, no. 4 (November 1971): 626-645.

Delmar, Serafín. *El año trágico.* Lima: Atahualpa, 1934.

Denegri, Marco Aurelio. *La crisis del enganche.* Lima: San Martí y Cía, 1911.

Díaz Ahumada, Joaquín. *Historia de las luchas sindicales en el valle de Chicama*. Trujillo: Bolivariana, 1962 [?].

Dunn, Robert W. *American Foreign Investments*. New York: Viking Press, 1926.

Dunn, William Edward. *Peru: A Commercial and Industrial Handbook*. Washington, D.C.: U.S. Bureau of Foreign and Domestic Commerce, 1925.

Eisenstadt, S. N. *Modernization: Protest and Change*. Englewood Cliffs, N.J.: Prentice-Hall, 1966.

"El azúcar peruana." *Informaciones Comerciales* (Lima), 2 parts, nos. 8-9 (August-September 1950), pp. 11-16, 8-17.

El esfuerzo libertador del comandante Jiménez. Lima, 1933.

El Perú centenario. Buenos Aires, 1922.

Empresa Agrícola Chicama Ltda. *Estatutos de la Empresa Agrícola Chicama Ltda., 1919*. Lima: Gil, 1946.

Enock, C. Reginold. *Peru*. London: Fisher Urwin, 1912.

Enríquez, Luis Eduardo. *Haya de la Torre: La estafa política mas grande de América*. Lima: Pacífico, 1951.

Espejo Asturrizaga, Juan. *César Vallejo: Itinerario del hombre, 1892-1923*. Lima: Mejía Baca, 1965.

Exposición de la Cámara de Comercio, Agricultura e Industria del departamento de La Libertad a los señores representantes a congreso de las labores hechas en defensa de los derechos nacionales y en particular de los de Trujillo, Salaverry y otros pueblos, seriamente amenazados con las concesiones otorgadas a los señores Gildemeister y Cía, para construir un muelle y un ferrocarril en Malabrigo. Trujillo: Olaya, 1917.

Exposición documentada, respecto a la usurpación de "El Cañal" por el Señor Fortunato Barúa, que hacen los hermanos Ríos Pinillos. Trujillo: La Razón, 1893.

Exposición que los productores de azúcar hacen al Congreso con motivo del proyectado impuesto de exportación. Lima: Masias y Cía, 1889.

Favre, Henri, et al. *La hacienda en el Perú*. Lima: Instituto de Estudios Peruanos, 1967.

Ferreyros, Alfredo. "Generalidades sobre el cultivo e industria de la caña de azúcar en el valle de Chicama." *Boletín del Ministerio de Fomento* 5, no. 11 (November 1902): 55-71.

Fitchett, Delbert Arthur. "Agricultural Land Tenure Arrangements on the Northern Coast of Peru." *Inter-American Economic Affairs* 20 (Summer 1966): 65-86.

Ford, Thomas R. *Man and Land in Peru*. Gainesville: University of Florida Press, 1955.

Gall, Norman. "Peru: The Master Is Dead." *Dissent* (June 1971), pp. 281-320.

Garbín, Raúl, et al. *Diccionario biográfico del Perú, 1943-1944*. Lima, 1944.

Garland, Alejandro. *El Perú en 1906*. Lima: La Industria, 1907.

———. *La industria azucarera en el Perú*. Lima, 1895.

———. *Las vías de comunicación en el Perú*. Lima, 1906.

———. *Reseña industrial del Perú*. Lima: La Industria, 1905.

Gillin, John. *Moche: A Peruvian Coastal Community*. Washington, D.C.: Smithsonian Institution, 1945.

González Prada, Manuel. *Horas de lucha*. Lima, 1908.

Guardia Mayorga, César. *Reconstruyendo el aprismo*. Arequipa: Acosta, 1945.

Guerra y Sánchez, Ramiro. *Sugar and Society in the Caribbean: An Economic History of Cuban Agriculture*. New Haven: Yale University Press, 1964.

Guillén, Alberto. "Haya delatorre ha dicho verdad." *Repertorio Americano* 17, no. 10 (September 8, 1928): 151.

Gutiérrez Vargas, Nilo. *Cuentos de Trujillo*. Lima: Rumbos, 1944.

Halsey, Frederic M. *Investments in Latin America and the British West Indies*. Washington, D.C.: Department of Commerce, Government Printing Office, 1918.

Hammel, Eugene A. *Wealth, Authority, and Prestige in the Ica Valley, Peru*. Albuquerque: University of New Mexico Press, 1962.

Haya, Raúl E. "Trujillo industrial de 1870 a 1920." *La Industria* (Trujillo), January 6, 1921.

Haya de la Torre, José Agustín. "Apuntes para la historia de la revolución de Trujillo." *Acción Aprista* (Trujillo), 2 parts, July 7 and 28, 1934.

Haya de la Torre, Víctor Raúl. *¿A dónde va Indoamérica?* Santiago: Ercilla, 1935.

———. "Autobiográfica." *Repertorio Americano* (San José, Costa Rica) 17, no. 4 (July 28, 1928): 50-52.

———. *Construyendo el aprismo: Artículos y cartas desde el exilio, 1924-1931*. Buenos Aires: Claridad, 1933.

———. *El antiimperialismo y el Apra*. 2d ed. Santiago: Ercilla, 1936.

———. *Espacio-tiempo histórico*. Lima: La Tribuna, 1948.

———. "Mis recuerdos de González Prada." *Repertorio Americano* 15, no. 6 (August 13, 1927): 84-85.

———. *Pensamiento político*. 5 vols. Lima: Pueblo, 1961.

———. *Política aprista*. Lima: Atahualpa, 1933.

———. *Por la emancipación de la América Latina: Artículos, mensajes, discursos 1923-1927*. Buenos Aires: Gleizer, 1927.

——. *Teoría y táctica del aprismo*. Lima: La Cultura Peruana, 1931.

——. "What Is the Apra?" *The Labour Monthly* 8 (December 1926): 756-759.

Heysen, Luis E. *El comandante del oropesa*. Cuzco: Ed. h.g.r.sc., 1931 [?].

Hidalgo, Alberto, et al. *Cantos de la revolución*. Lima: Atahualpa, 1934.

Hilliker, Grant. *The Politics of Reform in Peru: The Aprista and Other Mass Parties of Latin America*. Baltimore: Johns Hopkins Press, 1971.

Hopkins, Jack W. *The Government Executive of Modern Peru*. Gainesville: University of Florida Press, 1967.

Huntington, Samuel P. *Political Order in Changing Societies*. New Haven: Yale University Press, 1968.

Hutchinson, Harry William. *Village and Plantation Life in Northeastern Brazil*. Seattle: University of Washington Press, 1957.

Hutchinson, Thomas J. *Two Years in Peru with Exploration of Its Antiquities*. 2 vols. London: Sampson, Low, Morsten, Low, and Searle, 1873.

Irie, Toraje. "History of Japanese Migration to Peru." *Hispanic American Historical Review* 31 (August 1951): 437-452.

Johnson, John J. *Political Change in Latin America: The Emergence of the Middle Sectors*. Stanford: Stanford University Press, 1958.

Kantor, Harry. *The Ideology and Program of the Peruvian Aprista Movement*. Berkeley: University of California Press, 1953.

Klinge, Gerardo. "La agricultura en el Perú." In *Perú en cifras, 1944-45*, edited by Dario Sainte Marie S. Lima: Scheuch, 1945.

——. *La industria azucarera en el Perú*. Lima: Torres Aguirre, 1924.

Kubler, George. *The Indian Caste of Peru, 1795-1940*. Washington, D.C.: Smithsonian Institution, 1952.

"La gran industria azucarera del Perú." *La Industria* (Trujillo), August 7, 1915.

Larco Herrera, Carlos. *Hacienda Chiclín: Transferencia indebida de una acción social*. Lima: Garcilaso, 1927.

Larco Herrera, Rafael. *Aprovechamiento de las aguas del subsuelo en la costa del Perú*. Lima: Southwell, 1923.

——. *La obra social de Chiclín*. Lima: La Crónica y Variedades, 1930.

——. *Memorias*. Lima, 1947.

——. *Veintisiete años de labor en Chiclín: Reminiscensias y apuntes*. Lima: M. Moral, 1923.

Lavalle, Hernando. *La gran guerra y el organismo económico nacional*. Lima: Gil, 1919.

Lavalle y García, José Antonio de. *Las necesidades de guano de la agricultura nacional*. Lima: Gil, 1916.

León Echague, Félix. *Lo que ví y lo que se de la revolución de Trujillo.* Mexico City: Horóscopo, 1934.

Levin, Jonathan V. *The Export Economies: Their Pattern of Development in Historical Perspective.* Cambridge: Harvard University Press, 1960.

Maclean y Estenos, Roberto. *Sociología del Perú.* Lima: Gil, 1959.

McNeely, John H. "Origins of the Zapata Revolt in Morelos." *Hispanic American Historical Review* 46 (May 1966): 153-169.

Mariátegui, José Carlos. *Seven Interpretive Essays on Peruvian Reality.* Translated by Marjory Urquidi. Austin: University of Texas Press, 1971.

———. *Siete ensayos de interpretación de la realidad peruana.* 10th ed. Lima: Minerva, 1965.

Marie, Víctor. "La agricultura y la economía rural—valle de Chicama: Memoria presentada al Ministerio de Fomento." *Boletín Agrícola* (Arequipa), nos. 10-11 (April-May 1905), pp. 276-286.

Martin, Percy F. *Peru of the Twentieth Century.* London: Eduard Arnold, 1913.

Martinet, J. B. H. *L'agriculture au Pérou: Résumé du mémoire présenté au congrès international de l'agriculture.* Paris: Au Siège de la Société, 1878.

Martínez de la Torre, Ricardo. *Apuntes para una interpretación marxista de historia social del Perú.* 4 vols. Lima: Peruana, 1947.

Mathew, W. M. "The Imperialism of Free Trade: Peru, 1820-1870." *The Economic History Review* 21, no. 3 (December 1968): 562-579.

Mayer de Zulen, Dora. *El indígena peruano a los cien años de república libre e independiente.* Lima, 1921.

———, et al. *Conferencias pronunciadas en el centro unión hijos de Cajacay-julio, 1914.* Lima: El Inca, 1914.

Mazo, Gabriel del, ed. *La reforma universitaria: Documentos relativos a la propagación del movimiento en América Latina, 1918-1927.* Buenos Aires: Ferrari—Bme Mitre, 1927.

Mella, Julio Antonio. "La lucha revolucionaria contra el imperialismo: ¿Que es el Arpa? " *Amauta* (Lima) 4, nos. 31-32 (June-July, August-September 1930): 41-49, 24-37.

"Memoria presentada al supremo gobierno por el juez privativo de aguas de la provincia de Trujillo Dr. D. Enrique Guimaraes—1903." *Boletín del Ministerio de Fomento* (Lima) 1, no. 2 (December 1903): 89-107.

Memoria presentada al supremo gobierno por el juez privativo de aguas de la provincia de Trujillo Dr. D. Enrique de Guimaraes—1904. Trujillo: Haya, Verjel y Cía, 1905.

Memoria presentada al supremo gobierno por el juez privativo de aguas de la provincia de Trujillo Dr. D. Enrique de Guimaraes correspondiente al año 1905. Trujillo: Haya, Verjel y Cía, 1906.

"Memorial que en defensa de las clases trabajadoras presentarán al Parlamento Nacional las Sociedades Obreras de Trujillo." *El Derecho Obrero,* September 23, 1917.

Memorial que presenta el sindicato de la "Empresa del Muelle y Ferrocarril del valle de Chicama" a la representación nacional. Lima: Gil, 1917.

Mercado, Roger. *La revolución de Trujillo.* Lima: Fondo de Cultura Popular, 1966.

Merel, Juan de Dios. *Principios del aprismo.* Santiago: Ulam, 1936.

Mesones P., Manuel A. "El uso del agua, en relación con su valor Jurídicosocial." In *Anales del Primer Congreso de Irrigación y Colonización del Norte,* I, 743-756. Lima: Torres Aguirre, 1929.

Miller, Solomon. "Hacienda to Plantation in Northern Peru: The Process of Proletarianization of a Tenant Farmer Society." In *Contemporary Change in Traditional Societies: Mexican and Peruvian Communities,* edited by Julian Steward. Urbana: University of Illinois Press, 1967.

Ministerio de Hacienda. *Censo general de la república del Perú, 1876.* 7 vols. Lima: Imp. del Teatro, 1878.

———. *Memoria del director del crédito público-anexo.* Lima: Imp. del Estado, 1917.

———. *Resumen del censo general de habitantes del Perú, 1876.* Lima: Imp. del Estado, 1878.

Ministerio de Hacienda y Comercio. Dirección Nacional de Estadística. *Censo nacional de población, 1940.* 9 vols. Lima, 1944-1945.

———. *Extracto estadístico del Perú, 1940.* Lima: Imp. del Estado, 1941.

———. *Extracto estadístico y censo electoral de la república.* Lima, 1933.

———. *Memorias.* 25 vols. Lima, 1900-1925.

Mintz, Sidney. "Cañamelar: The Subculture of a Rural Sugar Plantation Proletariat." In *The People of Puerto Rico,* edited by Julian Steward et al., pp. 314-417. Urbana: University of Illinois Press, 1956.

———. "The Culture History of a Puerto Rican Sugar Cane Plantation, 1876-1949." *Hispanic American Historical Review* 33 (May 1953): 224-251.

———. "The Industrialization of Sugar Production and Its Relationship to Social and Economic Change." In *Background to Revolution: The Development of Modern Cuba,* edited by Robert Freeman Smith. New York: Knopf, 1966.

Miro-Quesada Laos, Carlos. *Sánchez Cerro y su tiempo.* Buenos Aires: El Ateneo, 1947.

Monguió, Luis. *César Vallejo: Vida y obra*. Lima: Perú Nuevo, 1952.

——. *La poesia postmodernist peruana*. Berkeley: University of California Press, 1954.

Moore, Barrington, Jr. *Social Origins of Dictatorship and Democracy: Lord and Peasant in the Making of the Modern World*. Boston: Beacon Press, 1966.

Moreno, Federico. *Las irrigaciones de la costa*. Lima: Imp. del Estado, 1900.

Moreyra Paz Soldán, Carlos. *Bibliográfica regional peruana*. Lima: Internacional, 1967.

——, and Carlos Derteano. "Evolución de la agricultura nacional en el siglo XX." In *Visión del Perú en el siglo XX*, edited by José Pareja Paz Soldán, I, 147-180. Lima: Studium, 1962.

Mostajo, Francisco. *Algunas ideas sobre la cuestión obrera: Contrato de enganche*. Arequipa: Quiroz, 1913.

Muñiz, Pedro Ernesto. *Penetración imperialista: Minería y aprismo*. Santiago: Ercilla, 1935.

——, and Carlos Showing. *Lo que es el aprismo*. Bogota: Cromos, 1932.

Naylor, Bernard. *Accounts of 19th-Century South America: An Annotated Checklist of Works by British and U.S. Observers*. London: University of London, 1969.

Nicolini, Juan Vicente. *La Policía de las aguas en el Perú*. Lima: San Marcos, 1919.

North, Liisa. "Origines y crecimiento del Partido Aprista y el cambio socioeconómico en el Perú." *Desarrollo Económico* 38, no. 10 (July-September 1970): 163-214.

Nuñez, Estuardo. *Viajeros alemanes al Perú: Cuatro relaciones desconocidas de P. Wolfgang Bayer, Friedrich Gerstaecker, Karl Scherzer, Hugo Zoller*. Lima: San Marcos, 1969.

Orrego, Antenor. "Panorama intelectual de Trujillo." *La Sierra* (Lima), nos. 13-14 (January-February 1928), pp. 26-28.

——. "Prólogo" in *El libro de la nave dorada: Poemas*, by Alcides Spelucín. Trujillo: El Norte, 1926.

——. "Prólogo" in *Trilce*, by César Vallejo. Lima, 1922.

——. *Pueblo continente*. Buenos Aires: Continente, 1957.

Osma, Felipe de. *Informe que sobre las huelgas del norte presenta al gobierno su comisionado don Felipe de Osma*. Lima: Casa Nacional de Moneda, 1912.

Pacheco, Julio Víctor. "Historia de la industria azucarera y su evolución." *La Industria* (Trujillo), April 10, 1922.

——. "Historia nacional: Fragmentos de la obra inédita; historia de los valles de Chicama, Chimú y Virú." *La Industria* (Trujillo), 2 parts, March 18 and 25, 1922.

Pan American Union. *The Peruvian Economy: A Study of Its Characteristics, Stage of Development and Main Problems.* Washington, D.C.: Pan American Union, 1950.

———. *Plantation Systems of the New World.* Washington, D.C.: OAS, 1959.

Parker, William Delmont. *Peruvians of Today.* Lima: Hispanic Society of America, 1919.

Parra del Riego, Juan. "La bohemia de Trujillo." *Balnearios* (Lima) 7, no. 281 (October 22, 1916).

Partido Aprista Peruano. *El proceso de Haya de la Torre: Documentos para la historia del ajusticiamiento de un pueblo.* Guayaquil, 1933.

———. *Llamamiento a la nación.* Lima: Minerva, 1931.

———. *Programa mínimo o plan de acción inmediata del Partido Aprista Peruano.* Lima: PAP, 1931.

Pasapera, Manuel S. *La ley de aguas con sus antecedentes: Expurgada de errores tipográficos y con algunos comentarios.* Lima: San Pedro, 1902.

Patrón, Enrique. *Leyes, decretos, resoluciones, reglamentos y circulares vigentes en el ramo de justicia: Legislación de aguas.* Lima: Torres Aguirre, 1901.

Payne, James L. *Labor and Politics in Peru.* New Haven: Yale University Press, 1965.

Paz Soldán, Juan Pedro. *Diccionario biográfico de peruanos contemporaneos.* Lima, 1917.

Paz Soldán, Mariano Felipe. *Diccionario geográfico estadístico del Perú.* Lima: Imp. del Estado, 1877.

Piel, Jean. "A propos d'un soulèvement rural péruvien au début du vingtième siècle: Tocroyoc (1921)." *Revue d'Histoire Moderne et Contemporaine* 14 (October-December 1967): 375-405.

———. "The Place of the Peasantry in the National Life of Peru in the Nineteenth Century." *Past and Present,* no. 46 (February 1970), pp. 108-133.

Pike, Fredrick B. *The Modern History of Peru.* New York: Praeger, 1967.

———. "The Old and the New APRA in Peru." *Inter-American Economic Affairs* 18, no. 2 (Autumn 1964): 3-45.

Poblete Troncoso, Moisés. *Condiciones de vida y de trabajo de la población indígena del Perú.* Geneva, 1938.

Porras Barrenechea, Raúl. "El congreso nacional de estudiantes del Cuzco." *Mercurio Peruano* (Lima) año 3, 4, no. 22 (April 1920): 311-312.

——. *Fuentes históricas Peruanas*. Lima, 1963.

Primer Congreso Nacional de Estudiantes reunido en la sede universitaria del Cuzco del 11 al 20 de marzo de 1920. Lima, 1920.

Prinsen Geerligs, H. C. *The World's Cane Sugar Industry: Past and Present*. Manchester: Norman Roger, 1912.

Puga, Pelayo. *Un proyecto de ley electoral: La falta de brazos para la agricultura de la costa del Perú*. Lima: Moreno, 1903.

Raimondi, Antonio. *El Perú*. 5 vols. Lima: Imp. del Estado, 1874-1913.

——. *Notas de viajes para su obra "el Perú."* 4 vols. Lima: Torres Aguirre, 1942-1944.

Ravines, Eudocio. *The Yenan Way*. New York: Scribner and Sons, 1951.

Rebaza Acosta, Alfredo. *Historia de la revolución de Trujillo*. Trujillo, 1934.

——. "La revolución de Trujillo: El ataque sobre el cuartel de O'Donovan." *La Antorcha* (Lima), December 17, 1933.

Rebaza Demóstenes, Santiago. *Conferencia pública: La agricultura en el valle de Chicama*. Trujillo: Comercial, 1899.

Renoz, M. Ch. *Le Pérou: Histoire, description physique et politique, productions, commerce, immigration et colonisation*. Brussels: P. Weissenbruch, 1897.

Rippy, J. Fred. "British Investments in Paraguay, Bolivia and Peru." *Inter-American Economic Affairs* 6, no. 4 (Spring 1953): 38-48.

——. "The Dawn of Manufacturing in Peru." *The Pacific Historical Review* 15 (1946): 147-157.

Robinson, David A. *Peru in Four Dimensions*. Lima: American Studies Press, 1964.

Rodríguez Dulanto, A. M. *El primer problema de la agricultura nacional*. Lima: La Industria, 1907.

Rodríguez Manffaurt, J. Leoncio. *Actuación del Capitán don J. Leoncio Rodríguez M. durante el movimiento revolucionario de Trujillo*. Trujillo: H. Cuba, 1932.

Romero, Emilio. *Historia económica del Perú*. Buenos Aires: Sudamericana, 1949.

Romero Paz, Carlos. "Estadística de la industria azucarera 1914." *Anales de la Dirección de Fomento*, nos. 10-12 (October-December 1915), pp. 1-38.

Rosenfeld, Arthur R. *La industria azucarera del Perú*. Lima: La Crónica, 1926 [?].

Rotary Club de Trujillo. *Monografía geográfica y histórica del departamento de La Libertad*. Trujillo: La Central, 1931.

Rowe, L. S. *Early Effects of the War upon the Finance, Commerce and Industry of Peru*. New York: Oxford University Press, 1920.

Ruillón, Giullermo. *Biobibliografía de José Carlos Mariátegui*. Lima: San Marcos, 1963.

Ruiz, Ramón Eduardo. *Cuba: The Making of a Revolution*. Amherst: University of Massachusetts Press, 1968.

Saco, Alfredo. *Programa agrario del aprismo*. Lima: Popular, 1946.

Sáenz, Moisés. *Sobre el indio peruano y su incorporación al medio nacional*. Mexico City, 1933.

Salazar, Jesús M. *El contrato de enganche*. Lima, 1910.

Salomón, Alberto. *Peru: Potentialities of Economic Development*. London: F. Southwell, 1920.

Samanamud, Pelayo. "El contrato de enganche." *Revista Universitaria* 2 (1912): 62.

Sánchez, Luis Alberto. "Aprista Bibliography." *Hispanic American Historical Review* 23 (August 1943): 441-456.

———. *El Perú: Retrato de un país adolescente*. 2d ed. Lima: San Marcos, 1963.

———. *Haya de la Torre y el Apra*. Santiago: Pacífico, 1955.

———. *Raúl Haya de la Torre o el político*. Santiago: Ercilla, 1934.

Sedgwick, Tomás F. *La industria azucarera en el Perú*. Lima: Imp. del Estado, 1908.

Seoane, Edgardo. *Surcos de Paz*. Lima: La Industria, 1963.

Seoane, Manuel. *Al pueblo: Peruanicemos el Perú*. Lima: PAP, 1930.

———. *Nuestros fines*. Lima: Rosay, 1931.

Smith, C. T. "Aspects of Agriculture and Settlement in Peru." *The Geographical Journal* 76, no. 4 (December 1960): 397-412.

Smith, Robert Freeman, ed. *Background to Revolution: Development of Modern Cuba*. New York: Knopf, 1966.

Sociedad Agrícola Casa Grande. *Estatutos 1899*. Lima: Gil, 1899.

Sociedad Nacional Agraria. *La situación actual del azúcar y los gravamenes que la afectan*. Lima: Gil, 1933.

———. *Provisión de brazos para la agricultura*. Lima: San José, 1902.

Solís, Abelardo. *Ante el problema agrario peruano*. Lima, 1928.

Spelucín, Alcides. "El departamento de La Libertad, fecundo campo de ensenañzas respecto a la acción imperialista de nuestro país." *APRA* (Lima), October 20, 1930.

Squier, E. George. *Peru: Incidence of Travel and Exploration in the Land of the Incas*. New York: Holt and Co., 1877.

Stewart, Watt. *Chinese Bondage in Peru: A History of the Chinese Coolie in Peru, 1849-1874*. Durham, N.C.: Duke University Press, 1951.

Stiglich, Germán. *Diccionario geográfico peruano y almanaque de "La Crónica" para 1918.* Lima: M. Moral, 1918.

Stuart, Graham H. *The Governmental System of Peru.* Washington, D.C.: Carnegie Institution, 1925.

Sutton, Carlos, et al. *El problema de la irrigación en el valle de Chicama.* Lima: Torres Aguirre, 1921.

Swirichi, Atilio. *Derecho indígena peruano: Proyecto de código indígena.* Lima: Kuntir, 1946.

Taboada, Daniel V. *La inmigración en la costa.* Lima: Liberal Unión, 1905.

Tauro, Alberto. *Diccionario enciclopédico del Perú.* Lima: Mejía Baca, 1966-1967.

Tella, Torcuato S. di. *La teoría del primer impacto del crecimiento económico.* Buenos Aires: Imp. de la Universidad, 1965.

———. "The Political Process in Latin America." Mimeographed paper. Berkeley: Center of Latin American Studies, 1968.

Thorndike, Guillermo. *El año de la barbarie, Perú, 1932.* Lima: Nueva América, 1969.

Tizón y Bueno, Ricardo. *Breve estudio geográfico estadístico del departamento de La Libertad.* Lima: Monitor Popular, 1899.

Ugarte, César Antonio. *Bosquejo de historia del Perú.* Lima, 1926.

———. *El problema agrario peruano.* Lima: Sanmartí, 1940.

Ugarte, Manuel. *El destino de un continente.* Nice, 1923.

Ulloa y Sotomayor, Alberto. *La organización social y legal del trabajo en el Perú.* Lima, 1916.

———. *Lineamientos de una legislación rural.* Lima: La Prensa, 1914.

U.S. Congress. Senate Committee on Foreign Relations. *United States-Latin American Relations.* Washington, D.C.: Government Printing House, 1960.

Valdizán, Hermilio. *Víctor Larco Herrera: El hombre, la obra.* Santiago: Nascimiento, 1934.

Vallejo, Santiago. "La vida en la hacienda." *La Sierra* (Lima) 2 parts, 1, nos. 2 and 7 (1927): 49 and 40.

———. *Trujillo en estampas y anécdotas.* Lima: Universitas, 1952.

Van Alsen, Mark J. "University Reform before Córdoba." *Hispanic American Historical Review* 51, no. 3 (August 1971): 447-462.

Vanderghem, George, et al. *Memorias presentadas al Ministerio de Fomento del Perú sobre diversos viajes emprendidos en varias regiones de la república.* Lima: C. Fabbri, 1902.

Vasconcelos, José. *La raza cósmica.* Mexico City, 1925.

Venturo, Pedro C. *Estudio de los ríos Chicama y Moche.* Lima: Pedro Berrio, 1908.

Vivanco, Guillermo de. *Legislación agrícola del Perú*. Lima: Gil, 1913.

Wiesse, Maria. "El Veneno." *Amauta* (Lima), no. 26 (September-October 1929), pp. 13-16.

Winkler, Max. *Investments of United States Capital in Latin America*. Boston: World Peace Foundation, 1929.

Wolf, Eric R., and Sidney Mintz. "Haciendas and Plantations in Middle America and the Antilles." *Social and Economic Studies* 6, no. 3 (1957): 380-412.

Womack, John. *Zapata and the Mexican Revolution*. New York: Knopf, 1968.

Zegarra, Jorge M. *Las lluvias y avenidas extraordinarias del verano de 1925 y su influencia sobre la agricultura del departamento de La Libertad*. Lima: Torres Aguirre, 1926.

Interviews and Letters

Cáceres Aguilar, Luis. Lima, June 10, 1967.

Cox, Carlos Manuel. Lima (Miraflores), May 11 and June 1, 1967.

Denegri Luna, Félix. Letter, June 9, 1969.

Gordon, Ronald M. J. Lima (San Isidro), April 14, 1967.

Haya de la Torre, Víctor Raúl. Lima and Villa Mercedes, July 20 and 23, 1971.

Moreyra Paz Soldán, Carlos. Lima (San Isidro), April 2, 1967.

Orbegoso Barúa, Carlos. Lima, March 30, 1967.

Pavletich, Esteban. Lima, October 1 and 10, 1966.

Pita Verdi, Leopoldo. Lima, March 21, March 30, and April 1, 1967.

Sabogal W., José. Lima, February 20, 1967.

Spelucín de Orrego, Carmela. Lima (Miraflores), May 29 and 31, 1967.

Newspapers and Periodicals

Acción Aprista (Trujillo), incomplete, 1934.

Amauta (Lima), 1926-1930.

APRA (Lima), 1930-1933.

Boletín de la Sociedad Nacional de Agricultura (Lima), 1900-1905.

El Agricultor (Lima), incomplete, 1875.

El Agricultor Peruano (Lima), incomplete, 1898-1914.

El Derecho Obrero (Trujillo), July 14-September 30, 1917, and November 9, 1919-June 20, 1920.

El Norte (Trujillo), 1923-1927 and 1931.

La Antorcha (Lima), incomplete, 1932-1933.

La Industria (Trujillo), 1900-1933.

La Prensa (Lima), October 10, 1917.

La Razón (Trujillo), incomplete, 1891, 1896, and 1912.
La Reforma (Trujillo), 1911-1922.
La Tribuna (Lima), 1931-1933.
Revista de Agricultura (Lima), 1875-1880.

INDEX

Acción Democrática: 152

Acción Republicana: response of, to Sánchez Cerro, 121; origins of, 121 and n.; candidate of, in 1931 election, 135-136

Agrarian Reform law of 1964: 155

agricultor: decline of, xvi, 53, 58, 60, 62, 65, 143, 144-145; traditional life of, 50, 52, 82; hardships of, 53, 57, 58 and n.-59 and n.; and polity, 61, 83-84, 124, 129; as *empleado*, 63-64. **See also** *comunidades indígenas*

Agricultural Credit Bank: 133-134

agriculture: modernization of, xiv, 15, 45; prosperity of, 4; decline of, 5-6

Albrecht Arias, Enrique: 104

Alianza Popular Revolucionaria Americana (APRA): regional character of, xiii, xiv, xviii, 136-137, 149 and n., 150; founding of, xiii n., 107-108; program of, xiii n., 108-109, 114; and Latin America, xiii and n., 109; and V. Haya, xiv-xv, 118; and economic changes, xiv, xvii, 142; strength of, as political party, xiv, xviii, 113, 114, 118, 122, 136; development of, xvii, 110, 118, 120, 137, 141, 149, 153-156; and reform, xviii, 135, 151,

155-156; and anti-American imperialism, 108, 109, 110, 112; appeal of, to popular classes, 109, 113, 141, 153; relations of, with regimes, 122 and n., 137, 154. **See also** Aprista movement; Partido Aprista Peruano

almacén. **See** *bodegas*

Alzamora, Guillermo: 9

Amauta: 114, 116

ambulantes: 67-68

Anarchists: 102

antiimperialism. **See** imperialism

"antiimperialist state." **See** *el estado antiimperialista*

APRA. **See** Alianza Popular Revolucionaria Americana

Aprista Congress: 124-125

Aprista movement: reasons for success of, xiii-xv, xvii, 115, 122, 127, 152; regional character of, xiii, 136, 148-150; and V. Haya, xiv, 46, 87, 146; origins of, 46, 87, 103, 120 and n., 146-148; ideology of, 108, 127, 128; in Latin America, 110 and n., 150-152; and Sánchez Cerro, 121, 137; and labor organization, 126, 154; since 1932, 152-156. **See also** Alianza Popular Revolucionaria Americana